Nature
Heals

Nature
Heals

The Psychological Essays of
PAUL GOODMAN

(Natura sanat non medicus)

Edited by
Taylor Stoehr

A Dutton Paperback

E. P. DUTTON / New York

Acknowledgments

The editor and publisher wish to thank the following for permission to reprint material included in this book:

Alternative—for "A Public Dream of Universal Disaster." Reprinted from *Alternative*, March 1950.

5 x 8 Press—for "The Golden Age." Originally appeared in *Complex*. Copyright © 1953 by the 5 x 8 Press.

Julian Press—for "The Anti-Social and Aggression." Taken from *Gestalt Therapy* by Frederick Perls, M.D., Ph.D., Ralph Hefferline, Ph.D., Paul Goodman, Ph.D. Copyright © 1951 by Frederick Perls, M.D., Ph.D., Ralph F. Hefferline, Ph.D., and Paul Goodman, Ph.D. Used by permission of Crown Publishers, Inc.

Kenyon Review—for "The Father of the Psychoanalytic Movement." Reprinted from *Kenyon Review*, September 20, 1945.

Liberation—for "The Children and Psychology," from *Liberation*, September 1956;—for "Great Pioneer, but No Libertarian," from *Liberation*, January 1958;—for "Designing Pacifist Films," from *Liberation*, April 1961.

New York Review of Books—for "Reflections on Racism, Spite, Guilt and Non-Violence." Reprinted with permission from the *New York Review of Books*. Copyright © 1958 *The New York Review*.

Politics—for "The Political Meaning of Some Recent Revisions of Freud." Reprinted from *Politics*, July and October 1945.

The Psychoanalytic Review—for "The Psychological Revolution and the Writer's Life-View." Reprinted from *The Psychoanalytic Review*, Vol. 50, No. 3, Fall 1963, through the courtesy of the Editors and the Publisher, National Psychological Association for Psychoanalysis, New York, New York.

Random House—for "Freud." Copyright © 1941 by New Directions;—for "Fever and Health." Copyright © 1972, 1973 by the Estate of Paul Goodman;—for "Novices of Art." Copyright © 1972, 1973 by the Estate of Paul Goodman;

Acknowledgments

—for "Manlike my God I make." Copyright© 1972, 1973 by the Estate of Paul Goodman. Reprinted from *Collected Poems* by Paul Goodman, edited by Taylor Stoehr, by permission of Random House, Inc.

Random House—for "The Fate of Dr. Reich's Books." Copyright© 1960 by Paul Goodman;—for "On the Intellectual Inhibition of Explosive Grief and Anger." Copyright© 1950 by Arts & Sciences Press;—for "On A Writer's Block." Copyright© 1952 by *Complex*;—for "My Psychology As a 'Utopian Sociologist'." Reprinted from *Utopian Essays and Practical Proposals* by Paul Goodman. Reprinted by permission of Random House, Inc.

Resistance—for "Freud's Theory of the Mind." Reprinted from *Resistance*, February 1954.

View—for "Sex and Revolution." First printed in *View* 1945, edited by Charles Henri Ford;—for "Eros, or The Drawing of the Bow." First printed in *View* 1946, edited by Charles Henri Ford.

Contents

III.
MODERN PSYCHOPATHOLOGY

IV.
WRITERS AND WRITING

V.
NOTES OF SELF-ANALYSIS

VI.
WHAT IS MAN?

Preface

This selection attempts to bring together Paul Goodman's best and most characteristic thought, from among the hundreds of things he wrote over a long and prolific career. Before the decade of his fame much of his writing was published in out of the way places and went unnoticed; even some of the more celebrated essays have been out of print since their first appearance. Although he rescued two or three volumes of miscellaneous pieces during his lifetime, they represented what he had on hand more than any retrospective view. This is the first attempt to collect his work systematically.

Goodman's favorite genre was the occasional poem. In prose too he always kept his eye on the present moment ("the kind of books these are, you're talking about the cases which are in *The New York Times,* no?"), so it is remarkable how well his work has held up. I have made no effort to prune the texts of dated material, but aside from a few references to other contributors in a symposium, other speakers from a platform, the reader will find little to remind him that these thoughts were not written yesterday. The issues he addressed are still with us, and his radical solutions are all the more appropriate as the problems persist and multiply. This applies to his literary as well as his social criticism; they were not so different.

Since this edition is meant for use, not for the record, its priorities vary from those of the usual "standard edition." Instead of the last text corrected by the author, for example, I have picked the fullest, strongest, and most characteristic version whenever more than one exists. To preserve rather than muffle their occasions, I have chosen to handle the texts as lightly as possible, letting idiosyncrasies of time, place and manner of publication stand. The inconsistencies (some magazines changed *tho* to *though*, *thru* to *through*, others didn't) reflect the tastes of editors, easy enough to live with. For similar reasons I have not worried about the few cases where Goodman borrowed whole paragraphs from one essay to use in another; it is interesting to see what he thought bore repeating. In short, the individual essays have not been trimmed, nor the speeches tidied up, except for punctuating a few tape-recorded sessions.

For the most part I have avoided reproducing much from Goodman's famous books—*Growing Up Absurd*, *Communitas*, *Gestalt Therapy*, *The Structure of Literature*—because they are still in print and likely to be widely available for a long time to come. Moreover, although readily excerpted, these books have a certain integrity and are best *read through*. Rather than a sampling of classics, I have striven after some sense of the range and development of his thought over several decades, with emphasis on the way he lived the intellectual life—his commitment to ideas. Whenever it has been possible, I have chosen writings that give a personal turn to the issues; and some selections have been included because you can hear Goodman's voice there, still sounding with his lively idiom.

For their suggestions and counsel I thank my fellow literary executors Sally Goodman, George Dennison, and Jason Epstein. Others too have been invaluable sounding boards for me as I wrote the introduction, especially Susan Goodman, Isadore From, Lore Perls, John Dings, Neil Hertz, and Ruth Perry. Maurice and Charlotte Sagoff made reading proof a pleasure, and Chuck Hamilton has proved what an advantage it can be to have a publisher who is an enthusiast.

T.S.

Introduction

When Freud died on September 23, 1939, Goodman wrote: "Herewith to many prose-works I prefix *In Memoriam Sigmund Freud*: not to rob the dead, and in love." Even more than Aristotle and Kant, the other heroes of intellect in his pantheon, Freud was his teacher and inspiration. His novels and stories could not have been written before psychoanalysis; his social criticism was a "psychopathology of everyday life," his "utopian essays" were a handbook of therapeutic technique.

Long before he took any professional interest in psychotherapy, Goodman was convinced that life-problems must be solved in the same way that art-problems are solved. What Freud taught him was that art and life are grounded in the same human nature, and he gave him a language to talk about it. "As a writer I do not 'apply' the findings of psychology; but I write as I experience, and I have been brought up to experience 'psychologically.' "

"Experiencing 'psychologically' " could be carried to astonishing lengths. I remember him saying once, to my puzzlement, that he used to masturbate with *The Interpretation of Dreams* open in front of him:

"What!?...Oh, you mean the case histories, a kind of voyeurism—"

"No, no, the ideas!" he said with that gleeful leer he had (age 12), "the ideas made me hot!"

At first I didn't believe him, but he told others the same story, it has to be taken seriously. "Dreams are the royal road to the unconscious"—ideas like that literally made his cock rise.

It is possible to say this more decorously—to wit, "the idea of the unconscious set fire to his imagination"—but we will never understand Goodman's power as a psychologist if we begin by making him palatable to those he wanted to shock. No doubt he liked being outrageous too much, but most of all he simply meant to look the facts in the face, and to rejoice in them if he could. And precisely what was there to be ashamed of?

The trouble with Freud was that *he* wanted to smooth over some of the embarrassing facts, even though it was he who had first brought them to light. Consider, for example, this passage from *The Problem of Anxiety*:

The separation of the ego from the id seems justifiable, is indeed forced upon us by certain findings. Yet on the other hand the ego is identical with the id, is only a specially differentiated portion of it. If in our thinking we contrast this portion with the whole, or if an actual disjunction of the two has come about, then the weakness of this ego becomes apparent. If, however, the ego remains one with the id and indistinguishable from it, then it is its strength that is apparent.

Goodman valued this insight as one of Freud's most important contributions to the theory of self, and he used this passage to begin his "war novel," *The State of Nature,* in which he argues that the lapse into the Hobbesian universe had been long prepared by the social order that celebrated the ego alone and repressed the id. Following Freud, Goodman's view was that "id" and "ego" was a false dichotomy, which led to the drying up of the well of spontaneity, the loss of instinctual powers, the loosening of fraternal bonds.

But Freud feared his own insight, according to Goodman, and could not accept its consequences. Only in childhood and in art was Freud ready to trust impulse; in the rest of life the instincts needed to be governed and sublimated. Civilization depended on it. Goodman imagined him saying, "At least the present system gives them such an outlet for their aggressive instincts that they do not destroy each other totally." *But,* Goodman goes on, "They were *already* fighting the war, organized in the system to destroy each other totally." Therefore Freud found it necessary to discover the "death-wish"; this was facing the facts too late, when there was no longer any choice but despair. Better to embrace our animal nature as the source of our strength, not as what we are reduced to.

Goodman had read Freud early, in high school and his first years at City College, and he continued to read widely in psychoanalytic theory all through the Thirties—Otto Rank, George Groddeck, Karl Abraham, Harry Stack Sullivan. By the time of the war the direction of his own psychoanalytic thought was clear, so that the discovery of the writings of Wilhelm Reich was not so much a turning point as a moment of self-recognition in his career. Most of all he found in Reich the confirmation of his own life-style, the choice he had made somewhere along the way to live by consulting his deepest impulse and following wherever it led. Freud, as he read him, justified this practice, but Reich came closer to making a science of it.

Goodman was perhaps the first of the New York intellectuals to "discover" Reich, whose *Function of the Orgasm* had been scarcely noticed when it was published by the Orgone Institute Press in 1942. Although Reich was living in New York by this time, he was unknown outside analytic circles. Goodman stumbled onto him in late 1944 when he reviewed A.S. Neill's *The Problem Teacher* for the *New Republic.* During the next few months two of Reich's major works appeared, *The Sexual Revolution* and *Character Analysis,* while a third, *The Mass Psychology of Fascism,* was circulating in proof and scheduled for the following year. These Goodman immediately read, along with *The Function of the Orgasm* and back issues of the *Journal of Sex Economy.*

Goodman had just finished writing *Communitas* with his brother Percival, and was in the middle of *The May Pamphlet,* his anarchist manifesto. He had recently been fired from a teaching job in a small progressive school—for trying to seduce his students—and was notorious in those circles that knew him at all, as a queer and a draft-dodger. Thus Reich's emphasis on liberating the sexuality of children and adolescents, and on the relation of "orgastic potency" to political behavior, were matters of everyday concern to Goodman. He began writing psychoanalytic essays of his own, using Reich for leverage.

The most important of these was "The Political Meaning of Some Recent Revisions of Freud," which Dwight Macdonald published in *Politics*. In it he compared the two main strands of post-Freudian theory, the social psychology of Erich Fromm and Karen Horney vs. the sex-economy of Reich. The failure of radical ideology to provide a rallying point for intellectuals during the war left the field open for psychoanalysis after it, and every psychoanalytic school was busy developing its explanation of World War II. Reich appealed to Goodman and his anarchist friends (many of whom soon became Reichian patients) because he had a theory of the war, fascism, and workers' politics that seemed to mesh with their own analysis. It was certainly more attractive than the static notion of "the authoritarian personality" put forth by the other main camp. In Goodman's view Freudian revisionists like Fromm and Horney were merely preparing the way for the coming "Sociolatry," blaming everything on the pathological Nazis while they peddled their own "ideal of 'adjustment,' which means the sterilizing and hygienizing of instinct in the interests of citizenship." Only Reich seemed to see "that cure could not depend merely on talk, revival of affect, and reconsideration, but must also pass over into practical behavior, and therefore must involve a change of the social rules so as to make such curative behavior possible." This was what Goodman called "the psychology of the revolution."

His essay was immediately attacked by C. Wright Mills and Patricia Salter in a sneering reply called "The Barricade and the Bedroom," where Goodman's "concept of freedom" was reviled as "the gratification of protoplasm." True enough, he had long held opinions that justified his own pan-sexuality, but merely to accuse him of suiting his theory to his practice was no argument against either. Mills, and the Marxist left generally, regarded Goodman as an *enfant terrible,* brilliant but wildly perverse, and addicted to the vices of bourgeois individualism—personalist politics, sexual deviance, mannerist art—without even the horse-sense to enjoy the standard of living that everyone else took for granted. Even more agitated were the doctrinaire *ex*-Marxists around *Partisan Review,* who had him on their black list. In 1940 and 1941 he had been one of their fair-haired boys; now they went out of their way to attack him publicly: "But if Goodman has misread Freud, Freud has already read him correctly: on several occasions Freud expressed concern that his theory, because of the prominence given to sex, would be debased and sensationalized by intellectual adventurers and playboys." And in private, so Goodman believed, Delmore Schwartz and Phil Rahv had begun a "whispering campaign about my past."

The outcry from the guardians of the public morals merely convinced Goodman he was on the right track, according to his "touchstone for the libertarian program" in *The May Pamphlet*: "does our program involve a large number of precisely those acts and words for which persons are in fact thrown in jail?" If not quite jail, public obloquy was the next best test. And after that, censorship. In the spring of 1945 two national magazines, the *New Republic* and *Common Sense,* had asked Goodman for reviews of Reich's new books, and then refused to print them. The *New Republic* explained that "we cannot subject our readers to such opinions on your authority," and *Common Sense* would not even give him back his manuscript (he sued them in Small Claims Court, and lost). Goodman had friends on the surrealist magazine *View* who would publish "such opinions," especially since they were interdicted elsewhere, but it was not the readers of *View* who needed to be sold on *The Sexual Revolution.*

If the leftist politicos objected to the importation of sex into the revolution, the advocates of a sexual revolution were just as distressed by the anarchist politics of their noisy supporter. Finally Reich himself called Goodman up and asked him out to the laboratory in Queens, where he demanded that his work no longer be linked with these mad utopian schemes. It was giving Orgonomy a bad name. He was worried too about his friend Neill. Summerhill had enough to contend with in its (undeserved) reputation for sexual permissiveness; Reich did not want to be responsible for tarring it with the anarchist brush as well. Of course Goodman paid no attention. "Really, Dr. Reich," he said, "what is it to you if we younger folk call you an anarchist or not?"

The truth of the matter was that Goodman had begun to construct his own Reich, as he had his own Freud, out of the ideas that he needed for his growth and development. Great scientific ideas, he believed, usually amounted to taking seriously some ordinary universal phenomenon, such as dreams, or the variations in a species, or falling bodies. Reich's one great idea was to study the orgasm and its function—or rather the failure of its function. He discovered that sexual deprivation led to neurosis not merely by way of the orthodox backroads of the sick psyche—punishment, fear, repression, guilt—but directly and simply as a result of the body's misery.

Freud made room for such an etiology in his distinction between "actual-neurosis" and "psycho-neurosis," but he had never developed the theory of actual-neurosis beyond the assumption that some real deprivation lay at the heart of every psychoneurosis. Reich proposed that the "actual-anxiety" continuously fed psychoneurosis, and that the key to treatment was therefore the restoration of orgastic potency.

Everything that Goodman admired in Reich came from this primary insistence on taking into account the ways in which the body suffers, retreats, and can be freed from the fortress-prison it creates of itself. There were other things in the Reichian psychology that he accepted, for instance, the emphasis on the neurotic character instead of the neurotic symptom. He was even willing to be convinced of the metaphysics—"I hope he did discover a new form of cosmic energy accumulable in boxes!"—but Goodman was really interested only in the side of Reich that helped fill out his own views. Reichianism was the rationale for his principle, Consult Your Deepest Impulse, and also offered new means of acting on it.

Early in 1946 Goodman submitted himself to Reichian therapy with Alexander Lowen, a young trainee of Reich who, coincidentally, had gone to high school with Goodman. "Submitted" is not quite the word for it, since Lowen remembers that his patient never let go of the reins. Nonetheless Goodman claimed to have gotten a good deal out of these sessions, conducted in an unheated hotel room in Greenwich Village. Lowen's technique was fairly orthodox vegetotherapy. Reichians never wasted much time in idle talk; Goodman learned how to induce involuntary vibration or shuddering in parts of his body by putting it under stress. But in following up the images and associations brought to the surface, he led

Lowen a merry chase, and did not even tell him most of his dis-
coveries, recorded only in pages and pages of notes he showed no
one. In short, he was more or less "in training" with Lowen,
learning the Reichian language of the body, and at the same time
was secretly engaged in self-analysis.

Recalling the experience from the perspective of the late
Sixties, Goodman praised Reich's invention of "a practical Yoga in
familiar Western terms and without drugs, so that it is possible to
tune in without dropping out, without having to lose one's wits,
although of course not without conflict and suffering." He claimed
to have gotten "great benefits from it both physically and emotionally," and this after a therapy of only four or five months. A
few years later when he began his own work as a therapist, he
sometimes adapted similar techniques to Gestalt purposes.

Much as he learned from his various contacts with the
Reichians, the "psychology of the revolution" seemed somewhat
barren in the long run—suited to the needs of the moment ("Orgastically potent people will not tolerate authority or present-day
industrial forms") but not rich enough to encompass alternatives
for human nature after "instinctual liberation." Reich's approach
considered the self too much in isolation, as the "self-of-the-body"
out of the full context of family, circumstance, work, political life,
etc. In the history of psychoanalysis the obvious bias of Reich's
early work was toward greater recognition of this context, but by
1946 he was permanently sidetracked in orgonomy, a dead end for
psychotherapy whatever vast possibilities might be there for cosmic
medicine. Goodman's next step would take him beyond Reich, to
the reformulation of "self as a process of structuring the organism-environment field." This was Gestalt Therapy, about to arrive
from South Africa in the persons of Fritz and Lore Perls.

Between them the Perls had had an extremely broad training in
psychoanalysis, including some work with Reich himself, and with
the Gestalt psychologists Gelb, Wertheimer, and Kurt Goldstein.
They also knew something of Yoga and Taoism, before it became
fashionable. Lore had integrated body-awareness techniques into
her style of therapy in the late Thirties and early Forties, not under
the influence of Reich so much as out of her own experience in
eurhythmics and modern dance. Fritz Perls' first book *Ego,*

Hunger and Aggression is a good example of his eclecticism—for he borrows from all these influences—and also of his genius for collaboration, since the book resulted from Lore's work as much as his own, though her name does not appear on the title page.

By the time the Perls emigrated the Gestalt approach had become even more central in their thinking, and Fritz had a manuscript of 100 pages attempting a new formulation. Furthermore, his real flair for technique had produced a whole practicum of exercises like those sketched in the second half of *Ego, Hunger and Aggression.* He arrived in New York looking for new collaborators and already planning the establishment of his own school of psychoanalysis.

The Perls had read Goodman's articles in *Politics* while they were still in Capetown. Fritz looked him up in his cold-water flat on Ninth Avenue, and after some further acquaintance he offered him $500 to turn the manuscript into a book. They quickly saw what they needed in each other. Perls hated to write, was balked and inept at it, but was exploding with ideas. Just as he paid little attention to where his brainstorms came from, he was unconcerned as to how they might be transformed in the hands of a collaborator. He was vain and eager for reputation but free of the compulsion to leave his stamp on every insight. Goodman was also full of ideas, though of a rather different sort. Whereas Perls saw things in terms of technique and methodology, Goodman had philosophical training and powerful literary gifts that brought theoretical implications into focus. He too found it easy to work with ideas borrowed from others, especially since as a writer he always made them thoroughly his own. His idea of co-authorship, for instance in his work with his brother, was simply to discuss the subject, and then to write out his own newly informed and energized opinions. The result was shown to his collaborator, revised accordingly, and published.

The writing went smoothly enough through the fall and winter of 1949 and the spring of 1950, but without the need for frequent discussions about the book, these two inventors of Gestalt Therapy would probably have avoided one another. Perls was too much the opportunist for Goodman; Goodman too much the carping queer for Perls. By the time the book was finished they were antagonists.

Meanwhile Goodman had gone into therapy with Lore Perls, who managed to preserve her own relation to him in spite of the fluctuations in Fritz's. Since his vegetotherapy Goodman had continued to work at self-analysis, doing the Reichian exercises and writing down his dreams and free associations. His family still remembers the snorts and groans that came from the little room he used as his "office." Although not a Reichian like Lowen, his new therapist also used breathing exercises, followed the resistances in the motor armor, and concentrated on psychosomatic symptoms like sneezing, stuttering, and piles. They made some progress, but any analyst attempting work with Goodman had to face one insurmountable obstacle: he wanted to run the show. In the long run she felt her main influence on him appeared in a gradual change in his style of communication—more patient; more interested in detailed experience, less set on shocking. Soon the therapy became training therapy, and then a sort of mutual consultation. He had begun to take patients himself.

Goodman always said that his own career as a therapist merely formalized the counseling role he already filled for his friends. People kept coming to him for advice, and it seemed reasonable to be as professional as possible about the responsibility. When asked what he would charge, he replied, "What does a good electrician get?" To some observers, this was another example of Goodman's incredible arrogance: he was neither trained nor fit for such a trust, even at only $3 an hour. Of course they had in mind his politics and his sexual reputation—nor did he ever pretend to keep the analytic relation "pure" of these contaminations. It was not a priesthood or a prophetic vocation, he argued. "A man should be as compassionate and wise as he can in society, and not otherwise with his patients. If others expect him to be other tnan his ordinary self, that is their lookout."

Somewhere along here Gestalt Therapy was born. A group of therapists, more or less Fritz and Lore's circle, began to see one another regularly at their apartment, to discuss work. Fritz pronounced it an Institute, and there began the recurring debate over whether minutes should be taken. Before long there were training groups established, and a branch in Cleveland. Workshops were advertised on topics like "The Problem of 'Psychosomatic Medicine' " (Paul Weisz), "The Classroom as a Laboratory for Psycho-therapy" (Elliott Shapiro), and "The Pathology of Speech and Writing" (Goodman). Everyone agreed that Goodman was "the theorist" of the group, while Fritz was "the technician." At the monthly meetings of the Institute the two of them often clashed, but much of the time Fritz was in Miami or Los Angeles seeing to his growing empire. In any event Goodman now had a set of true peers to consult in his practice. They sent him patients, screening out the pre-psychotics and other risky cases. He seems to have been considered competent to deal with a fairly wide range of neurotics; those that he felt were too precarious he referred back to his colleagues. Some of his friends graduated from patients to trainees, a metamorphosis implicit in Gestalt therapeutics.

The book itself came out in 1951, something of a breech-birth one might say, for the publisher insisted that the "examples" of technique come before the theory—since "how-to-do-it" books were popular. An acquaintance of Fritz, Ralph Hefferline, had used Gestalt exercises in his psychology classes at Columbia, and wrote up the results for the book. Fritz was more enthusiastic about them than Goodman; as *his* techniques they seemed to prove him the ultimate author of *Gestalt Therapy,* although he had actually written none of it.

Choosing a name for the book raised unexpected difficulties. Fritz's techniques had been called "concentration therapy" in *Ego, Hunger and Aggression,* but "concentration" was no longer a key term in the theory. Lore suggested "existential therapy," but given popular associations with Sartre and Camus, that was rejected as "too nihilistic." "Gestalt Therapy" was justified, they thought, by the framework borrowed from the Frankfort psychologists—but when intermediaries sent the manuscript to Köhler, he complained that the content though "harmless" seemed "almost cheap," and not seriously connected with traditional Gestalt psychology. Once again a reluctant mentor objected to the coupling of his name with Goodman's bold re-interpretation of his work.

Goodman's attempt to convince Köhler that the name was justified reveals something about why his heroes often preferred him as an enemy. After admitting that " 'almost cheap' is harsh but not unfair" if applied to Hefferline's half of the book—which he blithely assumes is all that Köhler has read—he goes on to explain how the traditional Gestalt psychologists have achieved the main issues but "not pressed them," so that *Gestalt Therapy* is "not irrelevant to Gestalt Psychology but a contribution *in* that psychology." This cool slap in the face is immediately followed by an aside to the effect that Kurt Goldstein "continually tends to defeat himself..." etc. And as a final ingratiating remark, he explains that although the Perls both "have connections of piety with Gestalt," he himself owes his orientation to Husserl and Dewey!

Yet he *meant* to be ingratiating, and in the last sentence of all he suddenly drops the polemic: "Personally, let me thank you for the formative influence of your books on me when I was a young man." This is certainly better than his "Really Dr. Reich..." five years earlier, but it came to the same thing. Goodman's pieties never distanced him from their objects. He really believed the doctrine of Gestalt Therapy, that growth "requires destroying the existing form to its assimilable elements, whether it be food, a lecture, a father's influence."

Of course Goodman knew perfectly well that the important comparison was not to Gestalt psychology anyway; the true lineage was "Charcot to Freud, Freud to Reich, and so forth." Gestalt Therapy was intended to take its place in this tradition by supplanting Freud and Reich. That was what Goodman meant in his letter to Köhler when he had the nerve to predict that "the traditional Gestalt Psychology will get more profit from our use of that language than our book will get from being called Gestalt Therapy."

Goodman argued the advantages of Gestalt Therapy in many places. Perhaps the most interesting comparison of its theories and methods to those of Freud and Reich is to be found in his lecture notes for training sessions that he gave under Institute auspices, for there he had his most important audience, the potential destroyers and assimilators of his own contributions. Here is a reconstruction of that overview:

Traditional Freudian symptom-analysis, especially as practised in 1950, had as its goal the sort of self-knowledge that would allow the patient to live happily adjusted to the social norms; its technique was to interpret whatever material the patient brought to the analysis; its only injunction was Don't Censor; one by one the neurotic symptoms were traced back to childhood and exorcised, leaving the mature adult ready to take his place in society, with all his impulses under control.

Reichian character-analysis rejected the social norms as themselves neurotic, and in their place posited an ideal of animal health. Instead of working with "what comes up," the Reichian therapist "attacked the resistances" (which represented the neurotic society's outposts in the patient's character); the rule was no longer Don't Censor, for the object was to "break the censorship" altogether, destroy the neurotic character structure, and recover the childhood spontaneity. Instead of *Know Yourself* the slogan was *Be Yourself.*

The problem with Reichian therapy was that it *did* break through to the underlying animal, without giving the patient anything to hold onto in the whirlpool of instinctual rebirth. The body was brought to life like Frankenstein's monster, without a world to inhabit or a world-view to give it coherence and direction. George Dennison used to say he could spot Reichian patients on the street, not blooming so much as bursting with animal health, and frowning anxiously at the impending explosion. The emphasis on "science" and laboratory experiment among the Reichians was supposed to identify a fundamental human nature, so that there would be some theory of health and some criterion for cure, but man is more than his physiology, as the Freudians tried to tell them. If *Know Yourself* meant adjusting to society, *Be Yourself* meant giving up that part of the self which is social; it was a way of glorying in powers not actually realizable in the world.

Gestalt Therapy rejected both approaches, since each lacked what the other had. The problem of the criteria for health (and accordingly the question of technique—what to work on) was solved by reformulating it. If neither social norms nor physiological fact could provide the grounds, then therapy would have to proceed on some new basis.

The impasse could be formulated as follows: either one chooses to live by the social norms, and thereby becomes a "well-adjusted person," or one turns his back on society and cultivates his own animal health, thereby becoming a kind of wild bear living in a state of nature. Ever since the beginning of World War II Goodman had considered himself in precisely this dilemma, and *Gestalt Therapy* was not the only book, nor psychoanalysis the only method through which he sought a solution. In *The Dead of Spring* for instance, volume three of *The Empire City*, written just before *Gestalt Therapy*, Goodman imagines a kind of paradigm case that clearly has the weight of psychoanalytic theory as well as personal experience behind it. His hero Horatio Alger, having fallen in love, is suddenly whisked off like K in *The Trial*, to face mysterious charges of treason—non-participation in the social order. The D.A. poses the dilemma which lies at the heart of the case: "If one conforms to our society, he becomes sick in certain ways. (I grant it, who can deny it?) But if he does *not* conform, he becomes demented, because ours is the only society that there is. *That* is the Dilemma."

Horatio's answer was "existential" in the way that Gestalt Therapy recommended: "Prosecutor, you present to this court a powerful, an irrefragable proof that I am demented, distorted and destructive. But I present a wonderful fact that makes your argument wither away. Here I am, scarred with such and such scars, but by ordinary grace, no doing of mine, I am in love."

Horatio's defense is not an appeal to Orgastic Potency, the healthy animal appetite that was the measure for the Reichians, nor to Romantic Love, the talisman of novel-readers, nor to the Caritas of Christian Humanism. Rather the source of his power is revealed as Eros ("hilarious Archer" the judge calls him at the end of this scene—Horatio: Horace: Eros are his names).

For Goodman, Eros was the symbol of the power of nature alive in us all. "*Natura sanat,*" Horatio explains, "Nature heals. What is needed from us is to stand out of the way, to allow a little freedom for the regenerative forces (no forces of ours), and in heaven's name, an abeyance, an abeyance of the pathological pressure." Horatio has been vouchsafed the grace to fall in love because his youth has been spent in freedom, a renegade from the sick society that the others conform to. He understands how to consult his deepest impulse. But just because he has avoided the schools, jobs, army, and jails that society has prepared for him does not mean that he has entirely abandoned society. In fact he grows up in the streets, learned to read from the headlines on the newsstands, he even had a job for a while, running a power drill, and he has made it his business, as Goodman advised in one of his political essays, "to live in present society as if it were a natural society."

Eros was nothing but the self come vividly to life, not the self as distinguished from society, not the ego as distinguished from the id, but the self as the on-going creative interplay of the organism and its total environment, including society. In Gestalt terms, the locus of Eros was the "contact boundary" of organism and environment. A whole set of alternatives to Freudian and Reichian therapy followed: the aim was neither adjustment to the social norms nor release of the animal instincts, but continuous integration of the two. There could not be any basic incompatibility between the instinctual and the social, for they were the givens of human existence. But if there was a bad fit, it was the social norms that ought to be looked to first, for they were at the further remove from nature.

It may now be seen why it didn't matter to the Gestalt Therapists that one could not rely on any particular theory of society or of instinct to define health; they had supplied an autonomous criterion, independent of any such theories, in the quality of the Gestalt itself, the field of organism/environment contact: "it has specific observable properties of brightness, clarity unity, fascination, grace, vigor, release, etc." Ideally every Gestalt would resolve itself into a vivid figure perceived against an "empty" background, not as a matter of self-conscious awareness but of absorbed activity. Thus, for example, "the classic therapeutic maxim is: 'The healthy man feels his emotions, the neurotic feels his body.' " This is the meaning of Horatio's defense at his trial in *The Dead of Spring*: in spite of his failure to conform to the social norms, he can point to an autonomous criterion for his own health—he is in love.

Obviously this is a very different sort of theoretical foundation for psychotherapy than Freud or Reich sought. Gestalt Therapists agreed with Freud that the aim was creative adjustment—but to what norms?—and with Reich as to the release of the lively instincts—but according to whose notion of human nature? Their answer was both very radical and very conservative. It was radical in that it abandoned theories of society and human nature in favor of ad hoc assessments of the quality of life in the patient's present moment (consult your deepest impulse). It was conservative in that it assumed that the job of the therapist (and patient) was "to stand out of the way." The best thing to do was the most conservative of all, nothing—let the organism regulate itself. How literally they took these notions varied with the situation—Goodman certainly had his theories of society and human nature, as well as his views of how best to treat individual cases—but the overall bias of their thinking is what counts here.

This was both a Taoist and an anarchist psychotherapy, and it should be clear by now that Gestalt terminology is not really crucial to its chief insight, the emphasis on context, "the irreducible unity of the socio-cultural, animal, and physical field in every concrete experience." Other terminologies would do as well, and the writings of Kropotkin and Lao-tse—and among psychoanalysts especially Otto Rank—were as important to Gestalt Therapy as those of Köhler and his colleagues.

It is still more difficult finally to assess the contributions of Perls and Goodman to this amalgam. If their previous histories tell us something about how their paths happened to cross, their subsequent careers reveal more of what they had at stake in their collaboration. Both became famous, Perls as a therapist and guru of the here-and-now, Goodman as a social critic and Dutch uncle to the youth movement. Curiously, of the two Goodman remained more faithful to the truths they worked out together, even though he no longer practised therapy or wrote much on the subject after 1960. Perls went from institute to institute, and if he did not totally renounce Gestalt Therapy, certainly he left it far behind in his frenzied adoption of new techniques and technologies—T-groups and sensitivity training, "the hot seat," "the empty seat," "It-be-coming-I," "never say 'should,'" and so on. Goodman on the other hand never revised the basic position he formulated in *Gestalt Therapy,* and in fact much of his later work may be taken simply as his attempt to be a therapist-at-large, exploring public ways and means of integrating the social norms and the animal instincts—

sometimes by suggesting what he liked to call "practical proposals" for new social arrangements (just as he liked to fix up his patients with jobs, dates, apartments), but more often simply calling on people to stand out of the way and let nature take its course. *Natura sanat non medicus.*

Taylor Stoehr

First thru the blooming fields of hell, among
the colored dreams, gay jokes, and gorgeous
mistakes, our guide had conducted us,
to where desire the dragon of my song
was flaming in his nether parts and tongue;
next were we exploring hideous
wastes of heaven, by salty pools of loss,
spiny anxieties, and gulphs of wrong,
even to the secret sphinx, the wish for death:
and here we halted with abated breath
—when suddenly dead, for all our hopes and fears,
is our guide across the air and deep:
this morning a surprise of mournful tears,
a friendly dream now I am asleep.

I

FREUD
AND
THE
GOLDEN
AGE

The
Father
of
the
Psychoanalytic
Movement

I.

"*T*he heavy burden," said Freud, "the heavy burden of psychoanalysis."

To a father a child is sometimes a heavy burden. Nevertheless he bears it and it rarely becomes too heavy. For the first blow of fatherhood is the hardest, when the helpless infancy is reborn also within the heart. After that is but the confirmation of the initial agreement to make all concessions. The father does not break down under the burden but simply wears himself out. If the child rebels, the burden is not heavier but merely harder to manage, like a bulkier box with the same contents.

But on the contrary! if the child does not rebel but precisely fulfills his father's will for him, then indeed the burden is heavier to bear, for the strength of the father is sapped from within. The old man would not have dared to conceive what the young one suddenly in fact does, as a matter of course, by his father's will. So he was trained.

Now further, we speak of a true thought or other gift of the spirit as a man's child; he "fathers" the thought, we say. But the analogy is a bad one. Such a gift is not a heavy burden. Rather, a man who has a true thought or a beautiful idea is borne up by strong wings. Easily he soars above the obstacles that stand in the way of other men. So easily that we often reverse the metaphor and say that the man is supported by the idea—but not as a son is supported by his father, but as an infant is lifted by a nurse, a mother: by a Muse who teaches him to speak and lifts him up with the lightness of infancy when easily one flew (otherwise dumb, helpless, and immobile).

What shall we say of our old teacher Sigmund Freud who came to speak of "the heavy burden of psychoanalysis"? He meant to say that the world, whose illness was being threatened by psychoanalysis, was resisting psychoanalysis and bent on destroying it. But this was absurd! for if this idea had spread so far and proved so strong from the beginning, why should it not—*crescit eundo*—be now stronger still? And bear up its professors on strong wings? Certainly when Freud was a young man, starting out, he would not have said, "The heavy burden of psychoanalysis."

Must we not say that our teacher was under the delusion that he was the father of psychoanalysis? (And truly, if any man could ever be called the father of an idea, Freud was the father of psychoanalysis.) That it was precisely because the child was following the father's will for him that the burden was becoming so heavy. In all directions the young ones were in fact doing, as a matter of course, by their father's will (so they were trained) what the old man did not dare to conceive.

What thought did he commit against his own father that he was thus constrained to assume the role of a grieving father? We know that his father said, "You will not come to anything"; then he said defiantly, "I *shall* come to something!"—until the helpless infancy began to be reborn also in his own heart.

No, what *withdrawal* did he feel toward his mother that he was ever unable, like a light infant, to be easily and joyously uplifted by such a smiling Muse?—and if ever a man could be said to be inspired by a Muse, Freud was inspired by psychoanalysis.

"The heavy burden of psychoanalysis"! Obviously we must distinguish between the idea of psychoanalysis and the psychoanalytic movement that consisted of congresses, publications, and the fight for recognition in the universities and asylums. It was the psychoanalytic movement that was the heavy burden. Yes, in these congresses and publications we know well that he was a loving father. Attentive, patient, helpful, encouraging; following the discussion in every detail and proudly summarizing what the boys had done; not without an ironic correction and even an occasional brusque reproof. This was a father! the father of the psycho-analytic movement—who overprotected the psychoanalytic move-ment—and did not break down under the burden but simply wore himself out.

In congresses and publications. Where, meantime, was the idea of psychoanalysis? It was in the needful patients, in the deep thoughts of ill souls, stammering their distress, their secrets, wounds. It was in the wounds and the ever-productive causes of nature. It was from the wounds of mankind, from discontent and war, and the productive forces in the soul, that sprang alive the idea of psychoanalysis. From dreams. Was Freud the father of these wounds and dreams?

On the contrary, he was a naturalist. And as we are told of Darwin that he sat for three hours with staring eyes while the bee visited the flower, so we may easily think of Freud, the attention crowding into his ears, listening to the voices of the wounds. Not a father, not a teacher, but a pupil and a child.

And as with Darwin, with Aristotle, and the others of the well-behaved observers of nature, one is not surprised that Freud also insensibly finds himself borne up by strong wings, easily, light as infancy. Then he is our guide through hell and heaven, through the fields of vivid dreams and flaming desire, by the salt pools of loss, to the sphinx of death. While he is attentive to the voices of the wounds. Is this "the heavy burden of psychoanalysis"? Also, while the physician heals. Also, bringing liberty and free conscience to all mankind—especially if we resist it! for he knows that the resistance is the way of the cure. Is this "the heavy burden of psychoanalysis"?

But if suddenly (the story goes) Freud, the Professor Extra-ordinary, this naturalist, burst out of the room and cried, *"Warum soll ich solchen Schweinerei aufhören?—why must I listen to such piggishness?"*!

Ah, *then* there is a heavy burden of psychoanalysis! (If true, is not this a revealing anecdote?)

Whipped, as by a scourge, to return to these wounds—to sniff this need; resisting it like the rest, and *still* his attention crowding into his lewd ears. (Many passages confirm this hypothesis.)

Making *himself* a heavy burden, when the mother tries to lift him up. Vertigo and vomiting. Ashamed to give himself to this ease.

Imitating the sobriety of his father and nevertheless maintaining a stoical calm and not crying out, but dutifully accepting the kiss. (As he has often seen it dutifully given and accepted in bourgeois homes.)

Meantime, he was the *first* one, and had to analyze himself. (He himself was one of his needful patients.) Against what could his resistance burn if not against psychoanalysis?

The father of the psychoanalytic movement!

Will not the child, in turn, make the burden heavier? not by rebelling, but on the contrary precisely by conforming to the father's will for him—doing as a matter of course what the old man did not dare to conceive. (So he was trained.) To try to liberate the war-sick discontented world. To say, *as a matter of course,* and not with sweat on the forehead, "It is highly instructive to learn something of the intensively tilled soil from which our virtues proudly emerge."

How much do we not owe to our dear dear friend and teacher that we can say it as a matter of course! What courage he had! What sadness he bore! *Therefore* let us not too feel guilty in turn, but make of it a brotherly festival.

(I for my part have only pleasure in it, if borne up by the strong wings of speech I can pay my debt to him by a memorial exclamation.)

No no, let us assume, what is certainly the case, that Freud too, attentively listening like a sage naturalist—like a cat, first cocking his ear in a new direction, then turning his head—he too wore a little smile; then he held his breath; then drew deep new breaths and even joyously laughed.

It was only when he came before the public, the psychoanalytic movement, before the congresses and in the publications, and he adjusted his hat and his tie, that suddenly his heavy heart smote him—for our sakes, as he thought! that we, not borne up by strong wings, must nevertheless put up with him, with it. With "the heavy burden of psychoanalysis."

Publicly one did not joke about it; privately there was a good

deal of laughter at the humorous impasses and witty improvisa-
tions. The excitement of being on the right track—yet making it up
out of the whole cloth as one went along. Yet it was necessary to
wear a hat and tie just as if psychoanalysis were not something
childish, just starting out, and much of it no doubt gibberish. What
humbug! "The heavy burden of psychoanalysis"!

Come, old teacher, do not feel so conscience-stricken before
your young friends. You with your "heavy burden of psychoanalysis"!

Don't joke. Our teacher is sad. The *fact* is, the simple fact,
that our teacher has grown very old. "The heavy burden of psychoanalysis"—To an old man *everything* is a heavy burden. I am
ashamed. How unbecoming it is for mere boys to scoff at gray
hairs. Rather say, Thanks! thanks—father! you *great* man: making
ourselves little boys in order that we may see him loom so huge. In
order to be lightly picked up.

He raises us high in the air: See!

How far one can see!

Is not the old man himself renewed, as Abraham, a hundred
years of age, had a second childhood in little Laughter? Where in
this picture is "the heavy burden of psychoanalysis"?

II. (*SEPTEMBER 24, 1939*)

Herewith to many prose-works I prefix *In Memoriam Sigmund Freud:* not to rob the dead, and in love.

The friendly man, our general friend, is dead. Now without a
possible addition, in books we read his careful conjectures, first
persuasive to the heart surprised, then recognized for even very
true. He proved freedom and good conscience to all men (most to
those who say the contrary but will be freed tomorrow). First he
explored the flowery fields of hell, then the fierce deserts of
heaven. An unfinished enterprise. His achievement is to be
achieved.

The donkeys braying as he went his way, I'll never name and
mar with sarcasm the sorrow for our dead companion.

III.

"I shall not publish this essay," wrote the old man in the preface to *Moses and Monotheistic Religion,* "but that need not hinder me from writing it.

"The more so," he went on to say, "since it was already written once before and thus only needs *re*writing."

This is by the author of *Symptoms, Inhibition, and Anxiety.* Is it not high comedy? "The more so since it is already written, and thus only needs rewriting!"

(To be sure, he did publish the essay.)

And the reason he would not publish the essay was that—it might offend (guess who?)—the Roman Catholic Church of Austria! This is by the author of *The Future of an Illusion.*

And then, says he, the Roman Church might—withdraw its support from—the psychoanalytic movement!

It is really necessary to put a dash of ironic anticipation before every phrase in these delicious remarks. This is by the author of *The Interpretation of Dreams.*

And the reason that he could publish the essay after all was that the Roman Catholic Church of Austria proved to be—a broken reed. This is by the author of *On Wit and its Relation to the Unconscious!*

Shame!

Meantime all the world, both west and east, had long been violently ill with the spreading war—though not yet so ill as it was still going to be.

Then some of the young men stormed to the old one and said: We must go down into the streets. The people are ill not in their thousands who come for treatment, but in their hundreds of millions who are about to tear the world apart.

Then Freud said: "At least the present system gives them such an outlet for their aggressive instincts that they do not destroy each other totally." They were *already* fighting the war, organized in the system to destroy each other totally.

"There is a wish to die," he said, meaning especially by this, I think, that *he* wished to die.

"Either you are totally wrong," he said, "or you alone must

bear the heavy burden of psychoanalysis!"

So. A man begins quietly, all unsuspecting perhaps, in a neat office with a few patients. Listening attentively to the voices of their wounds, he is all insensibly touched by the natural things that exist.

Next moment he is a free knight dubbed, wildly marauding (as it seems). On every side he sees monsters with the complacent faces of orderliness, purity, godliness, accumulation that are only masks for the savage resentment of sore wounds. But because he has come to admit the existence of something that indeed exists, he is no longer impressed by the things that do not exist. If there are sore wounds, he, noblesse oblige, will cure them; and he comes all gently, like a raging tempest, as it seems. In the twinkling of a few years, compared with the secular period of the institutions, an endless career lightens before him—a flash of lightning on the blue plain—to free his sisters and brothers! He has found a Royal Road to go into deep places. Muses smile him on. He is the champion of the freedom of the children. There are shouts that he is a black magician and he has invented the nature of children! "Only a Jew has such dreams!" Are not such shouts so many goads to the free knight, to lop more joyously away at the hideous growths that do not exist and listening attentively to the voices of the wounds, to speak a word that heals as it violates?

Meantime (here is the comedy) our knight has become the Father of the Psychoanalytic Movement. He is famous in congresses for his encouraging summations of what his boys have accomplished, not without an ironic correction and even an occasional brusque reproof. There are schemes for—official recognition. (It is really necessary to begin to insert dashes of sarcastic anticipation.) He is not so eager for the young men to campaign on their own, and be hurt, and hurt each other.

The question is, whether it is possible to be the champion of the freedom of children and the father of the psychoanalytic movement? That is, whether it is possible to be a free knight and a father at all?

It seems to me that Father Abraham was a knightly father. Would any one deny that he was a good father?

"I shall not publish this essay. To be sure that need not hinder me from writing it.'' The knight is now laying round him within the four walls of his private study.

"The more so since it is already written and thus only needs *re*writing.'' Rewriting, with the addition of some delicious prefatory notes. This is by the author of *On Wit and its Relation to the Unconscious.*

Father! pleaded some of the young men, lend *your* influence to help us when we go down into the streets.

"Either you are totally wrong," he cried, "or you alone must bear the heavy burden of psychoanalysis.''

So. Suddenly wherever one turns, to take a single step, one finds that the freedom and good conscience of mankind, and the joy of the children, have become—a heavy burden. It is not true that the thick-walled institutions do not exist. They exist! Even the Roman Catholic Church of Austria 1938 can be said to exist somewhat, if one exerts only a gentle kind of pressure. Perhaps the brothers and sisters can find refuge there.

(How becoming it is to scoff at the old man!)

Shame!

Shame not on Freud, but shame on the world for bringing our old teacher to this confusion.

The father of the psychoanalytic movement was overprotective toward the psychoanalytic movement. Then just because as a matter of course (so they were trained), some of the young men went down into the streets, he no longer even dared to conceive of it.

IV.

(The question, whether it is possible to be a free knight and a father at all.)

Now Abraham was a knightly father.

It is not likely that his boy, the Laughter of his old age, was a heavy burden to him. He did not feel guilty to murder Isaac because this was not his secret wish. Abraham was not overprotective toward Isaac because he did not wish to murder him, because Isaac was not a heavy burden to him.

On the contrary, father of the psychoanalytic movement! it is easy, in a knightly way, to murder one's child. The example of it is Abraham. All one need to do is to commit, step by step, dividing the steps and subdividing the divisions, the acts leading up to the murder. Thus, when God said: "Take now thine only son Isaac, whom thou lovest, and get thee into the land of Moriah, and offer him there for a burnt-offering on one of the mountains I shall tell thee of"—what did Abraham do first?—It says: "He arose early in the morning."

"He arose early in the morning and saddled his ass, and took two of his young men and Isaac his son; and he cleaved the wood for the burnt-offering, and rose up, and went."

The method by which it is easy, in a knightly way, to murder one's child who is not a heavy burden (one is not over-protective to him): all one need do is to commit the previous act and before that the act previously to that. Thus, "he arose early in the morning": that is to say, he got out of bed, washed, and dressed. That is to say, he awoke. He opened his eyes, first one eye, then the other—and saw that it was early in the morning.

God said, "Abraham!"

And he said, "Here am I."

But if the child is a heavy burden, then the last act burns too vividly before the mind and one cannot take step by step; on the contrary, then one is overprotective and inhibits the previous steps.

It is not the case, when there is a conflict of wishes, that one can will both of them at the same time. This is impossible. But on the contrary, it is easy, in a knightly way, freely, as a matter of course (so one has been trained) to take each step in turn; that is to say, to bring vividly before one's mind the idea of the next step, and thus to do it. This is called willing to do it.

"On the third day Abraham lifted up his eyes and saw the place afar off." That is to say, first he lifted up his eyes, which were presumably a heavy burden, then he saw the place. His eyes were downcast on the ground; then he brought vividly before his mind the idea of lifting up his eyes, *then* he lifted up his eyes, and *then* he saw the place. Is not this easy to do, in a free and knightly way, to think that it is about time that I brought vividly to mind the idea of lifting up my eyes?

"And Abraham said to his young men, 'Abide ye here with the

ass, and I and the lad will go yonder.' " See! what a wonderful advantage there is in starting out with three young men! What is extraordinary about it, to go on a trip with three young men? To have some one with, to converse on the way. Avoiding embarrassing silences. For the most part the boys talk to each other. Then afterwards, when the time comes, it is not hard to distinguish from the three the one. This is how to take each step in turn and eventually to murder one's only child. This is called willing to do it.

The boys talked about the things that were of interest to the boys, mainly sports and hunting. The old man concentrated on bringing vividly before his mind the idea of the next step. The ass bore the load of wood. We can judge by this that it was a treeless country with a bare profile of hills.

But *first* it was necessary to awake early in the morning. That is, to bring before one's mind vividly—presumably in the midst of some *other* dream—the idea of opening one's eyes, first one eye, then the other, and seeing that it is early in the morning.

"Abraham!"

"Here am I!"

This is the moment in the other dream that the father presents vividly to his mind the idea it is about time to present vividly to his mind the idea of opening an eye.

"Abraham took the wood for the burnt-offering and laid it upon Isaac his son; and he took in his hand the fire and the knife, and they went both of them together."

Abraham looked at his hand. It was empty. Then he presented vividly to his mind the idea of the knife being in his hand. Thus (in a flash!) he took it. This is easy! This is called willing to do it.

"Father!"

"Here am I, my son."

(Certainly, here he was! Was not this moment too the end result of the long process of time? Each moment had led easily, step by step, up to this step of climbing the mountain step by step.)

"Behold the fire and the wood; but where is the lamb for a burnt-offering?"

"God will provide Himself the lamb for a burnt-offering!"

The boy was not a knightly father! he found it hard to go just step by step, furthermore carrying a heavy load up the mountain. (Presumably he was trained obediently to carry such a load.) But

Abraham was a free knight; he committed it step by step and refused vividly to bring before his mind the idea of anything but the next step, for instance the idea of murdering his only son. Thus, a man is told that he may think of anything in the world except the idea "Q": the ordinary man finds this impossible to do; but if he would give himself freely to the next step, then it is easy to do—in a flash! This is refusing vividly! by giving oneself simply to the next step. It is the psychological method of what is called acting by faith.

Thus, it was easy to write the essay; why was it necessary to bring vividly to mind the idea of publishing it? The more so since it was already written and only needed *re*writing. One did not start in the first place with the idea of writing an offensive essay. But he was the author of *The Future of an Illusion,* and one offensive essay led to another. And the previous act was writing *Totem and Taboo,* a mere anthropological speculation: what was there offensive in that?

There was nothing offensive in bringing vividly to mind the idea of letting one's attention crowd into the ears, to listen to the voices of the wounds; and then—in a flash!—hearing them. This is called willing to do it. To *publish* the essay! To *lend* one's authority to the young men to go down into the streets. To go down into the streets! to liberate the war-sick world—not, at that time, yet *so* sick! Where in this picture is "the heavy burden of psychoanalysis"? But the father of the psychoanalytic movement overprotected the psychoanalytic movement.

Abraham was a knightly father. He did not feel guilty to murder Isaac because this was not his secret wish. He vividly refused to bring before his mind the idea of murdering him, because in a free and knightly way he was willing to take step by step. Borne up by the strong wings of each step by step. "God will provide Himself the lamb for a burnt-offering!"

"And they came to the place that God had told him of. And Abraham built an altar there and laid the wood in order, and bound Isaac his son, and laid him on the altar upon the wood.

"And Abraham stretched forth his hand, and took the knife to slay his son."

He stretched forth his hand, then he took the knife.

He looked at his hand. It was empty. Vividly he presented to his mind the idea of the knife's being in his hand. In a flash the knife was in his hand!

He noticed that his arm was lying by his side, and he vividly brought to mind the idea of stretching forth his hand. That is to say, he vividly brought to mind the idea of a tension in the muscles of his shoulder, first in one muscle, then in another.

That is, first one took a deep breath.

(This is called willing to do it and acting by faith. It is easy to do it, in a fatherly and knightly way, borne up by the strong wings of each act by act, if one commits first the previous act and before that the act previous to that.)

Is not each one of these acts also the end result of the long process of time? *Therefore* one can say, *"Here* am I."

So, in a flash!—for we must not think that just because it is possible to divide the knightly action and to subdivide the subdivisions, that all of it does not happen in a flash! In a flash awaking early in the morning! In a flash one goes down into the streets! In a flash freeing the children! In a flash we shall one day liberate our war-sick world.

"He *took* the knife to slay his son.

"And the Angel of the Lord called to him out of heaven and said, 'Abraham.'

"And he said, 'Here am I.' "

Certainly here he was. But I do not think that Father Abraham lifted his eyes to see where the voice was coming from. I think that his eyes were blinded with free, bitter, knightly, fatherly guiltless tears.

" 'Lay not thy hand upon the lad, neither do thou anything to him.' "

Then, "Abraham lifted up his eyes, and looked, and behold behind him a ram caught in the thicket by his horns."

That is to say, first he turned his head and then cleared his eyes (his attention was not crowding into his eyes); then he looked or allowed himself to see; then there was something to see that seized on his attention, *behold!* Shall we not say that his attention crowded into his eyes—away from his memory and other vivid ideas? But before this he was not in any haste to see, but that he slowly lifted his eyes?

Not with any feeling of guilt or as if expecting a reproof—but that it was no longer easy to take any step, to bring vividly before one's mind any idea at all.

(Now it must come from outside. One is no longer willing to do it.)

That to an old man everything is a heavy burden.

The question is, whether it is possible to be a free knight and an old man at all.

(It seems to me that Nestor was a knightly old man. He did not eye himself according to an unvarying standard.)

"And Abraham called the name of that place Jehovahjirah, as it is said to this day: In the mount where the Lord is seen."

V. SEPTEMBER 25, 1939

First thru the blooming fields of hell, among
the colored dreams, gay jokes, and gorgeous
mistakes, our guide had conducted us,
to where desire the dragon of my song
was flaming in his nether parts and tongue;
next were we exploring hideous
wastes of heaven, by salty pools of loss,
spiny anxieties, and gulphs of wrong,
even to the secret sphinx, the wish for death:
and here we halted with abated breath
—when suddenly dead, for all our hopes and fears,
is our guide across the air and deep:
this morning a surprise of mournful tears,
a friendly dream now I am asleep.

VI.

*"The aged lion, well on his way to being
a couch cover."* (Quoted by Hanns Sachs)

Freud was the first of the psychoanalysts and therefore had to analyze himself.

Resisting the analysis, he had no one to vent his hate on but himself.

Therefore Freud said, "The heavy burden of psychoanalysis."[1]

In this continuing analysis, that lasted too long, finally he came upon the wish to die.

Always eying himself! as if a man could never close his eyes.

He said, *"Ich kann mich nicht acht Stunden täglich anstarren lassen*—I can't let myself be stared at eight hours a day!" and he sat where his patients, his other patients, could not see him. Meantime he devised methods to eye himself also while he was asleep.

But always eying himself according to an unvarying standard, even when he became ill, old, and tired. After a while one cannot any more and comes to speak of "The diminishing of the creative powers that accompanies old age."

Every other person in analysis can burn with resentment against a son of the psychoanalytic movement and ultimately against the father of the psychoanalytic movement. The resentment is burnt out.

Then one dreams at one's ease, no need to watch out, some one else is watching it.

Soon one laughs and (living backwards) learns to smile.

But if Freud did not watch out for himself, who would watch out? His resentment was therefore not burnt out.

"These fools!" he said of his patients. (He himself was one of his patients.)

"Why must I always listen to such piggishness!" said Freud. "The heavy burden of psychoanalysis," he said. "These fools! I can't let myself be stared at for eight hours every day."

Eying himself for twenty-four hours a day for a quarter of a century; finally he saw there—the wish to die. When sleepiness began to overwhelm the eye of judgment, would not this be interpreted (by the eye of judgment) as the wish to die? To close one's eyes.

To relinquish the heavy burden of psychoanalysis.

All the same it is a logical contradiction to say "I wish to die." For the ground of any wish at all is the existence of the desires that express themselves in the wish; their existence cannot be the ground

[1] This excellent reason was suggested to me by Dr. Erich Kraft.

of their non-existence. Further, it is impossible to have a wish without an image, but one cannot imagine *oneself* as dead.

We must think of Freud as methodically eying himself for half a century, as a doctor does, and seeing that he had become old, ill, and tired. Or as a parent keeps an eye on a child who has a tendency to masturbate; what can the child do but get out?

It is possible that there is an universal inertia dragging all life back into matter, but this could not find expression as a wish. Perhaps what Freud meant to say was that there is a wish for a life of unconsciousness, to live *not* under the surveillance of the ego. But this is the A B C of psychoanalysis; why invent something new? To a person not eying *himself,* such a wish is by no means the wish to die, but precisely to live more freely, bringing the ego back into subordination to the instincts. (Also, this is "the strength of the ego.")

This was what Father Nestor did, when he danced with the dogs. It meant that the past with its curse was still blest. And had brought him at last to not less than he was. He did not eye himself any more; and he never had eyed himself according to an unvarying standard.

But we must think now of a man of great faculties and driving power, eying himself according to an unvarying standard (almost a public standard, with a hat and tie). He recognized by sure signs that his faculties were diminished and his power waning: was it not inevitable that he would interpret it, the sense of falling short of the measure, as the wish to die? (Also clinging to life all the harder—so that perhaps it was not apparent till the next year that he was ill.)

This is a mistaken interpretation: what one can one can; but one must not measure it according to an unvarying standard.

A new standard! no longer eying oneself, no longer rallying to the requirement.

To die without saying "I wish to die"! But "my resentment is burnt out."

Not overprotective toward the psychoanalytic movement, but to let the psychoanalytic movement go the way of the psychoanalytic movement.

Meantime the fact was that *everywhere* he looked in all the war-sick world old and tired, the *fact* was that indeed people wished to die. They had organized themselves into armies in order to carry out their wish without loneliness and guilt.

With unerring success millions have achieved their wish. In one city a million and a half. Four millions on one front, twelve millions on another. And thousands and thousands in the sea.

Every single one of these millions the object of grief and mourning. Numbers cannot dullen it.

O naturalist! here are plenty of wounds; what do their voices say?

"The Father of the Psychoanalytic Movement" was first published in *Kenyon Review* (Autumn 1945).

The
Golden
Age

I. FREUD AND THE EGYPTIANS

*T*he murder of the father of the primal horde, the angry aspect of the Oedipus-complex—for Freud this is the beginning of history, and he finds everywhere that history and culture is the reactive response to it. Nevertheless, there is never absent, in his thinking, the inkling of an "earlier" amiabl⌐ condition, "the only satisfactory relationship," as he says, that between the mother and her infant son. In mythology this condition is the Saturnian or Golden Age, a miraculous era of fulfillments, without scarcities or jealousies. But though Freud has much to say about the later mischances of the Saturnian race, the cannibalism and the emasculation, he does not tend to expatiate on the Saturnian peace. It is said, Happy is the people that has no history—where there are only finished situations as the seasons roll—and, conversely, there is no use of writing a history of happiness. Why *write* it?

Another example of Freud's avoidance of the deeper dream is his coolness to the theories and the occasional evidences of a primitive matriarchy. What a curious thing that Freud, of all people, should mention so rarely the ideas of Bachofen and the others! And when he does mention them, he derives the matriarchy, as a reaction, from the murderous sons' renunciation of the murdered father's women: presumably, these older women are identified with the dead man and are forbidden. But surely it is not far-fetched to think of the matriarchy as repeating also the primitive infantile joy.

I should like to suggest, however, that the strange speculation of Freud's last years, whereby Moses is made an Egyptian, is a more positive reference to the Golden Age of love. A hundred critics have explained that in this speculation, making Moses a "gentile," Freud at last takes vengeance on the Jews, on his father's religion so burdensome to himself. But this is superficial, for Freud does not make Moses a "gentile" at all, in the sense of a Christian gentile whose lineage he derives precisely as a reaction to the Jews. (His "vengeance" turns quite the other way.) Freud makes Moses not a gentile but an Egyptian, of the house of the Pharoahs. And what is this house? Its most salient character is that it is the royal incestuous family, and therefore divine. It is the house of the descendants of the wedded brother and sister. Elsewhere Freud speaks of "the most maiming wound" inflicted on mankind by civilization, the ban against incest; but the pharoahs did not suffer so severely from this wound as the rest of mankind. (And of course "royal" and "incestuous" are equated not only in Egypt.)

We must therefore conceive of the Freudian anthropology somewhat as follows: first the Egyptians, of divine lineage, civilized and sessile; then the wandering primal horde led by Moses; then the remorseful father-murderers, the Jews, reactively righteous in the Law; and then the Christians, rebelling against the constraints of righteousness. Add on to this the latest generation, the neurotics, and we have a respectable modern theogeny.

Why was Freud reluctant to explore the earlier, less gloomy condition, but dwelt only on the frustration and the murder? This is usually, and truly enough, attributed to his own character and behavior: he was paternal, filially-rebellious, stern, self-denying, law-abiding, the "father of the psychoanalytic movement"; or at a more impersonal remove, he was the conscientious voice of objective science (which he took to be "reality"), the rebel against established convention, banded with his brotherly co-workers, etc., etc. Finally, however, I think a more material, and *therefore* more ennobling, explanation can be given by Reich's conception of "primary masochism": that the tension of unfinished love tries to burst asunder the inner constraints to its fulfillment, and this is felt by the subject as a longing to be burst, punctured, injured, destroyed. The earlier dream is too anxious-making and dangerous to dwell with. The closer one comes to orgasm without giving in to it, and so it happens in "successful" classical psychoanalysis, the more violent become the sado-masochistic dreams of fire, slaughter, and cosmic explosion. Now in both himself and the patients he treated most successfully, Freud came to this deep place and saw these terrible things; he could not, or dared not, by his techniques break through. Naturally then he was obliged, as a good and honest observer, to say that the deeper you went, the more apparently you wanted to die.

Freud speculates in the grand philosophical style; he is free and easy with the theoretical formulations (for what difference does it make? theory is made for man, not man for theory), but in his context, and recurrent reference, he is always square in the center of present, obvious, and important experience, of his own behavior, his patients' dreams, the laws of the state. He dreams the sado-masochistic wish, fire and revolution in the social order, *and still the constraint and the self-constraint hold firm;* you can twist and turn it any way you want, but this is history, biography, and autobiography. This is what he is telling us in the famous chapter beginning, "Let us now envisage the scene of such a totemic meal." The plot is a fiction, but there is not a significant detail that is not obligated by what he found in himself, his healthiest patients' deepest dreams, and the mores of society.

When he became very old, on the other hand—the tension of longing less, and the need to rally less—and this is interpreted by the subject as "now I am succeeding in dying"—he dreamed a more inclusive dream and conceived of Freud-Moses as an Egyptian of the house of Pharaoh.

II. SEVEN WAYS OF COPING WITH THE FACT THAT WE DO NOT LIVE IN THE GOLDEN AGE

The first way is to deny that it is a fact, to forget that there was a terrible incident, and to go on. This method is so commonplace, it is almost our political constitution, that we have to remind ourselves how remarkable it is. It is alternatively expressed by saying, There is no Golden Age (it is utopian) or We live in a Golden Age. Forgetful, with varying degrees of conviction we rush or falter into one another's embrace.

It does not work out very well, for what is forgotten comes, precisely, to be remembered. The question is how it can work out at all. Let us still again recall the Story of Oedipus and Jocasta who embraced in wilful forgetfulness. (Speaking of Sophocles's play, Aristotle calls their ignorance an "improbability outside the plot"; but Sophocles, of course, has made their wilful ignorance just the essence of the motivation.) Jocasta slays herself and Oedipus blinds himself. Let us say that Jocasta slays herself in order to be again with Laius, whom she loves, for her pleasure with Oedipus has revived a deeper longing; she has come to mourn for the first time. And that Oedipus blinds himself in order not to look on with frustrated envy. *This* is the state in which we live and cope with the fact that we do not live in the Golden Age: somewhere there is an entranced fixation on a past happiness—not ours; and we flounder in darkness in order not to suffer intolerable envy.

ii.

Suppose, on the contrary, we proceed in full consciousness and have a society that is workaday and efficient like some of the primitives they write about. Certain compromises and drawings-of-the-line are necessary, perhaps most especially in the niceties of eating.

The mothers have diminished their loss by taking the place of rule. The men assume the old prerogatives and exercise their sexual prowess. By these compromises much damage of the past is undone. We are in the Golden Age; and also, in this daylight economy, it is as if the Golden Age had never been.

Nevertheless the feast must be periodically renewed in order to prevent forgetting and relapsing into the bad night of Oedipus. Our activities conform to etiquette and are circumscribed by taboos. Especially, I say, what concerns eating, eating something up, is limited by niceties and restrictions. And there are taboos about the mothers: for none of us must be allowed to loom in the age of omnipotence, since then once again father would exist, and the many fathers, grown equally strong, would tear one another limb from limb. But the mothers say: "Live at peace, love one another. If you embraced us, you would revive ancient delusions and it would be the end of us all. You may embrace freely, anybody in the *other* line." It is sad for them, not to have their own men around.

Our constitution is a game. The rules are devised to permit, to excite, the maximum of spontaneity, the most violent exercise possible without destroying the game. Also the rules are really changeable by us, but of course they are sacred and one pretends that they are not being changed. We play our game with serious joy and our etiquette is more important to us than morals.

iii.

Some of us do not deny the fact, but we defy it. We will not draw any lines and our games heighten into brawls. We live in the Cities of the Plain and take our pleasures variously and strike and kill.

We carry on in the face of the image of the Golden Age. Every gratification is ritually lawless, it is obligatorily unnatural, counter to what would come to be by growth. Obviously, as is told in the history of our cities, it is the angels who are most sought for, to debauch and kill; the daughters of Lot are not equally desirable. Each bout of love ending in murder blacks out the nagging past.

Contrary to what you imagine, our state of indiscriminate rapine is not impermanent, for it is intermitted by satiation and fatigue. Just because the ritual demands that every possibility be experimented to the extreme, our strength fails in good time and we faint away. We awaken again to desire.

Our fear—for unfortunately we are afraid, otherwise all would be well—is lest desire itself fail, the penis not be erect, the vagina frigid. We feel called on to bring it to the test, and so we anticipate the need; we suffer a stirring of desire before we are in the presence of anything desirable, and the sweat of effort stands on our brows.

But at least this hot fitful dream is better than the clear daylight of the goodies.

iv.

Disgusted with it. On the first day, ignorant; on the second hemmed round by rules and careful not to overstep the line; on the third, striving to the extreme, and finding that we fail. Rather finally accept the punishment and atone, and be received back into the Golden Age. The Great Mother says, "Give it up! give it up! We cannot have it, as men used to. He stands there, in your experience and mine, lifting his monstrous right. My children, I also feared and hated that Golden Age, as now it seems when I am deprived—for thinking back at joy, it seems to have been pain.

"Take a stone knife. Castrate yourselves. And then we shall live innocently together. Are we not again mother and infant, as in the Golden Age?"

We who have castrated ourselves constitute the priestly rule. We are by no means deprived of all pleasure; usually we eat well and are fat as pigs. We are pathically cleanly. Our rule is strict and cruel and gives us plenty of satisfaction. The taxes are high.

Yet there is no bloodshed or rebellion. Those who submit console themselves with the beautiful thought that we fathers are castrated. We who rule resent everything whatever and give plenty of cause for resentment. In place of the dead weight of guilt and loss, there is the continual friction of active resentment. This realm of universal love is very like the Golden Age.

The Great Mother smiles on her priests. It is not the case that she smiles equally on the others. From time to time she is given to fits of unpredictable cruelty that sadden one and all alike.

v.

Some of us, entrenched in academies, have elaborated the following Herodian conspiracy, saying: "Look, these young ones are again growing in strength and menace. Even now, just by existing and changing, they are forcing us into old age and death; by living, they force us out of life. Therefore let us be prudent and slay them while they are small and weak. In this way we can arrest the flight of time and be safe."

The inquisition of the elders is continuous and subtle. In order to survive it is necessary for the young to be born with the physiognomy of the aged. This is difficult but not impossible, and these communities based on infanticide have also proved viable.

For instance, there is a king who tells himself that he is young in spirit and he loves to surround himself wi+h the fresh faces and the spontaneous gestures and thoughts of children. He sends out his messengers and he fills his court with pretty girls and boys, and he takes pleasure in their sports. And these children, miraculously, do not change; they never, by growing up, remind the king that he is year by year older and is already an old man. For every year all the children are snatched away and destroyed and replaced by other identical children a year younger. It is easy to find other identical children; really all children are alike. So this king and his court live in the Golden Age.

So we teachers in universities do not grow old; we are young in spirit. But I, unfortunately, have found that after two or three years of it I have grown bored and prematurely old; for the new kids make the very same errors and it is I who have changed and cannot rally to the task again and again.

vi.

But whatever else we do (and some do one thing and some another), all of us repeat the heroic act by which Aeneas founded Rome. Fleeing from his burning homeland, Aeneas lifted his father Anchises from the ground and carried him on his shoulders.

At first he rode on our shoulders, like a burdensome old man of the sea. But we have learned, like Aeneas, to project him further, to throw him high into the sky. And when he rides the sky, he scarcely intervenes in our affairs.

This is the state that we presently see about us in America. He has become the rational truth in which we all believe; the truth does not intervene in our desires or in our wars: we take them where we wish, no fear. We understand them through and through. For us nothing is fearsome or guilty or at a loss, for we know what it is, and we say, "Aha! it is only this—"

It is *only* this: We live by the constitution that all things, and we are among the things, are knowable; we have displaced upward our Golden Age. It does not intervene in our needs; the truth has nothing to do with our needs.

Sometimes we explain it this way: there is an Objective World. This is a convenient formulation, for by becoming aware of every detail of this objective world (and we have techniques for becoming aware of any detail that you wish) we can circumvent the awakening in us of any concern. We are not afraid, we are not at a loss, we do not mourn, but we say, "It is (only) this." For there is an objective world, and what has that got to do with me?

Given this wonderful freedom, it is possible by new knowledge, safeguarded by more and more alienating intermediaries, to approximate as closely as we wish to the Golden Age.

The danger—but it is a small one—is that some one in an unguarded moment may directly touch on something real and be lost in love and anger.

vii.

We do miracles. These are deeds that are in the nature of things growing into the next moment. They are matters-of-fact. In the situation that there has been a terrible incident, and we do not live in the Golden Age, such matters-of-fact are called miracles.

For we are blind—then to do a matter-of-fact is a miracle. Or there are ritual rules—then to do a matter-of-fact is a miracle. Or we anticipate desire—then to do a matter-of-fact is a miracle. We are impotent—then to do a matter-of-fact is a miracle. Or the dead past has us in grip—then to do a matter-of-fact is a miracle. Or there is an objective world—then to do a matter-of-fact is a miracle.

Yet it *is* dark, there *is* an objective world, etc.; and nevertheless there continually come to be matters-of-fact.

It is as if a man should screw up his courage, close his eyes, take a deep breath, murmur a prayer—for a fearful dive into the abyss—and then proceed, with open eyes, breathing normally and humming a song, a next step on what is tolerably familiar ground.

In times of terrible violence, as in the woods at the end of March there is a swelling and cracking—I have been disgusted and horrified at it; but afterwards, one does think of those images as images of danger.

It is not that we do *not* live in the Golden Age and do not have to cope with that fact. On the contrary, who would dare to deny it—today! as the case is!—that a dead man is lying there? The miracle-workers do not disregard it but wail loudly; they beat themselves and tear their flesh and mix blood and tears and cry out: "Father! father! except for us the thread of the generations would be cut short."

This is a matter-of-fact. Except for us the thread of the generations *would* be cut short—as the lad said after he had done in papa and mama with his new home-made shot-gun.

III. ON THE QUESTION:
"HOW DID WE LAPSE?"

How did man first lapse from the Saturnian Age in which we were engaged and happy as one could be as a matter-of-fact—just how much that is is a matter-of-fact; how did we lapse from it into the misery of resignation and being beaten and brow-beaten? When we consider the many clever and arduous expedients that we are capable of, the puzzle presents itself how we are so wretched.

It is a classical question, and several different explanations are given. These explanations are not unsatisfactory and, especially if they are considered as operating dynamically together so that they heighten one another, they seem to add up to a sufficient reason. What is interesting about them, however, is that all of them imply an accident somewhere along the line; and this is unsatisfactory, for our misery seems so ingrained that it calls for an explanation from our essential natures.

It is likely, for instance, that because of some climatic or geological catastrophe, men were temporarily deprived of matter-of-fact necessities. They would then suffer from primary anxiety. In order to feel something again, they would, like primary masochists, seek out those who would punish and subdue them, perhaps provoking to it those innocent of any such need.

Or conversely—this is the usual theory of the foundation of states—a small violent and sadistic group might descend on an aboriginal population, rape its women and its wealth, and subjugate the majority to perpetuate its own prerogatives. The innocent victims are unversed in the arts of force and cunning necessary to protect themselves; they fall an easy prey. Now it is not unlikely that there should be such violent bands in the first place, for frustration leads to aggression and there are numerous chances of frustration.

These accidents, moreover, could have occurred so long ago that by the time there was a proper human species at all it could have been already formed to subjugation. Thus Freud and his authors speak of the Primal Horde as an original property of man: that is, a super-ego, the tendency to introject a super-ego, is innate in the species (as Kropotkin had already said that social mutual aid was innate in the species). And this opinion is likely, if we consider that human children are so long weakly and dependent, and learn what they learn by imitation. For children (such is the theory) have boundless desires and think they are omnipotent; they are wrong— their desires go far beyond their powers and they are frustrated; they then identify themselves with what is big and strong and frustrating. This sequence can be seen every day in nurseries, and it is likely that it is the nature of man.

Yet how puzzling, obvious as it seems! For how, by nature, can desire reach beyond power, since desire is adjusting of the state of things, one desires an environment that is one's own environment? One desires what in a sense one knows, and one knows only what one does; how then can one desire what one does not also potentially do?—there is of course such a thing as experiment or play. Surely it was by some accident that the children came to be "weak" and "dependent," granted that this accident might have occurred before the human species appeared on the scene.

So the various natural theories imply an accident somewhere along the line. As such they are not adequate to our despair. The theologians, however, insist that our misery is essential to us. This is intolerable to our hope. I should like to suggest that, as frequently, the theologians misinterpret the Bible text on which they build.

The Bible explains that it was the knowledge of good and evil that caused our lapse from innocence and soon the expulsion from paradise. Now this does not mean knowledge as such, as some have said, for in innocence Adam named the beasts. Nor does it mean the particular knowledge of sexuality, for Adam and Eve must have had sexual intercourse in innocence, altho the fact that they "knew that they were naked" was evidence of their guilt. Is then, as many have said, the fatal knowledge of good and evil to be contrasted with the ignorance of good and evil—to be ignorant is to be innocent? Surely not, for in the garden they knew every good thing and, in the usual commentary especially of the poets, they praised it as good. The meaning must then be: what was sinful was the *knowledge of good as cut off from other ways of living the good*. They fell from innocence when they knew and judged and did not act and enjoy. (So they knew they were naked and covered themselves rather than doing something else.) This interpretation is given by Kafka:

> We are sinful not merely because we have eaten of the Tree of Knowledge, but also because we have not yet eaten of the Tree of Life. The state in which we find ourselves is sinful quite independent of guilt.

The Biblical story puts us on the track of an answer to our question "How did we lapse?" *That* question, says the Bible, cannot be answered; every explanation must necessarily seem accidental and arbitrary. For by taking thought one cannot know anything about the Golden Age. It is taking thought itself that restricts us to the conditions of misery. The Golden Age is known only to the happy, and the happy do not devote themselves—how could they?—to the discussion of objective questions. To pose the question as we pose questions, as a problem of truth and evidence, is already to be sunk in the needs and functions of the Base Age. We have a kind of knowledge of the Golden Age, by way of dreams and hopes, but from these one cannot frame a compelling argument.

We see this in every detail of our experience. From our fears, inhibitions, disgusts and resentments, from our state-institutions and social mores, we can argue more or less compellingly to a terrible incident, we froze, we murdered the father of the primal horde, we wear a rigid armor, our children imagine an infinite destruction, etc., etc. From the data of the objective world, external and internal, we can prove hypotheses less and less relevant to our concern in the present moment. These are typical functions of the Base Age. But from our flashes of happiness and our flushes of concern we do not find that, using words in a rational way, we can conclude anything at all. Conversely (what a blessing!) we do not find that by the rational use of words and evidence we can convince a man to fall in love, to feel concern, to be happy or unhappy. Our happiness consists simply in matters-of-fact, miracles.

"How did we lapse?" is not a meaningful question; but there is a related question that is meaningful, "Under what conditions do men seek to answer the meaningless but necessary, and necessarily meaningless question, 'How did we lapse?' " "What is the meaning of life?" is not a meaningful question; but there is a meaningful related question, "Under what conditions do men ask themselves the question, 'What is the meaning of life?' " If I had the learning, I should explore these questions. For my own part, this much learning I have, I come to them when, attempting to be quiet and at ease, I consult my memories and my plans, instead of giving way to the cries of anger and pain that would otherwise overwhelm me.

"The Golden Age" was first published in *Complex* (Winter 1953-4), the magazine that Goodman edited off and on in the early Fifties.

Eros,
or
the
Drawing
of
the
Bow

"Mesonuktiois pot' horais—"
Anacreonteia

In the middle of the night
when the Bear already sinks
toward the hand of the Plowman,
and all the tribes that speak
lie overwhelmed in sleep:
then halting, Love did pound
upon my bolted door.
"Who bangs upon my door?
My dream you have divided."
But Love said, "Open up!
Only a child—don't fear;
I'm wet; I've lost my way
thru the night without a moon."
When I heard it I took pity
and taking up the lamp
I opened wide: a child indeed
I saw: he had a bow
and wings and a quiver.
He stood beside the hearth
warming the palms of hands
and shaking the wet water from his hair
But when the chill was past,
"Come," said he, "let us try
this bow, whether the string
is hurt by being wet."
He stretches it and smites me
full in the breast, and stings;
and now he leaps and laughs,
"O friend," he cries, "rejoice!
My bow it is unhurt!
but you will ache at heart."

So in these Trials of the Bow a man returns to his wound, both received and given; and joyfully puts his fear of castration to the test. In this first Trial he is a child again: to make all the world tiny, and be safe.

I. THE HISTORY OF EROS

This poem is the archetypal dream of the followers of Anacreon. It is a late dream, the result of a long repression. Eros has become a child again; he is no longer the powerful Archer of Homer. The older Desire was not helpless in the grown-up social world, but was one, not the least, of the forces of constructive and destructive action; his acts were so strong and direct that one did not need (to describe Love) to look for him in one's feelings, in the sting of the heart, but could depict an objective dramatic scene. But by the time of the followers of Anacreon the social action of Desire was moderated, kept within bounds; then one inquired into the feelings of this Eros. Nevertheless, there was as yet no illusion, for there was as yet no repression of the pleasures of Love, but only of all its grown-up social effects. On the contrary, the experience was nothing but pleasure (and pain), and was never released into constructive and destructive, and self-destructive, action. Clinging, all the rest given up, to this pleasure. Then speculating on the polymorphous pleasures that one felt, one came easily to discover the polymorphous child within.

Now later most of these pleasures themselves came to be denied, and even pleasure itself: then one ceased to picture Love as one's real self at all. Instead people developed the illusion of an ideal object, a Mother, close to the original object itself but forgotten and untouchable; then the boy Cupid shrank to the size of an infant, who still decorates our calendars. (And what shall we say of the most recent years when a man, fostered in school till his late adolescence, thinks that Love is an adolescent like himself, of female sex?)

"In the middle of the night"—when business is intermitted, especially the Anacreontic business of alcohol and roses, and polymorphous pleasures; one is alone.

Then one does not speak, but instead dreams: images, already the mode of thought of early years, but still concerned with grown-up business.

"Then on my bolted door"—for the mind is purposely shut fast against its depths. Yet the child is halted there behind: arrested.

"You have interrupted my dreams!" Surely! for this child is not himself a dream, a dream-thought; but the fact itself, the cause of thought.

It is only a child, no fear. It is the very child that one was. He is wet: new-born. He comes from the dark night: one had no acquaintance there. He was lost, but now he has halted, arrested. In the Anacreontic day, many an experience might occur by which the child within might suddenly be summoned, and stand arrested.

"Pitying—" these are the idle tears, I know not what they mean, that are shed for oneself. For whom else are idle tears shed? But taking the lamp: now one will know.

So often, opening a door, one sees something framed in the doorway.

A child indeed. The bow and darts are the small penis erect. Winged: for easily a child soars aloft, borne in his mother's arms. This is why the childish Cupid is winged.

Warming himself: for he has come from the cold world of the dead. So it must always seem in the actual hour, that the past is cold and dead. Now reborn dripping, so he must be dried like a newborn child. Soon he is accustomed to the warmth of the present hour, and he looks about.

We must think of this child as about six years old, in the full maturity of childish sexuality, before that sexuality has been blotted from the mind. Is his power lost? this is the question. This is the trial of the bow.

His power is not lost: he stretches the bow. How easily this experimental masturbation must become the rivalry, penis for penis, of the trial of the bow in the *Odyssey*! As yet it is the self-love of childhood; next the love of a man for this little rival within himself. Will he not discover rivals outside himself?

As for the child, he rejoices, says, "Rejoice *with* me!" as if, a new discoverer, he was the first to find how to give oneself pleasure.

But the poet returns to his wound. This is the deepest thing he wishes, to return to his wound. His wound is the weak-point in the armor of his ego; it is through the wound that stream the forces from the depths. To return and look into this deep spring. His wound is not the child, but that the child stands there arrested, that he could not merge into the present hour and vanish. That he torments one from the past. This sting leaves a rankling wound. It is a familiar experience, that we try to fill up this void, like a quicksand, with the pleasures of the followers of Anacreon. Also, on the contrary! there streams to us from this void such power and action as we do have. We loose another dart, and still the quiver is not empty.

II.

"Toxou thesis"
—*Odyssey, xxi.*

Penelope said that "whoever could easily bend the bow in his hands and shoot the arrow, with him she'd go, quitting her nuptial home so fair and full of the means of life (which she thought she remembered as in a dream)."

The suitors could not bend it, tho they warmed the bow at a fire and greased it well. But their hearts ached not because of the woman, they said, but because the people would call them feeble.

But Odysseus (disguised), when he took the bow, turned it all ways and tried it here and there, lest it had been harmed in the absence of the king. "See how he handles it, as if he had such a thing at home!"

This bow that his boyhood friend Eurytides Iphitus gave him. He did not take it to the war on his black ship, but he kept it at home as a memento of his dear friend. There he used to carry it.

Taking the great bow, he looked about him on all sides, then, "as a man skilled in music and the lyre easily stretches a string around the peg, so hastily Odysseus bent the mighty bow."

He thumbed the string and it moaned like the swallow. A great ache entered into the suitors' hearts and their flesh crept.

This Odysseus did not have a wound, but the healed scar of a boar that attacked him when he climbed Parnassus with the boys of Autolycus.

Stripped of his rags, "Now this contest is over!" he cried to the suitors, "let us try another not yet proposed, so grant it me Apollo!" And he aimed the arrow at Antinoös.

It is the same penis-rivalry, play and earnest, that we met with in the poem of the follower of Anacreon. But now it is not the child who bends the bow, but the man himself. This is the heroic expression of Love in constructive and destructive action; it is not necessary to linger in the description of feelings.

The man carries not his wound, but the scar of his wound. By this we know him for the king. One has become a whole (scarred) man, with full power (such as it is). But it is worthwhile to mention also the hero Philoctetes, who was suffering a live wound, but then he did not shoot his bow.

"He looked about him on all sides"—posing: so the mutual contest turns into an exhibition of oneself. He exhibits first his scar, then his prowess.

The bow that his dear friend gave him, and the wound that he took in the company of the sons of Autolycus: we have not to do, as previously, with childhood, but with the sexuality of adolescence. From this wound one indeed recovers, and this bow can indeed be turned to slay one's fellows, after all have drifted apart.

At least Odysseus did not carry his bow off to the war: I take it to mean that Odysseus was not one of your vindictive warriors whose aggression is nothing but the result of homosexual frustration.

"As easily as a musician"—so says Homer! For Homer, to be sure, this prowess and this exhibition are very easy. This handling—this power to stretch as if lifeless the audience of the song.

> my hand is strong, has turned to fire
> the arpeggios of the lyre,
> and elsewhere we love carelessly
> who closely love Saint Harmony.

At the climax of his poem (we may picture the scene), the poet Homer compares his hero with—himself!

"Stripped of his rags"—Odysseus is not stripped naked; on the contrary, bristling with sword and spear. An armed love. And Antinoös, when the king looses his arrow, is about to lift the goblet to his lips to drink wine: "death was not his concern, among many feasting men," says Homer—these are the brothers sitting together, but no longer in trust and amity, but selfishness and greed.

"The doors were bolted"—it means that there is no opening into this conscious slaughter for any access of deeper love. For yes!

there is a free and natural love, a mutual aid among all mankind, deeper than these Trials of the Bow.

III.

I have so far omitted the most striking passage.

The son Telemachus spoke up among them: "Zeus has made me crazy. My dear mother in her wisdom says that she will follow another and leave this house, yet I laugh and am happy, like a madman. Come, suitors, since this seems to be the prize, she's not the only woman in Greece. What difference does mother's fable make to me? But I *myself* shall try the bow, if I can bend it and shoot! Not to my sorrow would the lady my mother leave this house and go with another, when I'd be left behind alone to take father's prizes."

He stood on the platform and tried the bow. Thrice he made it tremble, straining with all his might. Thrice his strength failed him. But the fourth time, he strongly bent it.—But Odysseus shook his head and prevented him from shooting.

The prince mad, and pretending to be mad, at once puts us in mind of Hamlet. The difference is that Hamlet's father was dead and returned to him from within, to stay his hand. No longer a prince of epic destruction, but of tragic self-destruction, and then even, as Goethe said, a prince of feelings rather than acts. But Odysseus has returned alive to Telemachus: there he sits (the doors are not yet bolted), one of the suitors, just one of the suitors. Why should not Telemachus also try the bow?

We may say that Telemachus looked for his father in three ways: (1) in order to *find* him, so as to have a secure father instead of the rout of suitors among whom he grew up—and we may imagine his hostility; (2) in order *not* to find him, to be free finally to make up his own mind; and (3) to *hunt him down*—for the Trial of the Bow. Well, now he had hunted him down.

"She's not the only woman in Greece—" What an astounding statement for the son to make! what a lie of despair! Does he not hereby include himself among the frivolous suitors?

"When he should be left behind alone, in father's place"— blotting them out of the picture one and all, including Penelope, like a child affirming himself after he has agreed to take every fatal loss.

"Thrice he made the bow tremble!" So one grows up through childhood, boyhood, and adolescence. (By this time many sons have already won, or lost, the trial of the bow; but Odysseus has prudently absented himself for the full twenty years.)

"The fourth time he stretched it!" He is now twenty or twenty-one years old. It is a contest between grown men. This is the most unusual feature of the *Odyssey*, it is the essence of the *Odyssey*: that there is a father who has not struggled with and identified himself with, and succumbed to, his child at some childish age—two or six or thirteen—but he stayed away until it was a manly contest, in which a father has some chance of victory.

"But Odysseus shook his head and prevented him from shooting." So? Is this indeed what took place? And if Telemachus had let fly? And at what would the first arrow be let fly if not at Odysseus, the chief of the suitors?

What a surprise for Odysseus! to come home after twenty years to this young arrow! And as the blood gushes from his nostrils, is there not, nevertheless, a flashing glance of recognition, and love, from the eyes?

But Telemachus has not suffered a wound, therefore he lowers the bow.

These are the three trials of the bow. The trial of the child within; the trial of the boyish rivals; the trial of the father and the son.

The first is the lyric trial; the second the epic trial; and the third would have been the tragic trial.

But indeed, there is a free and natural love, mutual aid among all mankind, deeper than these Trials of the Bow.

First published in the Surrealist magazine *View* (May 1946).

When the strings are loosed can the clear song sound?
when the tendons taut from the reins to the neck
against scrutiny and a blow in the back,
and the belly hard against the inward wound
of anxious love? and the thighs tightly bound
to jump with fear, and the forehead black
with counter-thinking?

        The leashes all are slack
on which from the third year I used to pound
the iron voices with a scratching nail.
I touch them: the box is almost still.

"Breathe! and fill with even breathing
the body of tubes that tremble and blow:
and sometimes suddenly they sound, unheeding,
organ-tones—that one must hear to know."

II

REICH
AND
HIS
ENEMIES

[Freud's
Theory
of
the
Mind]

*I*n Ernest Jones's excellent biography
of Freud, of which the first volume has just appeared, there is
important new evidence for the development of Freud's "theory of
the mind." A striking trend in that development is: that as Freud
deepened his explanation of the mental processes, he more and
more gave up the contact of "mind" and "external world"; he
tended toward a closed system, the individual acting out a mental
drama on an isolated stage.

I have tried to show elsewhere (in *Gestalt Therapy*, part II, ch.
3) that "mind" is an abstraction from the felt contact of the field
of the organism and its physical and social environment. This
abstraction is necessary, and is felt as a real thing, under certain
conditions: namely, a chronic low-grade emergency in which
proprioception (the sense of the body) is diminished and selectively
blotted out; there is a hypertension of muscularity; there is a split in
the unity desired-perceived because of frustration, danger, and
resignation; habitual deliberateness and unrelaxed self-constriction
color the foreground of awareness and produce an exaggerated
feeling of the exercise of "Will"; the safe play of dream and
speculation is maximized; and so forth. I need hardly point out to
38   readers of this magazine how these conditions obtain in our

societies. But it is instructive to show examples in Freud's theorizing of how he progressively comes to the "mind."

Just before the *Interpretation of Dreams,* Freud wrote and rejected a physiological psychology on a neuronal basis, a kind of thinking-machine. There is one major difference between this and the model of the mind in the *Dreams*: in the earlier work he held that sensory stimuli imparted a *quantity* of energy to the neuronal system, later he held that such stimuli merely "excite" and "qualify" the mental apparatus. That is, the earlier view allows for a psychology of growth—the environment is novel and nourishing and the organism survives by creatively adjusting, changing and changing the environment. On the later view, the drama is all internal. Therapeutically this comes to mean that a cure does not depend essentially on finishing an unfinished emotional situation in actual current experience, but simply on a reshuffling of the conflicting cathected ideas; there is no "real" conflict but only "inner" conflict. But the case is, I think, that essentially all inner conflict is a real conflict and there is no cure without current environmental change, providing new nourishment. There can be a release of dammed-up affect only by a real object or its real absence. In clinical practice Freud, of course, understood this perfectly when he laid so much stress on the transference to the therapist; but he then interprets the effect of the transference as a revival of an old illusion, whereas the truth is, I believe, that the effect comes from a new experimental try with a real person. As if embarrassed by the importance of the therapist, Freud tries in every way to make the actual man completely unobtrusive and shadowy; but this is blinking at the facts.

It was at this same period, again, that Freud first held a theory, evidenced by an astonishing unanimity of memory of all his patients, that hysteria was specifically caused by the seduction of the very small child by some adult. Soon he had to give up this spectacular bright idea, for it turned out on closer investigation that the "memories" were only fantasies, wishes, a form of infantile auto-erotism. Of course they were; but what is astonishing is that Freud does not at once follow up with the next question: why should children have such a fantastic wish? The explanation must be that they have been starved in the social environment; they have previously been denied a necessary close contact with the other people; frustrated, they dream it up, in terms appropriate to their later similar starvation. One does not need to look far to find the conditions of community-starvation in Vienna 1895. But Freud took this social "reality" to be the nature of things.

Another example of the splitting of the soul from its environment was Freud's cooling toward his theory of "actual-neurosis," imperfect current sexual gratification, as the core of psycho-neurosis. Freud never quite abandoned this view, but he came to lay *all* the stress on mental repression. But supposing he had pursued the earlier view: it would have become increasingly evident to him, would it not, that cure could not depend merely on talk, revival of affect, and reconsideration, but must also pass over into practical behavior, and therefore must involve a change of the social rules so as to make such curative behavior possible. Obviously Freud was not willing to make any such frontal attack on the moral and economic institutions.

Skipping a few years to the *Three Contributions to the Theory of Sex* (this is further on than the period covered by Jones's first volume), we find a peculiar anomaly in Freud's theory of infantile sexuality as mainly under the control of the erotogenic zones—skin, mouth, anus, genitals. On the one hand, like the great biologist he was, he insists that these zones, and the entire sexuality, are "anaclitic," that is that they lean on, and support, vital life functions, of nourishment, excretion, etc. On the other hand, he increasingly insists that the infantile sexuality is essentially auto-erotic, self-contained, and only in the course of time includes the world and the others. But this latter view cannot make fundamental sense, for the very material nature of the erotogenic zones—sensitive mucous membranes—shows us that they are organs of *contact*, perceptual and chemical; their auto-erotic employment must be secondary. When he makes this secondary employment primary, he must inevitably come to the curious language of calling the infantile sexuality "polymorphously perverse."

To sum up the tendency evidenced in these examples, splitting the soul and the world, instead of regarding their unitary interaction as the context of psychology, Freud came to regard the original "primary" process of thought as totally "unrealistic." But this is against all the evidence of the animal kingdom—for how do the animals who have, I suppose, only that primary process, nevertheless manage so well? And then Freud came to the contradiction between "pleasure-principle" and "reality-principle," and his consequent gray and stoical view of culture and society.

Two things strike one here: First, that as Freud's insight became more concrete, daring, and far-ranging, even to anthropology and religion, he more and more withdrew into himself and limited the "possible" sphere of direct environmental contact; conversely, from this secure vantage-point he forged the extraordinary practical weapon of the psychoanalytical movement. But secondly, the most important later advances by others, in theory and technique, have been able to go back precisely to ideas (and hopes) that Freud resigned on the way.

This review of Ernest Jones' biography of Freud was untitled when it first appeared in *Resistance* (February 1954).

The Political Meaning of Some Recent Revisions of Freud

In the following remarks I trust that I can keep differentiated those judgments that depend on general social and cultural awareness from those that require special clinical experience, which I do not have. I am not a psychoanalyst. But the social role of analysis has recently come so much to the fore, and the new revisions of the Freudian doctrine are so politically tendentious—mostly to the right, but in one excellent case (Reich) to the left—that I feel the readers of this magazine should be informed of what is at stake.—P.G.

There are at least four causes for the current enormous interest in the social role of psychotherapy. (1) The staggering number of psychological rejects in the draft both before and after induction into the army; and the even greater number of those who are suffering or will be suffering from what is now euphemistically called "war neurosis." (2) The consequent reflection on the conditions of peacetime existence that generate the "neurotic personality of our time." (3) The manufacture of propaganda for psychological warfare for both domestic and foreign consumption, whence studies of the "character structure of the Japanese" etc. (4)

And more specially, the attempted analysis, particularly by middle European refugees, of the psychological framework of the Nazi state. These causes have led to new practices and new theories. What is alarming is not their deviation from the orthodox Freudian sociology and implied politics, in which a good deal is faulty, but the fact that most of these deviations lead step by step to a psychology of non-revolutionary social adjustment that is precisely the political ideal (by no means the political action) of the New Deal, the Beveridge Plan, Stalinism, etc.

I.

First, briefly, apropos of new practices, I should like to comment on a recent paper by Franz Alexander, director of the orthodox Chicago Institute for Psychoanalysis.[1] Dr. Alexander finds that "particularly in acute and incipient cases, briefer methods of psychotherapy can be successfully utilized," e.g. fewer interviews and repeated interruptions rather than the orthodox two years of daily analysis. This means, of course, giving up the infantile recollection. For this the doctor would substitute the "emotional training of the Ego" that "takes place in that experimental personal interrelationship between the patient and the physician which is called transference." "The goal of psychotherapy is to increase the Ego's efficiency in fulfilling its task of finding such gratification for a person's subjective needs as is in harmony with the standards and ideals of the person and with existing conditions." (The same renunciation of the infantile recollection, plus an even stronger intervention of the analyst, is advocated *a fortiori* by those who revise the theory as well as the practice.)

This position is certainly un-Freudian. "It is nonsensical," Freud said in his last major work, "to maintain that psychoanalysis is practiced if these early periods of life are excluded from one's investigation."[2] Those analysts, again, who emphasize the role of the analyst and base their treatment on following up the resistances to treatment, but who *insist on the primacy of instinctual gratification,* insist also on the primacy of the infantile scene. I doubt

[1] "New Perspectives in Psychotherapy," *The New Republic,* Jan. 8, 1945.
[2] *Moses and Monotheism* (1939), p. 114.

very much whether Freud would have called instinctual gratification "a person's subjective needs." As I understand it, the point of the infantile recollection is not merely to live out the emotional distress involved in the early associations but also to give to the Ego, thru understanding, a *control* of these associations, in order then to face the existing situation unimpeded, the instinctual drives being part of the objective situation. (Whether or not even this control constitutes a cure is a question.) There is here no question of "harmony," but of enlightened choice and if need be struggle. But it is just this concept of harmony between the subjective personality and the objective conditions that we shall soon discuss in its full political efflorescence.

But the real bother with Dr. Alexander's argument is the social reasons he assigns for the briefer treatment. First, he says, these emotionally disturbed and incipient cases are walking around active in life as foremen, laborers, statesmen, lawyers, etc. etc., and have "an incalculable effect on society." Second, "life in our machine-age is becoming more and more complex," setting up an unbearable conflict of interdependence on the one hand and competitive rivalry on the other; therefore "to help contemporary man to find his place in this structure without falling victim...is the great future function of psychiatry." Thirdly, in the face of the imminent huge number of cases, if the qualified therapist does not "acquire methods which can be applied on a large scale...there will be a fiasco of the first magnitude."

Is it possible to draw any other conclusion from this reasoning than that the goal of therapy is the smooth running of the social machine *as it exists*? What a fantastic proposal, when a society creates emotional tensions, to reorient not the society but the people! as if indeed it were possible to change the people without changing the daily pattern and therefore both the economic relations and the nature of the work. And what familiar name shall we call a "therapy" that pretends to create harmony on a mass scale? I take it that Dr. Alexander does not really know what he is asserting.

The need does exist in its millions—and there are, for instance, 250 Freudian analysts in the United States! Given all schools of psychiatry and all the new methods you will (including the Army's narco-synthesis), there will be a fiasco; but the society that has maneuvered itself into two world wars is used to fiascos. Who can deny that the only practical mass method is to strike at the institutions and inhibiting mores and to give our sick generation, if not an era of peace, at least a war of liberation?

II.

Let us now turn to a new revisionism in theory advocated most popularly by Karen Horney and with the most intellectual influence by Erich Fromm. Many of the propositions of this school look like the ancient deviation of Adler, but their principle is different and their conclusions, as I hope to show, aim at adjustment not so much to existent society as to the kind of rationalized sociolatry towards which the imperialist nations are headed in their *domestic* policy. (Let me reintroduce the Comtean term, *sociolatry*—i.e., "religion of society"—to refer to the ways in which natural energies are absorbed, sublimated, and verbally gratified in our corporative industrial states.)

To state their position in the most general way, Horney and Fromm diminish the role of instinctual drives to the vanishing point; they find that character *directly* reflects the social pattern and that the source of neurosis is "irrational authority"; they explain anxiety, which with the Freudians they consider the central point in neurosis, solely as fear of such authority; and they regard mental health as the "free" and "spontaneous" action of "personality." I shall try to show that, from a revolutionary standpoint, even when the political slogans resulting from this position are unexceptionable—so that even sound anarchists like Herbert Read have been taken in by them—they are purely *formal*; they have been deprived of all psychological dynamism; and when we examine the concrete social applications, to find a content for the forms, we find nothing but a roseate New Deal both in peace and war.

Both Fromm and Horney are still at the stage where they find it necessary again and again to show where Freud is in error. In summary:[3] (1) Freud was too biologically-minded to understand

---

[3] This summary is from E. Fromm, *Escape from Freedom,* pp. 290ff., but it is identical in Horney's *New Ways in Psychoanalysis,* passim.

that differing cultural patterns lead to differing character-structures. (2) He was physiological and hedonistic and traced everything to pleasures and frustrations. (3) He was individualistic and considered man as "primarily self-sufficient and only secondarily in need of others to satisfy his instinctual needs." But "individual psychology is fundamentally social-psychology—the psychology, as Sullivan would say, of interpersonal relationships." (4) Freud misinterpreted the relation between character-structure and the infantile life, the erogenous zones, etc., when he thought that the latter caused the former. (On the basis of this critique, Fromm and Horney reject the importance of infantile sexuality, the sexual Oedipus complex, the Freudian characterology and analysis of the perversions, the therapeutic recollection, the psychic apparatus of the Id and the Ego, the theory of the libido, the importance of the unconscious in healthy persons, etc., etc. Yet still they insist that Freud is their great inspirer, etc.)

Without following Freud in every detail, I think it can be shown that every part of this general indictment is either wrong or absurd. But the upshot of it is that, after all the retrenchments and rejections have been made, Horney and Fromm commence their own psychologizing with the following residue: (1) On the one hand the inherited instincts are much diminished; in a remarkable passage Karen Horney "equates" the "Freudian instincts" with what she calls "neurotic trends."[4] (2) But on the other hand there exists a "personality" apparently sprung from nowhere—for I do not think that any one would say that a speechless child had a personality, and yet they reject the meticulous Freudian history of the forming of personality from the data of prehistory and the cradle.

Now Horney and Fromm—the latter especially moved by the memories of Nazism—turn to the neurotic personality of our time, and they find the key in "irrational" authority. The threats of "irrational" authority put the "personality" in fear of his self-expression; this rouses anxiety; and subsequent behavior is the attempt to regain security by various means, for instance submissiveness, will-to-power, competitiveness, renunciation, suffering, etc.[5] Let me quote:

[4] *New Ways*, p. 77.
[5] These devices to regain security constitute the successive chapters of K. Horney, *The Neurotic Personality of Our Time.*

Freud states that the Oedipus complex is justifiably regarded as the kernel of neurosis. I believe that the statement is the most fundamental one which can be made about the origin of neurosis, but I think it needs to be qualified and reinterpreted in a frame of reference different from the one Freud had in mind. What Freud meant in his statement was this: because of the sexual desire the little boy, let us say, has for his mother, he becomes the rival of his father, and the neurotic development consists in the failure to cope with the anxiety rooted in this rivalry in a satisfactory way. I believe that Freud touched upon the most elementary root of neurosis in pointing to the conflict between the child and parental authority and the failure of the child to solve this conflict satisfactorily. But I do not think that this conflict is brought about by the sexual rivalry, but that it results from the child's reaction to the pressure of parental authority, the child's fear of it and submission to it. Before I go on elaborating this point, I should like to differentiate between two kinds of authority. One is objective, based on the competency of the person in authority to function properly with respect to the task of guidance he has to perform. This kind of authority may be called rational authority. In contrast to it is what may be called irrational authority, which is based on the power which authority has over those subjected to it and on the fear and awe with which the latter reciprocate.[6]

But why does the child *fear* the parental authority if not because he is being deprived of something? What he is being deprived of is continuous attention, breast-feeding, loud shouting, immediate elimination, the opportunity of being continually present and prying, (later) masturbation, etc. All this is the motor of the Oedipus complex, but it is the instinctual life from which these authors resolutely turn away. To Freud the "root" is not in the rivalry, but in the repression, as is proved by his repeated statement that in every psychoneurosis there is a core of *actual-neurosis*, the term applied to anxiety that is the direct transformation of repressed libido.[7] Consider a child in a tantrum: would one say that this is fear or rage at frustration? It is just the energy of the frustration that explains the energy of the fear. One does not see that a small child fears a big man with a gruff voice any more than he would a tree, until he comes to associate the image with a deprivation. The neurotic, says Horney in a typical passage, seeks desperately to be loved because he thinks, if you love me, then you will not hurt me.[8] Yes, says Freud, but this is because it was

---

[6] Fromm, "Individual and Social Origins of Neurosis," *American Sociological Review,* August 1944, p. 381.

[7] E.g., *The Interpretation of Dreams,* 3rd English Edition (1933), p. 165.

[8] *Neurotic Personality,* p. 96.

originally the fact that they didn't love him that hurt him, and he is trying not only to be safe now but even more to make up for the past deprivation. If the inheritance of the infant, as I have been arguing, is socially colored thru and thru—and this must follow from the fact that the human child is so long helpless and yet has managed to survive—then every withdrawal of love or continuous attention must gravely wound not the personality (that comes later) but the whole body of the instincts. This is just what Freud expresses when he says that very many of the instincts are erotic; eros is the impulse of object-union even prior to the organization of the Ego.

The child's free personality, say Horney and Fromm, is endangered by the irrational authority, therefore he is anxious. On the contrary, says Freud, there is as yet no definite personality, but deprivation is inevitable by *any* authority, rational or not and whether embodied in single persons or not; the result of these very deprivations is that now the Ego, retrenching to avoid further suffering, is constituted as a closed system *against* the instincts, by repressing the instincts. Hitherto the Ego was a part of the Id, it was the agent, the artist, the informant, and the social-interpreter of the instincts: this is "the strength of the Ego." Now, having repressed the instincts, and especially when it has incorporated the external authority into itself (the super-Ego, heir of the Oedipus complex), it fears the instincts foreign to it: this is "the weakness of the Ego."[9] Neurotic anxiety is the threat against the Ego by the instincts that burst free from repression.

According to Fromm, the obstacle to general psychological health is the presence, in the family and the culture, of irrational authority. According to Freud, the obstacle is the presence, in all civilization—so he thinks—of instinctual deprivation.

The "Free Personality" as the Social Unit

What then is mental health? Practically, according to Freud, it is the opening-out of the Ego, and the relaxation of the demands of the super-Ego, sufficiently to come to recognize the irrepressible instinct as its own. Ideally—though I do not recall that Freud goes this far—it would be the opening out and flexibility of the Ego to

[9] Freud, *The Problem of Anxiety,* p. 29.

recognize every demand of the unconscious and adjudicate its claims, remembering always that it is only an agent.

According to Fromm and Horney, mental health is primarily the absence of irrational authority; what is then given is "independent personality," a "free character structure." Since I am not sure what this means, and since it is the jumping-off point for the social philosophy, let me quote some further descriptions. It is "a person who has emancipated himself from oppressing authority, who does not submit nor is an automaton conforming to other people's expectations; he has attained the strength and integration to be himself."[10] He has "a conviction of his own integrity and thereby his identity, based on a self which is unique and indestructible because it is rooted in his own genuine and 'original' act of being."[11] (Is not this narcissim?) "The individual's greatest strength is based on the maximum of integration of his personality, and that means also the maximum of transparence to himself."[12] He is spontaneous: "Spontaneous activity is free activity of the self.... Only if a man does not repress parts of his self, only if he has become transparent to himself, is spontaneous activity possible."[13] (Are we to conclude from these sentences that the free person has no unconscious? This is indeed the end of psychoanalysis!) As *examples* of free character-structure, Fromm mentions artists and uninhibited children; but these examples are preposterous: what artist would say that his good work is *his* work or that, as a creator, he is transparent to himself? and what is more clear, in the behavior of a child, than that it wells from the unconscious and is not "integrated"?

But if the Id, with its dark infinity, is absent from the psychic apparatus of the free personality, where is the *content* rather than the form, of the spontaneity to come from? In Freudian terms, spontaneity—e.g. spontaneous wit—is the emergence of contents of the id called forth by and transforming some objective reality;[14] this is a process familiar to every artist. But the "free personality" is known through and through.

"A character-structure characterized by freedom." Now it is

[10] Fromm, "Faith as a Character Trait," *Psychiatry,* August 1942.
[11] Ibid.
[12] *Escape from Freedom,* p. 249.
[13] Ibid., p. 258.
[14] Freud, *On Wit,* Ch. 6.

axiomatic with both Horney and Fromm that a character-structure and its attitudes can be defined independently of past causes (e.g. sadistic-anal); and likewise independently of present acts; thus "love is a lingering quality in a personality which refers in its manifestations to certain 'objects' but which is not brought into existence by these objects."[15] Then, apart from causes and effects, what is the free character as such? It is free, spontaneous, capable of love and productiveness; it can promise and contract; it is imbued with rational faith. Freedom is—to depend on oneself. And spontaneity is—to be oneself. Love is "the passionate affirmation of another on a basis of equality with mutual respect for each other's integrity";[16] does not this sound like loving oneself? But on what else could love crystallize if we have severed the arc extending from the unknown past through the self into the present? To promise is—to remain identical with oneself. Ah, but the proper object of rational faith is the triumph of the democratic ideals![17]

So it is this independent personality, this pure freedom, absolutely without a past and conceivably without a present, characterized neither by bodily traits nor by social experience, without an unconscious and transparent through and through, and with a very thin collection of instincts (for the "Freudian" instincts are neurotic trends)—it is this figment that is the unit of a free society? With what content is this negation to be filled?

"Rational Authority" and "Democratic Ideals"

Let us turn to the rational authority which is congenial to the free character-structure. It is "objective, based on the competency of the person in authority to function properly with respect to the task of guidance he has to perform." The acceptance of his leadership is rooted in "the conviction based on their own thinking and critical appraisal of the ideas presented." Further, "there is no

---

[15] "Faith as a Character Trait."

[16] Ibid.

[17] Lest the reader think this paragraph unfair, let him ponder on this sentence of Horney: "Generally speaking, the striving for reassurance not only may be as strong as instinctual drives, but may yield an equally strong satisfaction." That is to say, the satisfaction it gives is of the order of an orgasm. Can one avoid calling "personality" a narcissistic object? *The Neurotic Personality of Our Time,* p. 105.

society, and could scarcely be one, without authority and leadership."[18]

First, how is a child supposed to decide on the competency on objective grounds? Children are certainly very astute and intuitive in assessing affection and even honesty, but this is done by emotional rapport (it is just here that adults, more inhibited, go astray); surely an objective test is beyond them: to them a rational authority is simply an authority. But secondly, when the authority is far off, hedged round with special and technical knowledge, in a system beyond any one man's experience, does even an adult feel that he can decide competency? We are recently well acquainted with authorities that on objective grounds of military expediency, or the grounds that careless public criticism might create international complications, have been unable to present their "ideas." Does the free personality still extend his trust? *for how long?* But are we to assume that Fromm is speaking of simple matters, in everybody's ken and which a frank fearless gaze cannot fail to penetrate? Not at all! "The Nazis," he says, "will presently discover that the modern industrial system is incompatible with irrational kinds of faith."[19] It is the *modern industrial system* in which a free personality is supposed to put his trust in competent authority! a system which in itself, under whatever authority, would be tolerated for a moment only by such long habituated maniacs as ourselves. Is not the content of the free character-structure becoming familiar?

There is only one kind of matter that the frank fearless gaze of a child or of a sane man can infallibly penetrate: his strong desires and daily acts. Is he hungry? sexually satisfied? is the work of his hands immediately satisfactory? It is the direct action of these immediate instincts that has the power to make a revolutionary change; there is no need to mediate these things through the formal questions of whether the authority is rational and whether one is technically free. The social cohesion exists prior to the delegation of authority. Authority is delegated *pro tempore* whether to a man or to a system of institutions. Freedom consists not, as Fromm says, in the agreement to participate as an equal member in a vast social system, even if it were known through and through (which it

[18] "Faith as a Character Trait." And see likewise, "Individual and Social Origins"; these two papers are complementary.

[19] Ibid.

is not and will not be), but in the continuing revolution of new demands and ideas as they emerge from the depths, called forth by and transforming the reality, including the institutions. A free society is one that is peacefully permeable by this revolution.

"As long as mankind has not attained a state of organization in which the interest of the individual and that of society are identical, the aims of society have to be attained at a greater or lesser expense of the freedom and spontaneity of the individual. This aim is performed by the process of child-training and education. . . . It is the belief of the progressive forces in society that such a state is possible, that the interest of society and the individual need not be antagonistic forever."[20] What is the desirability, or the meaning, of having the interest of an individual and a society *identical*? But the important point is what to do about the antagonism: is there not the possibility that masses of people might regain freedom and spontaneity, full of content, by resisting the greater or lesser exploitation? In such a case might it not be, from time to time, precisely the disorganization of society, rather than the increasing organization, that is called for? Why do the aims of society *have* to be attained? I am not raising an idle question, for the answer to it determines, for instance, the curricula of different progressive schools. And is it not really an error to speak of men and Society, with a big S (I am not referring to the natural societies of families and friends), as equipollent?—for the freedom and spontaneity of men are natural, but the institutions have been made.

What, according to Fromm, is the social structure that would make possible a free character-structure? First, he says, we must have the Rights already achieved: "the fundamental right of representative government"—the Bill of Rights—and the new right that "society is responsible for all its members; no one shall be frightened into submission and lose his human pride through fear of unemployment and starvation." A psychologist who lays all his emphasis on the relation of man to society, finds that representative, not direct, government, is a fundamental political act! And a progressive who looks for the end of the exploiting system finds that society is responsible for its members and not that they must learn to be responsible for themselves!

[20] "Individual and Social Origins," pp. 381, 384.

Secondly: "The irrational and planless character of society must be replaced by a planned economy that represents the concerted effort of society as such. Society must master (!) the social problem as rationally as it has mastered nature." This is the language of an anti-authoritarian. "Today the vast majority of people have little chance to develop genuine initiative at the particular job they are doing. Only in a planned economy in which the whole nation has rationally mastered the economic and social forces, can the individual share responsibility and use creative intelligence in his work."[21] This is simply false. The experience of anarchist groups, wherever they have had a chance, disproves it.[22] What he pictures is Stakhanovism. If he gave the slightest thought to actual conditions of industry he would realize that the initiative and ingenuity of the individual worker require precisely the loosening and decentralizing of the economy, which in most ways is already overplanned. "Unless planning from the top," he goes on to say, "is blended with active participation from below, a planned economy will lead to renewed manipulation of the people."[23] Why need there be a blend? Why cannot the economy be primarily and progressively managed from below, as in the proposals of the anarcho-syndicalists? (Is one supposed to think that Fromm is honestly ignorant of such possibilities?)

The System of Sociolatry

The method of Fromm and Horney is to empty out the soul and then fill it. It is filled with social unanimity and rational faith: "The aims of the individual and society are identical."

By deciding in principle that character-structure is the institutional pattern, rather than the effect of conflict between instinct, including social instinct, and the institutional pattern, it then becomes easy to conceive a "free society" that does not oppress the "free personalities." Easy, so long as the discussion is purely formal and juridical. But: (1) what if the political content of the structure then proves to be the Four Freedoms and "modern

[21] *Escape*, pp. 271ff.
[22] E.g., cf. *The Spanish Labyrinth*, by Gerald Brenan.
[23] *Escape*, p. 275.

industrial life''? And (2) what meanwhile has happened to the revolutionary dynamism of instinctual conflict to bring about any institutional change at all?

On the one side we have the free personality: by definition it is not neurotic, for it has neither conflict nor dream. Its desires, such as they are, are transparent, for they are just what institutional approval keeps in the forefront of consciousness; another institutional pattern would alter their number and intensity; there is little in them that is natural, irreducible, or culturally dangerous. But *on the other side,* the social bond itself is nothing but the mutual reflection of these self-secure integrities. Recall the definition of love. Is not this the very picture of a small academic? Where is there a place in this hall of mirrors for either personality or fraternity?

What is rational faith?

To survive man needs faith. To survive in the world of the present and the evolving future, every one will need rational faith. It is only in a social order in which the democratic ideals are being more and more fully realized that the needed rational faith can develop and prevail.

In the course of the development of mankind the objects of faith have become more and more rational and have come into an increasing close relation to practical questions of social and political organization.

While solidarity and mutual obligation receive considerable stress in time of war, the tendency in peace time has been to develop irresponsible egotism. [24]

We need not go far, I think, to find what is meant by rationality, solidarity, and responsibility (where have we heard this word?): it is what the democratic regimes have more and more been tending toward on the whole, and the wartime morale that you may feel by stepping outside without a raincoat is a quite good sample.

What is the content of rational faith? it is the extension of the *attitude* of freedom. And what is the act of the attitude of freedom? it is the *attitude* of participation in the social solidarity. And what is the goal of the attitude of participation? it is the *attitude* of mutual respect for each other's integrity. . . . At no point in this rigmarole is there *ever* any content!

Meanwhile the content is clear as day: *it is the continued and more efficient working, without nervous breakdowns, of the*

[24] "Faith."

modern industrial system, war and peace. This is taken for
granted!

Now nearly a century ago, in the time of Louis Napoleon, the
heir of the revolution of '48 (yes! just as the Super-Ego is the heir
of the Oedipus complex)—a great man, Auguste Comte, with far
more psychological inventiveness than your Fromms and Horneys,
conceived of his *System of Sociolatry,* a rational faith for the
spiritual organization of men, so that the modern industrial system
could continue to work more efficiently, war and peace. Compared
to the Sociolatry, Fromm's system is as yet a pale imitation.

III.

What a pleasure it is to turn from this philistine ethical culture
to a Freudian deviation to the left! I am referring to the work of
Wilhelm Reich, expelled in 1933 from the International Psychoanalytical Association because of his insistence on carrying into
social action the obvious implications of the original instinct theory
(along with related revolutionary economic demands). This insistence has not endeared him to the Marxists either, though he is a
Marxist. Whether or not one follows Reich in all his theoretic
deviations—and it seems to me that, lacking in Freud's beautiful
intuitive centrality among the sciences of Man, he misses the point
of the complexity of Freud's discussion of the psychic apparatus—
nevertheless, in what refers to immediate social agitation, he
applies what is so fundamental and undeniable in Freud to evils
that are so glaring in society, that one must agree absolutely.
Considering the appalling proportion of neurosis on any criterion,
and which on his own criterion of "true orgastic potency." and the
orgasm reflex includes the *vast majority of the population,*[25] Reich
shows the futility of medical treatment of a few cases; he argues
that analysts who do not lend their authority to immediate general
sex-liberation in education, morals, and marriage, are no true
doctors. He demonstrates in case reports that persons restored to
sexual health and animal spirits simply will not tolerate the
mechanical and routine jobs they have been working at, but turn
(at whatever general inconvenience) to work that is spontaneous
and directly meaningful.

[25] Wilhelm Reich, *The Function of the Orgasm* (1942), p. 169.

If the work in which they were engaged lent itself to the absorption of real interest, they blossomed out. If, however, their work was mechanical as e.g. that of an employee, a merchant, or a clerk, it became an almost unbearable burden. The difficulty which now made its appearance was hard to overcome. For the world was not geared to a consideration of human interest in work. Teachers who, though liberal, had not been particularly critical of present-day education, began to feel the usual manner of handling children as painful and intolerable.

The changes occurring in my patients were both positively and negatively ambiguous. Their new attitude seemed to follow laws which had nothing in common with the usual moral concepts and demands, laws which were new to me. The picture presented at the end by all of them was that of *a different kind of society*.

The individual with a "moral" structure appears to follow the rigid laws of the moral world; in fact he only adjusts outwardly and rebels inwardly. Thus he is exposed in the highest degree to an unconscious compulsive and impulsive anti-sociality. The healthy self-regulated individual does not adjust himself to the irrational part of the world and insists on his natural rights. [26]

He concludes that the repression of infantile and adolescent sexuality by family, school, and church, and by such conditions as inadequate housing and economically forced abstinence, is *the direct cause of the submissiveness of the people to present political rule of whatever kind;* but that unrepressed people will provide for themselves a society that is peaceable and orderly enough; more generally,

The participation of the industrial workers in the *management* of production and distribution, in contrast to a representation of their interests by parties or trade unions, in which the workers themselves remain passive. [27]

How does he come to all this?

First he returns to Freud's original observation of the libido-economy: *the energy of anxiety is the energy of repressed sexuality.* In the condition of actual-neurosis (brought on e.g. by habitual interrupted coition or a sudden renunciation of masturbation) it is the entire cause of the anxiety, and in every psychoneurosis there is a core of actual-neurosis. This is the position that Freud later declared to be, not false, but of secondary importance, [28] when he

[26] Ibid., pp. 150-156.
[27] "Living Productive Power," *Journal of Sex Economy,* Oct. 1944, p. 161.
[28] *The Problem of Anxiety,* p. 105.

came to lay the emphasis on the fearful perception of the punishing authority and the systematizing of the Ego against the instincts (and Horney, as we have seen, took this second position and left out the cause of the fear). But Reich argues as follows: it is the *core of actual-anxiety* that makes vivid the anticipation of punishment, for one cannot have a vivid *image* without a source of energy from within; then the fearful anticipation leads to a repetition of the inhibition and this of course redoubles the actual-anxiety, and so forth; thus, actual-neurosis leads to psychoneurosis.

To turn the fright of a really experienced punishment into an habitual state of fearfulness and submissiveness takes very little deprivation to begin with, *unless the circle is broken by positive gratification*. It is not sufficient to reduce the unconscious associations; unless the patient has positive sexual satisfaction, if only by masturbation, the cycle of anxiety will recommence. To avoid the inner tension and the anxiety, the child then tenses his muscles and holds his breath and literally constructs a character-armor against his sexuality: this becomes, as many thicknesses are added, the "moral character" described above.[29] Therefore, by an analysis of character and neurosis, we see how Reich must be led to consider the vast majority as sick, and to hold that there must be a revolution in morals and economy, perhaps especially with regard to adolescence, for it is then that the instincts resurge through the armor and give the possibility of real gratification. Likewise, in medical therapy itself Reich adds to the Freudian goal of uncovering and reliving the conflicts, the absolute need of actively effectuating orgastic potency and gratification. A moment's reflection will show how profoundly this must alter the role of the physician.

(In order to base a "different kind of society" on instinctual liberation alone, Reich gives a picture of the instinctual life which, it seems to me, is excessively simple and Rousseauian. But *at the present moment* this picture is perfectly adequate as a kind of "minimum demand" that broad masses can unite on.)

IV.

Let me summarize the argument of this essay: I have tried to show how, in the present situation of admitted mass neurosis, three

[29] *Function*, pp. 109-129.

different theories of neurosis directly imply three different political philosophies:

1. HORNEY-FROMM: The core of neurosis is the defeat of personality in the conflict with irrational authority; therapy is the reduction of such authority; and free society is the competent rule of representatives of free personalities. The instincts are largely out of the picture. We saw that such a society is only formally desirable; that like any juridical formula it is true as a negative check, e.g. against exploitation; that such content as is indicated seems very like the ideal of the industrial status quo; and all revolutionary dynamics to bring about any change has vanished. This is the psychology of the coming sociolatry. (In Freudian terms: *erotized Ego.*)

2. REICH: Here the core of neurosis is in the deprivation of instinctual satisfaction, and the aim of therapy is to give instinctual satisfaction. Orgastically potent people will not tolerate authority or present-day industrial forms, but will instinctually create new forms. The role of the judging and deciding Ego is left largely out of account, and the instincts are considered correspondingly simple and compatible. At present, such a theory is acceptable in every *positive* detail (though not always in what it denies); it has enormous revolutionary dynamism. It is the psychology of the revolution. (*Rationalized Id.*)

3. FREUD: The core of the neurosis is the defense of the Ego against the instincts, and the aim of therapy is to make the Ego again part of the Id. Good society (as we shall immediately discuss it) is the maximum of happiness possible to the non-rational Id, whose instincts are part social, part anti-social, part inventive, part archaic; culture is an art and science of the Ego as the interpreter of reality. But in fact, Freud should but does not say, such an art is possible only *after* a thorogoing liberation has set free natural alternatives to choose from. This is the psychology of the post-revolution. (*Ego as part of Id.*)

POSTSCRIPT: FREUD'S POLITICS

I want to say something about the political writing of Freud. There is a startling, almost uncanny, apparent contradiction between the therapeutic goals of Freud and his explicit theory. His therapy is to liberate the instinct and to clarify all transferred and transformed eros to its original form. His politics emphasizes the need for repression of instinct (for even more repression than exists!) and for the sublimation of eros into the social bonds of brotherly love. But first, let us remember this: the environment of the therapy was a quiet conversation between a wise physician and a patient becoming wiser; then one might trust in reason to draw on nature. And the environment of the politics? *Civilization and its Discontents* appeared in 1929, when the Nazis were getting their forces; when it was clear that the Russian revolution, for which Freud had had high hopes,[30] was failing *from within*; when war was coming, yet still there was a struggle, for a formula of peace. Then Freud, an admirer of Lenin, could say that Capitalism had at least the advantage that it was a not absolutely fatal outlet for hostile drives! He was 74 years old, and we know that he was ill and tired.[31]

Freud was a poor observer of our culture-patterns; one feels that his experience of social facts was second hand, as if from newspapers. All the more clear was his wonderful central reflective feeling for the vast human culture that does not change with dynasties, but must be read in anthropology and the history of religions. Of course, by serious standards, he was not a scholar at all; I am not attempting to say that his speculations are correct; but that he knew, unlearned, by genius, the *kinds* of facts that were relevant, and the *weights* to be assigned; so that serious scholars employ Freud's categories. Now this kind of wisdom is useless in the practical affairs of the world, as things are; now there are crying abuses and we must turn to Reich. But they will be invaluable when one day there is peace and nature, just as they are invaluable today to artists and poets, who work with inner peace and nature. Then the problems of politics will be to increase the richness and deepen the color of happiness (the very happiness of which Freud despaired); then there will be no use for the simple formulas of a Reich, and we must turn to Freud. Let me give an example. Reich says we are to trust our liberated love: this will

[30] *Function,* p. 183, but cf. *Civilization and its Discontents,* pp. 87ff.

[31] The earlier work, *Mass-Psychology and the Analysis of the Ego,* to my mind contains most of what is valuable in all the books on the psychology of authoritarian states.

make a "society of a different kind." Good! True! But consider, for instance the case of Oedipus and sibling incest. Could there be a very elaborate culture if great masses of the people were incestuous and cemented with complete satisfaction the ties that already bind them so close to home? would they ever then really stir abroad? This great privilege of gods and pharaohs must perhaps then *not* be trusted, but sublimated: "The most maiming wound," says Freud, "ever inflicted through the ages on the erotic life of man." "Culture," says Freud, "obeys the laws of psychological economic necessity in making restrictions, for it obtains the great part of the mental energy it needs by subtracting it from sexuality. Culture behaves toward sexuality like a tribe in a population that has gained the upper hand and is exploiting the rest to its own advantage. Fear of a revolt among the oppressed then becomes the motive for even stricter regulation."[32] This is not the wisdom needed today, but is it not useful for a people who are rational and natural *enough,* and want to live better still?

There is still another melancholy reason for the defects in Freud's political thought and action. He was the father of the psychoanalytical movement—how much a loving but somewhat awesome father one may surmise by the violence and hostility with which some analysts broke with him (like Adler); the euphemistic laudations of others (like Horney) at the very time that they are turning everything upside down; and the touching reverence of others who try to prove they agree even when they disagree (like Reich). From the beginning psychoanalysis was the object of bitter attacks and personal slanders by the whole barrage of the social institutions it undermined. Freud protected his child; it was inevitable that he would over-protect it, imagining that it could survive by caution rather than by standing witness to the truth. Even when he was over eighty years old (1938), he was afraid to publish *Moses* in Vienna, lest the *Catholic Church* withdraw its "support" and crush the movement![33] This by the author of *The Future of an Illusion*! Would one not say that he was demented? Shame not on Freud, but shame on the world for bringing their old teacher to this confusion!

[32] *Civilization,* p. 74.
[33] *Moses,* p. 85.

A RESPONSE BY C. WRIGHT MILLS
AND PATRICIA J. SALTER
THE BARRICADE AND THE BEDROOM

For a long time conservatives have stressed the biological immutability of man's nature, whereas progressives have emphasized the social plasticity of his character structure. Conservatives have tried to buttress every status quo by appealing to the biological instincts of man. Now Paul Goodman seeks to overturn a particular status quo by appealing to the apparently same instinctual nature.[1] He presents us with a metaphysics of biology in which he would do no less than anchor a revolution.

The difference between Goodman's metaphysics and, for example, Max Eastman's ("Socialism Doesn't Jibe with Human Nature") is that Eastman roots the existing economic order in his biology, whereas Goodman uses his as a lever to overturn capitalism and institute anarchism. If, says Eastman, current institutions, especially private property, are upset, "the techniques of modern industry and education are left at the mercy of the naked instincts of a savage tribe." If, says Goodman, man's instincts, especially the sexual, are released, he might not be neurotic and indeed might build a new heaven on earth: "Unrepressed people will provide for themselves a society that is peaceful and orderly enough." There is, writes Eastman, a "drive" . . . a "veritable passion . . . for regimentation and discipleship, for being lead, for obeying and conforming . . ." etc. And regardless of "how much they may be repressed or directed by training" such "drives reappear in the

[1] Re: Paul Goodman's "The Political Meaning of some Recent Revisions of Freud," which appeared in *Politics,* July, 1945. Most of Goodman's discussion is in criticism of Fromm and Horney. We are not here concerned with their defense, although in passing we must note that most of what Goodman criticizes is his own misunderstanding of their position. We wish, rather, to examine his positive assumptions, the theories upon which he tries to stand and which he uses as a critical lever. Fromm and Horney are part of a general drift in current research and theory which moves toward a historical and a sociological psychology. We agree wholly with that drift and with its positive political relevance. It is the political meaning of this general drift—which Goodman opposes—rather than details in the work of these particular writers which we discuss here. C.W.M. & P.J.S.

original form." Goodman, on the other hand, drawing from Reich, thinks that the direct cause of "the submissiveness of the people to present political rule of whatever kind" is the "repression of infantile and adolescent sexuality." On the basis of the uninhibited release of such sexuality he would rest genuinely free and humane (not savage) institutions. You choose your biology and you get your political order.

The key tactic of these political appeals to biology is the masking of ethical choices by a metaphysics of biology. The confusion of moral choices with theories of the biology of personality development is an underlying inadequacy of Goodman's essay.

The speculative insight that man's social existence determines his consciousness has been continually verified by modern social psychology. Goodman admits to difficulties in understanding the sociological theory of personality-formation. He states that if personality is not developed according to the Freudian model, it must be "apparently sprung from nowhere." Thus, he does not see types of childhood, biography, and social structure in their intricate and sophisticated inter-relations. He apparently fails to understand that *social* integrations of impulse and feeling in one phase of the psychic structure may not be adequate to meet the *social* demands of subsequent roles. But, of course, it is from such socially created tensions that neuroses, as well as many psychological capacities for social change, may arise.

There is a general continuity between the Fromm-Horney sociological revision of Freud and the anti-psychologism of Marx. One aspect of this continuity is the idea that the problems of a particular social structure—including the neuroses of its members—cannot be reduced to those of man's biological nature. To assume that the biological organism can be used as a basis for judgment about an existing social structure, or a wished-for one, is simply to biologize the social contract theory of the state and of institutions in general.

The capitalist market cannot be derived from a study of the economic man, nor can the frustration which it causes be understood by examining man's *formal* biological equipment. Indeed, the specific impulses which sustain economic man are shaped by their operations on various types of markets. Impulses are given *content* only by the participation of men in given institutions. The content of frustrations—and the severe political directions which they may take—are dependent upon the particular institutions men create.

Goodman is concerned lest a sociological psychology lose "the revolutionary dynamics of instinctual conflict to bring about institutional change at all." He believes that "it is the direct action of these immediate instincts [sex, hunger, etc.] that has the power to make a revolutionary change." Thus, he locates the dynamics of revolution in a tension between biology and institutions, and rests his hope for revolution upon a mass biological release.

This gonad theory of revolution would be the more amusing if Goodman attempted to interpret any known revolution with it. Then, the historical dynamics of class structures, the gap between tantalizing aspirations and deprivations socially rendered, the sudden defeat of mass armies, the grip of ideologies, the slow growth of counterloyalties—all the shifts in institutional structure, as well as the distributions of power, property, and prestige, Mr. Goodman would have somehow to pull, like historical rabbits, from his biological hat. Apparently the positions held and the interests assumed by class members are not relevant to revolutionary dynamics. Thus, if the capitalist managers of GM become "orgastically potent," they would be as likely to overthrow the institution of private property as would "released" and organized workers.

The dynamics of revolution go on within institutional structures. The motives of individual men engaging in movements for or against the status quo must be understood in terms of the differing positions they occupy within these structures, and in terms of the biographies they seek to live out within and beyond the circles of their society. The locus of freedom, and of the historical dynamic, is not the gonads but the political and economic order.

The sphere of erotics is not connected with the economic and political order in the direct way, and certainly not in the direction, which Mr. Goodman apparently believes. Although no general rule governs the relation, it would seem that political energies more frequently go with sexual asceticism; and lack of sexual inhibition with lack of political initiative. One can easily compare sexually free and easy characters with sexually ascetic revolutionary leaders.

In modern society, man, when alienated from his work may well turn to "sex." Dr. Reich may have implemented in various cases this secular process and given it his authoritative approval. But "sexually released" men do not turn against the institutions which ruin one of their major chances for self-expression—creative work. On the contrary, given current institutions, what Durant has called, "the machinery of amusement" seizes precisely upon "sex" and exploits it as the central value of "fun" and "glamor." The circle of "orgastic potency" is much more likely to be from bedroom to bedroom, than from bedroom to barricade.

"Orgastic potency" is not the key to "freedom"; much less is it the lever of revolution. Within the broad range of sexual expression open to the species, the freely rational man will "place" sex in his life scheme as one value among others. Since many men, as formed by contemporary institutions, are neither free nor rational, they are not fully capable of so locating sex. Victor Mature and Betty Grable are thus the current images of "orgastic potency." We do not see what their antics nor those of their imitators have to do with freedom or with revolution. As values in a style of life for free men and women, they are more likely to lead away from serious concern with political injustice.

Historically, as Max Weber has noted, sex has frequently been socially and psychically linked with religion and magical orgiasticism. Sex is among the great irrational forces, and when it is cultivated, either by certain types of psychoanalytic therapy or by any other ideological manipulation, it may become eroticism:.an end and a value in itself.

The enhancement of sex into eroticism as a central value in modern culture must be understood in connection with the social structure of feudal honor and vassalship. Later forms of this development, including the rationalist development of modern vocational man, would have to be studied for the full picture. In short, what role "sex" plays in the development and lives of different types of men is in very large part a problem of the sociological history.of the values attached to sex.

"The kingdom of freedom" of which Marx and the left in general have dreamed involves the mastering of one's fate. A free society entails the *social possibility* and the psychological capacity of men to make rational political choices. The sociological theory of character development conceives of man as capable of making such choices *only* under favorable institutional conditions. It thus leads to an emphasis upon the necessity of changing institutions in order to enlarge man's capacity to live freely. But to root freedom in the release of biological instinct denies to man this capacity for rational freedom; it turns freedom over to the gratification of protoplasm. If we accept Goodman's concept of freedom, the cultivation of biological "release," freedom becomes identified with the fixed irrationalities of the leisured and private life.

Rationality and freedom are values which must be socially achieved. But in the Rousseauian conception, which Goodman apparently holds, freedom is "naturally" given to individual men. To flower, it needs only release from institutional bondage. But, in fact, it is a freedom which would make man a slave to biological instinct and deny the rational component of freedom as social achievement.

Freedom does have as its condition specifiable institutional arrangements. But its locus is not between man's biological impulses and institutions. In all societies of which we know, these impulses are structured and defined in their content by whatever values prevail for given men. Men in society learn to will what is objectively required for the enactment of institutionalized roles. And values and slogans legitimize these roles and the trained impulses which sustain their enactment. Freedom lies in choice of roles being open to individuals and to classes of individuals. Its locus is the institutional arrangement of these roles, not the absence of conflict between biologically given drives and the structure of institutions.

The psychological problem of a socialist movement is not how to release the "orgastic potencies" of men but how to make men rationally and critically aware of where their interests lie and how they may realize them collectively.

A socialist view of human nature will recognize fully that man is a historical creature. It will not mask its humane scheme of values by a metaphysics of biology. It will recognize the collective conditions of work which exist under capitalism and which will continue to exist in any modern industrial society. It will see in immense detail how the institutions of such collective work, pegged upon bureaucratized private property, make for the alienation of man from one of his key chances to contact reality creatively. It will see that the chances of individual men rationally to work out their life plans are increasingly expropriated by the spread and clutch of corporative institutions. The goal of a socialistic movement and the ideology it will seek to develop, will be fitted to these facts.

It is because of the dependence of individual man's "innermost being" upon institutions that he should be given this chance to plan what shape these institutions may take, for only by changing his social structure can he collectively change his individual self. The problem of freedom cannot be adequately stated in terms of the unhampered expression of the individual's biological instincts. Freedom, as well as other values for which we should strive, must be viewed in terms of institutional structures and the opportunity for rational social planning. Leave Mr. Goodman with his revolution in the bedroom. We have still to search out the barricades of our freedom.

C. WRIGHT MILLS AND PATRICIA J. SALTER

REPLY:

These authors confound two different issues: (a) the "biological" vs. the "social"; (b) "human nature" vs. "historical character." On the first point it is the Freudian view that our inherited nature is social thru and thru; this also is the view, e.g., of Proudhon and Kropotkin and Marx and Engels; all these are therefore social-psychologists rather than individual-psychologists; they develop different, but mostly quite compatible, pictures of the original social nature. For instance, Marx and Engels regard cooperative production as the biological determinant of the emergence of our species and therefore they correlate the erect posture with the freeing and perfecting of the hand; Freud, laying more stress on reproduction, correlates erect posture with the loss of the sense of smell, the primacy of sight and hearing, the exposure of the genitals. Now communication is inherited; the dependency and educability of infants is inherited; the forming of the ego on the exemplars that gratify and deprive, and conversely the merging of the mother's ego with the infant's; and the extraordinary parallel development of pleasure-zones and object-choices, resulting in the connection of seeing, embracing and copulating—all this elaborate pattern of social function must be inherited. But furthermore, for Freud, there is no such thing as pleasure except in function—pleasure, as he says, is "anaclitic"—therefore it is reasonable to regard uncoerced desire as a social force. These propositions are commonplace, but I fail to see how they are trivialized by quotations from Max Eastman. One does not "choose" one's biology. Certainly I may be omitting or wrongly estimating certain biological facts, but this must be shown biologically, not by dismissing biology from the argument.

The authors have a curious misconception of my political position, and, I may say, of the libertarian position in general. We are not asserting that the liberation of instinct will of itself produce a "heaven on earth"; good institutions are cooperative inventions, they come to be as adjustments and transformations of historical conditions, they are certainly not inherited. But we assert that the repression of instinct makes good institutions unattainable. And by and large, since the instincts are elaborately organized, the repression of some will entail the repression or violent reaction of others. The importance of sexuality especially can be wrongly estimated: when it is free, it is only one among several productive forces; but when it is repressed it is the most important destructive influence that there is. I should certainly agree that "political energies go with sexual asceticism": these are precisely the energies that we see in the sadism and masochism of monolithic parties and in transitional dictatorships that become permanent. Let me refer the authors who blab so glibly about "pulling historical rabbits out of a biological hat," to Reich's brilliant history of the sex-reform movement in Soviet Russia, 1919-1935 (in *The Sexual Revolution,* 1945).

To turn to the second issue, human nature and history: in general, "human nature" refers to a potentiality and as such can only be observed in its acts, which are historical. Human nature is inferred positively from great achievements, from the lively promise of youngsters, etc.; it is inferred negatively from the dire effects of obvious outrages. "Conservatives," say these authors, "have stressed the biological immutability of man's nature, whereas progressives have emphasized the social plasticity of his character-structure." Now I hoped that I had made it clear that original nature was different from character-structure, which is in every case a good or bad organization of one's experiences, conflicts, and opportunities: good when the organization implements and actualizes one's powers, bad when it depresses them. Then is it the fact that radicals—not "progressives"—have emphasized the plasticity of original nature rather than cried out precisely against the outrages against it? I need not mention the anarchists and utopian-socialists who have drawn especially on the French revolutionary word Fraternity, the eros that creates institutions. But is it so sure that Marx and Engels believed that there was no original nature or that it was unimportant? Is it not their position that we must destroy class institutions just in order that true humanity, with its tragedies, can assert itself? Let me cull a few quotations (they are in Venable's *Human Nature: the Marxian View,* which I happen to have to hand): "These Londoners," says Engels, "have been forced to sacrifice the best qualities of their human nature—a hundred powers which slumbered within them have remained inactive, have been suppressed . . . The dissolution of mankind into monads, of which each one has a separate principle, is here carried out to its utmost extreme . . . One shrinks from the consequences of our social state and can only wonder that the whole crazy fabric still holds together." The manufacturing division of labor, says Marx, "cuts at the very roots of the individual's life;—to subdivide a man is to execute him . . . The subdivision of labor is the assassination of a people." It makes the worker "a cripple, a monster, by forcing him to develop some highly specialized dexterity at the cost of a world of productive impulses and faculties." Again, is not the Marxian meaning of alienation the divorce, under the pressure of commodity-institutions, of man's consciousness from his nature? Lastly, in the glorious passage in the Gotha critique that goes "in a higher phase of communist society, after the enslaving subordination of individuals under division of labor, and therewith also the antithesis between mental and physical labor, has vanished; after labor has become not merely a means to live but has become itself the primary necessity of life; after the productive forces have also increased with the all round development of the individual"—is not Marx returning, in a higher phase, to something like the "character-structure" of primitive communism, and indeed to the original biological emergence of the species as cooperative producer?

On the other hand, is it not just the fascists—not the "conservatives"—who have most relied on the notion that by fear, repression, and coordination a man can be made to conform to any symbols whatever? I am not implying that the authors are fascists, but that they are indeed progressives—not radicals. I wonder, however, since we are not to speak of inherited powers and their realization and cultural perfection, exactly on what do these progressives base their "humane scheme of values"? *Where do they find the motives for their Sociolatry?*

As to the points the authors make by the way, I confess that most of them seem to me to be rubbish. "The machinery of amusement seizes upon sex and exploits it as the central value of fun and glamor"—what on earth has this to do with liberating the sexuality of children and 13-year-olds? On the contrary, would the exploitation of sex be possible except for the prior inhibition? One cannot create popular culture except on the basis of desire, and "glamor" is just the flaunting of the mysterious and habitually forbidden. I am sure that we are all grateful for the newsy item from Max Weber, especially for the bashful fact that sex has frequently been socially linked with religious orgiasticism. What do you know? By all means let us keep the role of "sex" well within quotation marks, for it is by the sociological history of "values" that we procreate the race. It is also, no doubt, by the "institutional arrangment of the social roles" that my thumb freely opposes its four fingers. And certainly it must have been only after a close study of unnecessarily centralized technology, the subdivision of labor for profits, the sabotage of invention and inventiveness, the discipline of the timeclock, and the premiums on wasteful planning, that the authors assure us that "the collective conditions of work which exist under capitalism will continue to exist in any modern industrial society"—for do they not also exist in the Soviet Union, and didn't they beat Japan?

PAUL GOODMAN.

When this iconoclastic essay was published in *Politics* (July 1945), it irritated many leftwingers as well as orthodox psychoanalysts. C. Wright Mills and Patricia Salter wrote a long attack on it for the October issue, to which Goodman responded. Even Reich himself complained—of being linked with the anarchists (see the Introduction above).

Sex
and
Revolution

Wilhelm Reich is perhaps the most brilliant of the generation of psychoanalysts after the first World War. He was the leader of the Technical Seminar that devoted itself to the problems of actual analytic practice and evolved the now widespread notion of the neurotic character rather than the neurotic symptom. A Marxist, he became convinced, through work with German youth-groups, of the political importance of psychotherapy. With the reaction of the U.S.S.R. against the sexual revolution, he broke with the Communists. And his insistence on the need for analysis to play an active social role led also to his expulsion from the International Psychoanalytic Association, in 1933. In Scandinavia, during the thirties, he led the movement for sexual reform (contraceptive information, etc.), attracting a certain mass following for his Sex-Economic program. Now in this country, he seems to be devoting most of his attention to bio-electrical experiments on which, as yet, no competent judgment has been passed, to my knowledge.

The two works now put into English by Dr. Wolfe date from the twenties and thirties; they are in the line of standard psychoanalytic investigation and do not draw on the new biophysical principles. *The Sexual Revolution* is a compendium of "Sexuality and the Cultural Struggle" and much of the substance of "The Fiasco of Sexual Moralism," "The Sexual Struggle of Youth," and "Mass Psychology of Fascism." Whatever criticisms or reservations one might make in essaying this work, its thesis is so simple and direct, so immediately applicable to family-life and pedagogy and yet so revolutionary, that it cannot be disregarded or evaded. Since American readers, however, are mostly ignorant of Reich's work, I here devote space to summarizing his position.

It is not sufficient, says Reich, for parents and educators to have a liberal attitude toward the sexuality of children, and educators to teach the facts of life and preach that sex is natural and beautiful. The children and adolescents must enjoy actual sexual pleasure according to their ages and desires. Every permission must be accorded them; in the present state of social prohibition there must be active encouragement, such as the provision of private quarters to adolescents. *The issue is not one of attitude but of physiological sexual stasis or flow.* Continence as such is harmful in the young.

Reich returns to the old libido-economy contention of Freud that the core of all psychoneurosis is "actual-neurosis," anxiety caused simply by dammed-up libido. This anxiety it is that heightens the fear of the repressing forces, leads to further repression, more damming-up, more actual anxiety, and more psychic fear. The result is a character lacking in initiative and independence, prone to accept authority, and masochistic or sadistic as influenced. Reich sees this character as a necessary condition and even a cause of fascism. Further, by means of the coercive monogamous family this character recreates itself from generation to generation and nullifies the progressive revolution in politics and economics: "the revolution in the ideological superstructure fails to take place because the bearer of this revolution, the psychic structure of human beings, has not been changed." Thus, according to Reich, the Leninist revolution degenerates into a new political submissiveness and a compulsive-anal attitude toward economic work, instead of the spontaneous cooperation of true communism.

On the other hand, those who have been sexually liberated and enjoy "orgastic potency" at once show a new productiveness in interesting work but refuse to continue with dull, routine, or meaningless jobs. (For such cases, see Wm. Reich, *The Function of the Orgasm,* 1942.) Politically, Reich is a syndicalist.

According to Reich's standards of "orgastic potency"—which he distinguishes sharply, for instance, from erective potency—the great majority are neurotic. There is therefore little use in curative psychoanalytic procedure, but we must revolutionize the institutions of family and school. This is the insistence on bringing analysis out of the consulting-room and down into the streets that led to Reich's expulsion from the International Psychoanalytic Association in 1933, coincident with the rise of Hitler who nevertheless did not prove exactly a friend to analysis.

In arguing his central thesis of the need for actual sex-gratification, Reich wittily presents the dilemma of the liberal parent who tries to be permissive, honest, and informative on sexual matters and nevertheless, in the interests of "decency" and social conformity, wants the child to bide his time. The result is a mental confusion and anxiety in some ways worse than the effects of the older total prohibition; the imperfect repression results in problem cases familiar to progressive educators. Reich presents a brilliant critical review of the popular sex educational literature current in Germany in the twenties, similar to our own advanced writing on this subject. But probably the best thing in the book is the history of the sex-reform movement in Soviet Russia, the description of sex-life in the kindergartens and the communes, the analysis of delinquency and the so-called "work therapy," the resistance of both peasantry and proletariat, up to the calamitous return of the anti-abortion laws, the abolition of co-education, the persecution of homosexuals, the enforcement of monogamy, etc.

In general, Reich holds that on the genital level self-regulation cannot lead to anti-social acts; that sadism and other anti-social acts are the results of repression; that in free genital characters the pre-genital sexuality is either incorporated into genitality as fore-pleasure or readily sublimated; that free genital characters spurn casual relationships but also refuse to remain in marriages that are no longer gratifying. He does not hold with Freud that culture depends on sublimation, but rather that gratification releases productivity. As a substitute for the patriarchal family, he urges a return to collective domesticity as a means of socializing the Oedipus complex. Against educators like Anna Freud, he holds that the super-ego, the internalized parental or social authority, is useless (and impossible) for free people.

One must distinguish between Reich's self-governing "genital character" and the "free personality structure" of Fromm and Horney. All these writers primarily analyze neurotic character rather than neurotic symptoms; and Fromm, like Reich, but later (and both of them after Freud's great study of *Mass-Psychology and the Analysis of the Ego*), interpret the Fascist as a sado-masochistic character. But Reich, having broken through the neurotic character by hammering at the resistances, then proceeds to dissolve the infantile incest which is the original cause of inhibition, and lastly he seeks to liberate the sexual stasis by establishing genital potency. He remains with the historical method of Freud and the "genital character" has a concrete and definable content. But the "free personality" of Fromm and Horney, so far as I can understand it all, is a purely formal entity that can be adjusted to any social content if the juridical forms are observed.

It is just because Reich wants to set free the forces native to each individual, which, in adults at least, are beyond the influence of advertising slogans and political propaganda, that his thought has such enormous libertarian dynamism.

In terms of the future culture and achievement of free social groups, his thought has grave defects; compared with Freud, or Rank, he seems strangely narrow and even inhumane. One is not clear how his proposals for child-care differ from the institutional bleakness of crèches and day-nurseries. When he speaks of the "structure of the Id," we begin to lose the underworld of Freud, archaic yet still endlessly inventive of social combinations. Like most of the analytic writers—especially the women!—he has a male bias; if motherhood is nothing but the secondary instinct he speaks of, one wonders how the race came to survive.

Nevertheless, this book must be squarely faced: it places the responsibility on parent and teacher in their daily acts.

This review of a couple of Reich's reprinted books was first written "on assignment" for the *New Republic,* but the editors turned it down as unsuitable for their readers. *View* (November 1945) then published it.

The
Fate
of
Dr. Reich's
Books

I.

We are here concerned with the fate of Dr. Reich's books, banned by the Food and Drug Administration. The relation of theory and practice, of a scientific theory and its applications, is a thorny one; but it *must* in every case be decided in the direction of absolute freedom of speculation and publication, otherwise it is impossible to live and breathe. The practical policing of therapies is not an author's responsibility. The Administrator's reasoning in Section 5 of his injunction is intolerable; if it cannot be struck down, it must be flouted—we must applaud the republication (by Farrar, Straus) of some of the banned passages, and the forthcoming publication of *The Function of the Orgasm*.

The forbidding of "statements pertaining to the *existence* of orgone energy" is simply ludicrous. The Administrator of the drug law is not the Creator of the heavens and the earth; he is not even the Pope in Rome. Is he quite sane, to write such a proposition?

His notion of the books as "constituting labeling" is more interesting; for no one can candidly read *The Function of the Orgasm; The Cancer Biopathy; The Sexual Revolution; The Mass-Psychology of Fascism; Listen, Little Man;* or *Character Analysis* in any edition, and regard them as labels or advertisements. In the first place, the very vulgarity of such a conception makes one

75

smile—and wince. The Administrator has been moving too much in the racketeering circles of the drug companies, the medical journals, and certain members of the A.M.A. who were recently under Congressional investigation for their plugging and pricing. But my guess is that the Administrator's lack of candor betrays a different intent. The real objection to Dr. Reich's work has little to do with orgone energy, but is to its whole drift as pedagogy, social science, and perhaps medical science; and *therefore* his books are banned and any convenient pretext is seized on to impede their circulation. Dealing with strong universal drives and terrible real situations, Dr. Reich's theories cannot easily be disregarded or explained away. They generate their own propaganda. Therefore it has been convenient to try to silence them altogether by treating them as commercial plugs for a contraband commodity. How American!

II.

Consider a fair analogy to the Administrator's high-handed procedure in banning the books with the box. Let us compare Reich and Volta. At the end of the eighteenth century, Volta was able to make available electrical energy of any potential by wrapping some metal sticks in wet rags, a device as primitive as Reich's box. Now suppose that—inspired by his colleague Galvani's jumping dead frogs, and perhaps by Mesmer's "animal magnetism" (which we here analogize to Freud's "libido")—Volta or somebody else hit on the electro-shock therapy for "lunacy." (This therapy was highly esteemed among us ten years ago, is still in use, and has certainly done more damage than all the orgone accumulators, though nobody has gone to jail.) And suppose again that, like mesmerism in France, this electro-shock therapy was banned:

According to the logic of the Administrator of the drug law, all traces of Volta's battery, his equipment, his reports, his theory of differential potentials, should then be expunged from the face of the earth. They are labels for the illegal therapy. And the *existence* of flowing electricity must henceforth never be mentioned.

Whether or not Reich was a Volta, I don't know; but how in the devil is a bureaucrat to decide the question? It is the kind of thing that must be determined by generations of scholars and their experiments, with free publication and no holds barred. Naturally, as a human being, I hope that Reich was right and that we have discovered something new and wonderful, whatever the applications.

III.

Let me say something about a few of these banned books. (I am writing from memory, if the reader will pardon me.)

The Function of the Orgasm is a classic almost by definition, from its title. For here Reich seized on a phenomenon of universal occurrence and obvious importance, definite, observable, and experimentable, which had nevertheless never been seriously studied. Simply making the obvious metabolic, electrical, and muscular observations and experiments, and fitting the findings into standard modern psychology and his own character-analytic methods, the doctor produced a great book. Why should not such a book exist? To answer this question I submit to the philosophical reader the following puzzle: How is it possible that this subject had to wait until the second quarter of the twentieth century to get a halfway adequate treatment? Indeed, the puzzle is still with us. E.g., in the Kinsey reports, although Reich's relevant studies are mentioned in the bibliography, the statistics are nevertheless collected by counting undifferentiated and unstructured "climaxes," as though Reich's careful anatomy and physiology did not exist. Naturally Kinsey says many absurd things.

Quite apart from its ingenious cancer theory, *The Cancer Biopathy* is a remarkable work. For what Reich does again is to seize on problems and approaches that are important but are precisely swept under the rug or frowned on by modern medical orthodoxy: e.g., abiogenesis, the frequent embarrassments of the germ-infection hypothesis, and especially the factors of susceptibility and resistance of various patients to various diseases. It is the hallmark of genius to pay attention to such dark and *suppressed* areas, and to find connections among entities that tend to be neglected. But it is not to be expected that the orthodox will shout for joy about it; nor that they will much respect the simple-mindedness and dumb-bunny apparatus of a primary researcher. At the same time, Reich's work is full in the stream of important cancer problems, e.g., the virus or nonvirus etiology, and the puzzling relevance of sexual organs and sexual types. It is a pity that the research reported never seems to be informed about Reich's hypotheses. It is not a field in which we can afford to burn books.

Listen, Little Man I remember as the anguished and somewhat frenzied outcry of a high-aspiring and inwardly oppressed strong soul caught in a petty and apathetic world. Not unlike a chapter out of Dostoevski, and exactly the kind of thing that should be reprinted in anthologies like the recent *Identity and Anxiety: Survival of the Person in Mass Society.* Why it should be banned and burned is beyond me, unless with the spiteful aim of blotting out a man's memory.

Character Analysis is a universally admired text, powerfully influential in modern clinical practice; and I am told that it is now legal "for professional use." It deals with character resistance, the muscular defensive "armor," and methods of active therapy.

The Sexual Revolution and *The Mass-Psychology of Fascism,* finally, are excellent studies in the application of psychoanalysis to politics and history, in the wake of Freud's *Mass-Psychology and the Analysis of the Ego* and *Totem and Taboo,* and no more exceptionable than the similar attempts of Fromm, Kardiner, etc. Like the others, Reich is concerned with the authoritarian character and especially, as an ex-Marxist, with the psychology of cultural lag. *The Sexual Revolution* contains a beautiful history of the reaction in the Soviet Union under Stalin and is, to my mind, invaluable for the understanding of that country. Both books, however, are practical in intent and prescribe, among other things, the sexual freedom of children and adolescents as absolutely essential for the restoration of social health. I am convinced that this is the explanation of the antagonism to them. (E.g., the liberal *New Republic* commissioned and then banned as scandalous a review of them that summarized their arguments.)

Such, roughly, are the actual contents of the books which have been banned and burned as "labels" for orgone accumulators! All six books are interesting; a couple are perhaps great. (I am not acquainted with the other, shorter, pamphlets on the banned list.)

IV.

I feel impelled to make a further remark to the Americans on this issue. We are living in a precarious time. Let me mention two aspects of it.

During the last months before the execution of Caryl Chessman, there were several polls of public opinion. By and large throughout the country, opinion ran more than 70 per cent against him. (The pacifist *Catholic Worker* reported with astonishment that *its* readers were 75 per cent for immediate execution!) But the significant thing was the tone of this opinion, as expressed in very many letters. It was violently, sickeningly sadistic, pornographic, and vindictive; and this on an issue not of momentary indignation, but after several years of discussion and debate. Now, the justice meted out to one individual is important; the question of capital punishment is important; but the tone of such a majority was, to my mind, the frightening and portentous fact about that case. It means that when I walk down the street, I am not safe, for these are the thoughts and feelings that seethe just beneath the surface in the majority of my fellow citizens. My friends and I, who want to live productively and sexually, must live here; and it is in this insane asylum that I have to bring up my children.

It was to the terrible reality of this "emotional plague," as he called it, that Dr. Reich directed his efforts, according to his lights. I do not know if he had the cure for it; but he accurately named the disease; and certainly no less radical prescription than his can possibly be of any avail. Our government jailed him and burned his books; but if he is not allowed to speak out, none of us will be allowed.

Secondly, on a world-wide scale many human beings are manufacturing bombs that can blow up the world; they are poisoning the atmosphere testing them; they are impressing the best brains of mankind in the study of how to develop them and best launch them. Meantime, the rest of the human beings, in the "advanced" nations, are acquiescing in this, paying for it, and de facto approving it. All this may explode any day. Such lunatic behavior and catatonic paralysis are not new things among us, but there has never been a time when the behavior was so dangerous and so universally admitted to be universally catastrophic, and when, therefore, the paralysis of people was so evidently irrational.

It was against this trend toward mass suicide that Dr. Reich evolved and, rather desperately, tried to apply his theory of primary masochism. Just as Freud spoke in despair of the need for Eros, and others of us are willing to risk other desperate alternatives like anarchy, *ahimsa,* and wooing the creator spirit. It is not a good time for Administrators to put obstacles in the way of freedom of the spirit. Get them out of the way.

This attack on the U.S. government's "burning" of Wilhelm Reich's writings was written for a special issue of *Kulchur* planned for Winter 1960-1 (the intention was to create a test case by publishing some of Reich's banned work, but nothing came of it because Farrar, Straus had already contracted with Reich's heirs to bring out several of the suppressed volumes. Goodman's essay lost none of its sting from the government's finally backing down; it still has it today.

Great
Pioneer
But
No
Libertarian

I.

*D*iscussion of the work of Reich is not only appropriate and important, but essential for our integrity, since Reich has been subjected to a disgraceful conspiracy of silence and overlooking. (But he always did have a favorable press in *Resistance* and I would exempt our group of "radicals and libertarians" from Calhoun's cry of shame.) It has been a conspiracy in the sense of an identical reaction-formation in many individuals; and the conspiracy has taken the form of silence because that is the only weapon against disturbing thoughts that are stimulating and that everybody knows to be true. Everybody knows, for instance, of the sexual misery of adolescence and that it is an artifact of our mores, but people cannot relax these mores without intolerable anxiety to themselves; or everybody knows of the sexual misery of our marriages, but we cannot simply alleviate it because we are in the throes of our inherited Oedipus-complex and its jealousies. Now nobody wants to hear painful home truths, and especially if his guilt is the stronger because he turns away from difficult remedies that are offered. Nevertheless it is shameful not to listen anyway and suffer. Our inner conflicts we cannot help avoiding, but this conflict we need not avoid and some good will come of it. Let me give an example or two of the silence—the book-banning from "interstate commerce" (!) that Calhoun mentions speaks for itself.

Direct Censorship. In 1945 *The New Republic* gave me the page-proofs of *The Sexual Revolution* and *Mass-Psychology of Fascism* to review. Since I felt that the point of view would be brand new to liberal readers, and since I found *The Sexual Revolution* a masterly piece of historiography, I limited my review strictly to reporting the contents of the works, without further appraisal. My review was promptly rejected on the grounds that "we cannot subject our readers to such opinions on your (!) authority."

Scientific silence. In the past decade there have appeared in the science columns of the press many reports of "pioneer" experiments and hypotheses on abiogenesis, the relation of certain cancers to sexual deficiencies, and so forth. There is never a hint of the fact that Reich had already published the identical experiments. It looks as though the experiments in isolation are mentionable, but when Reich combines them in a remarkable intellectual synthesis, they become unmentionable.

Negligent treatment. Consider the Kinsey report and the publicity it received. The statistics in the report are based on a counting of "climaxes" in various circumstances. Now Kinsey was well aware—in his introductory chapters of the first report—that it is the quality and dynamism of the orgasm that defines the sexual phenomenon; his reported qualitative descriptions in the introduction are simple-minded but not far off-base. Further, he includes in his bibliography the works of Reich which give the complete and correct explanation of these qualitative differences and their significance. There is then simply no reason to neglect this most essential aspect; yet he and his associates proceed throughout the rest of the reports as if no such descriptions of their own cases could exist and as if the indispensable prior work of Reich did not exist. Naturally the counting leads to numerous absurdities. This is disgraceful overlooking. (I do not mean that the Kinsey report is not a useful thing, but I wonder if the Americans would have been so receptive of a Kinsey report a little closer to the uncomfortable facts of life.)

I doubt that Reich left us, as Don Calhoun says, a "great new glimpse of reality." But in his praise, several things seem to me beyond dispute. First, he was, almost by definition, great as a pioneer. For he hit on a topic of the first importance throughout the animal kingdom and man: the orgasm and its function; a topic that was easily observable and could be experimented; and that nevertheless had been neglected. Any such subject is a gold mine. It is like dreams, or the variations in a species, or the falling of bodies.

Secondly, by returning to the early Freudian conception of "Actual Neurosis," that there is a pathological residue from undischarged sexual stimulation itself, that sexual gratification is therefore an hygienic necessity, Reich has forced the entire psychotherapeutic and progressive educational enterprise to a much more pragmatic, prescriptive, and revolutionary task; he has made them face an either-or. This is the subject of Calhoun's paper.

Again, in the technique of psychotherapy, actively working on the "muscular armor" and seeking for vegetative streaming, Reich gathered together and systematized, and made teachable, a body of techniques that have been transforming and will continue to transform professional practice. My impression is that not much of this technique nor attitude is Reichian as such; but by his energy, his simplicity, his outspokenness, and his flair for upsetting the applecart, Reich put the technique across. It is not the Alpha and Omega of psychotherapy; it works badly with some kinds of patients, and in general it falls short (in my view) of achieving the most worth while ends of education and re-education; yet I myself as a Reichian patient (of Alexander Lowen) got great benefit from it both physically and emotionally, and I certainly make use of it as a therapist.

More specifically, the hypothesis of primary masochism is great: that repressed libido at a deep level appears as a wish to be pierced, exploded, killed, humiliated; that the "masochist" does not want to be hurt or dominated, but freed from his own repressing wilful self. (Is not this evident in child and sexual behavior?) This concept is historically of the first importance, because it is the only one that does full justice to the clinical findings and intuitions that led Freud, in the richness of his experience, to speak of repetition-compulsion and to postulate a death-wish and write *Civilization and its Discontents.* The other psychoanalytic rejections of these thoughts of Freud seem to me to be pious mental hygiene. The Reichian conception involves, however, actual potency and its gratification, and the moral and social environment to permit this.

Finally, let me add a sentimental proposition in praise of Wilhelm Reich. He was a scientist in the old style back to the 17th and 18th Centuries. In these days of multi-million dollar equipment, IBM tabulation of thousands of empty questionnaires, and specialist scientists who are also organization-men who avoid the dirty conflicts of the world which happen to embody all the relevant reality, what a heart-warming thought of this doughty round man working with shoestring apparatus and a few transference-devoted disciples, with lively material and free-wheeling speculation, ranging everywhere, poking his nose into the business of the body politic and continually getting rapped for it! Whatever else it is, *The Cancer Biopathy* is a lovely intellectual construction full of dumb-bunny experiments easy to repeat. I hope he did discover a new form of cosmic energy accumulable in his boxes! and that he made living matter. After all, Volta first controlled electricity with nothing but a couple of sticks in some acid soup.

II.

In candor, however, I must take exception to some of Don Calhoun's propositions. It was not necessarily through our ignorance that we libertarians did not "feel a kinship" with Reich, and did not "rally spontaneously to defend him." (It did not occur to one that he would die.) Reich was not a libertarian; he did not have the humor, good sense, sense of perspective, humane culture, call it what you will. He was a very dogmatic man. I doubt that he was one to take good advice, and he was badly advised, or he would have known that contempt of a court-order is a very different thing from murder or rape or dissemination of painful ideas, for this is the structure of the State—they cannot overlook it—and if one intends to fight it, one must consistently attend to this kind of dynamite and not go single-mindedly after "biological cores" and (by projection) cosmic bombardments. The Reichian movement has always been stupidly sectarian, and Don's paper breathes a little of the same: it is narrow-minded and fanatical in the sense of saying "Only one thing is necessary," and other things and people must be subordinated to this thing. For there is no such thing.

Let me tell a personal story. In 1945 Reich 'phoned and asked me to call on him. I was pleased and puzzled, and fondly hoped that this remarkable man would put me to some activity. (My need for such direction and permission is my problem.) But what he wanted was for me to "stop linking his name with anarchists or libertarians"—he had perhaps read a laudatory notice I had written of him in *Politics*, July 1945. I was astonished at his request; after all, I said, his main points were anarchist points and we needed him, and he never said anything we strongly disagreed with, though he made careless formulations. He denied my statements—it became clear that he had never read Kropotkin; charmingly his face fell in childlike surprise when I mentioned some pedagogic commonplace from *Fields, Factories, and Workshops*—I was immensely impressed by his openness to a simple feeling of surprise. "Really, Dr. Reich," I said finally, "what is it to you if we younger folk call you an anarchist or not?" He explained, this time to my dismay, that Neill in England would find it doubly hard to keep his upperclass kids in Summerhill, the progressive school, if the movement was tagged as anarchist *too*. My guess was that the doctor was suffering from the understandable paranoia of the refugee from Hitler.

The Reichians are so high-minded and moral; it is in Don's paper too. They always make me feel I don't know how to behave at all, at all.

There are some places in Reich's writings where he says, "There ought to be such and such a law"—instead of this antisexual law, some other anti-anti-sexual law. These are perhaps trivial lapses grounded in ignorance; the bother is that the particular kind of ignorance is raised to a dogma. Reich was great when he proceeded as a naturalist and a passionate physician; he was moving when, as a man, he cried out how he was hounded and how little were the little men; but he and his associates were a pain in the neck when they made like an authoritative central planning-board for the good society, and when they engaged in a tedious scientism that fell prey to the identical obsessions that the orgasm was supposed to have freed them from.

In my opinion there is a grave defect in the Reichian theory. He regards the organism as much more insulated and self-contained than it is. Psychologically, this comes to thinking of the self as the self-of-the-"body," whereas it is more profitable to think of the self as a process of structuring the organism-environment field. Reich's error is explicit in an important model he uses: the organism as a bladder with a system of homeostatic tensions to be relaxed. But the organism is much more open to the environment than that, and its tensions are importantly used in the integration of new material and in growth. The Reichian theory does not offer a convenient explanation of growth and change, and it is hard to conceive of an explanation of creativity. For Reich, the surface tends to be superficial and therefore, starting from the surface, one must proceed to the deep core. True, as far as it goes; but the surface is also a contact-boundary, apt for exploring and manipulating, and whose mechanisms for adaptation to emergency should by no means be taken as neurotic. Reich does not accept the surface, he "attacks" it. Now the result of rousing the deep feelings while not integrating the surface, is projection, fantasying entities that answer to the deep feelings. Most religion is this and it is a fine thing, but it is what it is.

With this biological theory and the attitude underlying it goes a humorless anthropology, as if the Trobriand Islanders were the model of the human enterprise. And worse, a scientism that is not what just today we are hungering and thirsting for.

Then, good: as a Joshua to lead us into the Promised Land, I should not vote for Reich or a Reichian. But in our situation as it is, when the problem is to live, Don Calhoun is right, we need at least the Reichian program. The way is direct expression of feelings. As I said in *Alternative*, a fist-fight and some good sex are the best ways to diminish the chance of war; and I got this wisdom from Wilhelm Reich.

These reservations were published in *Liberation* (January 1958), along with a more purely laudatory essay by Don Calhoun. The reference at the end to Goodman's piece in *Alternative* should be compared with the original ("A Public Dream of Universal Disaster") for an example of *libertarian* censorship.

Fever is beautiful the twinkling
campfires of the resistance
the scorched earth and the strait pass,
though it is terrible to watch
the history of the disease
and the wrong banner flying.

But the loveliest thing the violent stars
roll as they rush is animal health!
the three gaits of locomotion
and the fourfold gamut of song
and practical syllogism
and hammering and careless love.

III

MODERN
PSYCHOPATHOLOGY

Unpublished
"Editors'
Note"
for
First
Issue
of
Complex

*I*n our society we do not use intelligence to get us the most obvious fundamental goods, personal happiness, social peace, the efficient production and distribution of wealth, etc. In the pursuit of these things our energy is dissipated, our means are ingenious but inefficient, direct simple goals are lost sight of, we expend effort in directions that lead to personal dissatisfaction, war, waste of wealth, etc. All this is obvious to any reflective observer. Indeed, viewed with a certain detachment, our ways of living must seem not merely stupid but idiotic.

There are forces compelling the inhibition and abuse of intelligence, preventing solutions of urgent problems and perverting inventiveness. Traditionally these forces have been located in the institutions of society, the economic and political institutions, the moral, religious, educational, and domestic institutions. And one can easily see where these institutions cause our woes. Yet on the other hand, we acquiesce in these institutions, support them, further their functioning; we constitute these institutions and are formed by their pattern. Therefore large among the maleficent irrational forces we must name the characters, fears, and anxieties of ourselves.

There is need thus to play light on just these psychological difficulties and especially on the places where they interact with social institutions. This is clearly not a function of medicine, in the sense of being the private business of a doctor and his patient; for all are generally involved (few are medical patients) and, more importantly, *changes* in institutions and ways of living must spring from us all in our social, not medical, relations. There is warrant for airing these issues publicly in a non-technical magazine; the issues are often deeply personal, but they are not private.

Lastly, it has been the faith of most psychoanalysts that awareness of the meaning and the springs of behavior is itself a means of liberating behavior from bondage. This faith is no doubt justified. But in dealing with those matters of institutional behavior, we hope that our writers will carry their analysis also to a point where the concrete details of everyday life and political exercise will have been so clarified that feasible practical action is indicated.

To Our Writers

Our social ways are *very* unsatisfactory. It is shameful, dangerous, and even unbearable to go on as we are. This urgency must inspire us to call a spade a spade and risk touching sore spots. It is in principle impossible to deal seriously with the subjects that must be dealt with without giving offense and rousing resistance.

The editors have, of course, their own opinions, but as editors they are non-sectarian. Any important contribution to our subject, from whatever school, will be welcomed. Any idea, strong, clear, and to the point, will be printed unedited; if we consider it wrongheaded we shall refute it, if we can.

Articles would likely cover any or all of the following phases:

1. *Observation*, of concrete manifestations
2. *Explanation,* or socio-psychological diagnosis
3. *Practice,* action against social-neurotic manifestations in feasible, concrete practices.

In the Spring of 1950 a young libertarian, Sander Katz, who had just been released from a year in prison for refusal to register, decided to start a "magazine of psychoanalysis and related affairs," and persuaded Goodman and Gertrud M. Kurth to be editors with him. Although it lasted only a few years, and most of the issues were not edited by Goodman (he dropped out after two, came back for the ninth-and-last), he published quite a bit in *Complex*. The selection printed here is an "Editors' Note" that was apparently rejected by the other editors in favor of quotations from Thomas Mann and Sigmund Freud, which served as an epigraphic indication of the aims of the magazine.

A
Public
Dream
of
Universal
Disaster

We have in America a combination of unexampled general wealth and unexampled civil peace. Economically and sociologically these are beneficent causes of each other, the more civil order the more production, and the more wealth the less incentive to destroy the civil order. By civil order here is meant not the absence of crimes of violence, but the pervasive safety of both city and country. Compared with other ages, travel is without danger anywhere and at any hour; there are almost no brawls, riots, or armed bands. Madmen do not roam the streets, disease is quickly isolated in hospitals; death is never seen, childbirth rarely. Meat is eaten, but no one in the city ever sees an animal slaughtered. No such state of non-violence, safety, and sterility has ever before existed. Concerning our wealth, again, I need only point out that none of the debated economic problems has to do with subsistence; the unions demand better hours, wages, and security, the capitalists demand fewer controls and better conditions of reinvestment; a single case of starvation is a scandal for the press. Less than 10% of the economy is concerned with elementary subsistence. Never in history have there been so many comforts, luxuries, and entertainments.

Psychologically the picture is more dubious. There is little frustration but there is little satisfaction. General bafflement and insecurity of individuals in the too-big society destroy self-confidence and initiative, and without these there cannot be active enjoyment. Sports and entertainments are passive; the choices on the mass-market are passive; people make nothing for themselves and do nothing for themselves. The quantity of sexuality is increasingly great and approaching adequacy, but the de-sensitization is extreme. It used to be felt that science and technology and the reform in mores would bring an age of happiness. This hope is disappointed; everywhere people are disappointed. Even so far, then, there is evident a reason to smash things, to destroy not this or that part of the system (e.g. the upper class), but the whole system en bloc; for it offers no promise, but only more of the same. And considered more deeply, we have here the condition almost specific for the excitement of primary masochism: continual stimulation and only partial release of tension, unbearable heightening of the unawares tension (unawares because people do not know what they want nor how to get it), and finally the desire for orgasm interpreted as a desire for total self-destruction. It is inevitable that there should be a public dream of universal disaster, with explosions, fires, and electric-shocks; and people pool their efforts to bring this apocalypse to an actuality.

At the same time, however, all overt expression of destructiveness, annihilation, anger, combativeness, murderousness, is suppressed, in the state of civil peace. To a large degree the *feeling* of anger is suppressed and even repressed. People are sensible, tolerant, polite, and cooperative in being pushed around. But the occasions of anger are not minimized. On the contrary, just the situation of substituting for the large movements of initiative the competitive routine of offices, bureaucracies, and factories, produces continual petty frictions, hurt feelings, being crossed. Small anger is continually generated and never really let out; big anger (that goes with big initiative) is repressed. The result is the projection of the angry situation afar; we find big distant causes adequate to explain the accumulated anger that is certainly not explicable by petty frictions (and that is largely self-hatred). In brief, one is angry with the enemy.

This enemy is also cruel and hardly human; there is no use in treating with him as tho he were a human being. Why is this? The aim of American love, as is proved by the content of all popular cinema and literature, is sado-masochistic; but the love-making itself is not, in general, sado-masochistic (for that would be anti-social and indecent). Therefore it must be "some one else" who is sadistic.

In civil society, the cluster of aggressive drives is "anti-social," but fortunately in wars they are not "anti-social." That is, one can wage wars against enemies who indeed anger, and fascinate, by their beastliness and sub-human strength. But it must be remembered that the ultimate aim of these wars is universal explosion and disaster; satisfaction at last, and the end of civil peace.

The mass-democratic army, further, is excellently apt for the needs of the people. It gives security, removes one from the jobs and homes that give no great pleasure and rouse feelings of inadequacy; and it organizes one's efforts more actively toward sadism and primary masochism.

People observe the catastrophe approaching: they receive rational warnings and make all kinds of resolutions. But energy is paralyzed for one is fascinated by and really desirous of the dangerous prospect. One is eager to complete the unfinished situation. People are bent on mass suicide, an outcome that solves most problems without personal guilt.

In these circumstances any pacifist propaganda without adventurous revolutionary social and psychological action is worse than useless: it solves no problems and increases personal guilt. To refuse war in a society geared to war is a salutary shock, but the shock is useful merely as a means to further releases of anxiety and aggression; as such a good fuck or a fist-fight is equally useful.

This was Goodman's statement in a symposium of political and cultural radicals on the H-Bomb, printed by *Alternative* (March 1950). (Compare the passage from *Gestalt Therapy* reprinted on pages 162-165 below.) *Alternative* was distributed free by the Committee for Non-Violent Revolution, which included, among others, Sander Katz, the founder of *Complex*, and Dave Dellinger and other founders of *Liberation*. In November, *Alternative* was barred from the mails for its advocacy of draft resistance (the Korean War was on). Some of the editors felt that Goodman's article, with its "four-letter word," had something to do with the post-office's action.

The
Children
and
Psychology

What is most significant, it seems to me, is the earnest attention paid to the Children and Family as a subject, the desire of parents to be informed and thereby do their best, rather than following their wit and impulse; or to say this another way, what is significant is the importance assigned in our society to Psychology itself, for Psychology is still by and large the family-psychology that Freud made it, discussing the problems of jealousy, infantile dependency, authority submissiveness and rebelliousness, and sibling competition; and problems of spite, moral prejudice and other reaction-formations springing from instinctual deprivation. This interest in the Children is of course hopeful, for the increase of wisdom cannot fail to remedy abuses, and has already done so quite spectacularly.

But this interest is also itself a symptom of an unfortunate social situation. Earnest folk pay such special attention to the children, and in general to their Interpersonal Relations, because there is not enough objective man's work or woman's work to put themselves to. I do not mean that there is not enough absolutely (it's a large universe); but in our present social and technical arrangements there are not enough exciting and *available* and unquestionably self-justifying enterprises, where a lively human being can exercise initiative and use his enormous psychic and physical powers to anything like capacity. This problem goes, I think, deeper than any of the current differences in political or economic arrangements, and I cannot think of any immediate change that could alleviate it. We are in a phase of collective enterprise that does not, and probably cannot as yet, much use and stimulate such remarkably gifted animals as individual people, especially if we consider them (as children) before they are discouraged and become rusty, and in addition to our powers all the knowledge and equipment of our culture. So more and more are likely to blow off steam in religious exploration; and the brunt of the burden falls on preoccupation with the Children and Interpersonal Relations, for these at least are things that one can individually try to do something about.

Good parents work to preserve-and-give more available energy to their children; the children in turn grow up and find they have not much field of action for this energy, but they can expend some of it on their children.

The helping of children has the prime advantage that it can be disinterested, compassionate, and *noblesse oblige*; it is our nearest equivalent to the old chivalry. The bother is that, except for those who have a calling, who are born teachers, it is stultifying as a steady occupation. We also need some dragons to kill and planets to visit, or goods to produce that people unquestionably need. A psychiatrist friend of mine says that the right care of children is: Let them alone and be around; where "be around" means, I suppose, to provide safety, audience for the exploit, consolation for the hurt, suggestion and material equipment for the next step, and the answers when asked. This simple formula will not fill up a twenty-lecture seminar on Children.

THE FAMILY AS BATTLEGROUND

As our families are, the children in both their present satisfaction and the free growth of their powers, are certainly crushed, thwarted, pushed, hurt, and misled by their hostile and doting grown-ups. Frankly, I doubt that you can find one child in a dozen who is not being seriously injured, in quite definite and tangible ways, by his family. I would say this indignantly, as an indictment of the Family and *ecrasez l'infame*, let's fight to get rid of it! if I thought that the available substitutes were not even more disastrous. But consider also the other side, that the parents are tied to and tyrannized over by the little Neros. You cannot put them in their places for several reasons: 1. you can't, try it; 2. it's bad for them to slap them down, and if they are injured it bounces back on you in the end; and 3. most fundamentally, in the good cases you can't deny the imperious demands of the children because most, and perhaps all, of the hard things they really want are justified: they want space, excitement, sexual freedom, noble models to grow up to, wise saws of experience, real arts and crafts to learn, animals to hunt, an unknown to explore, and comprehensible answers to direct questions. But it is not the case that our housing, our economy, our style, our frontiers, and our sciences are amenable to these justified childish demands. Our arrangements have become so objective that few grownups and no children any longer have an available objective world. So a sensitive parent feels justly guilty; he tries anxiously, in impossible conditions, not to rob the children of their natural rights as the free heirs of nature and man. Do not many of us suffer from what we could call the Lear-complex? We are abashed by the free unspoiled power of the very young, we have no right to withstand it, we resign and give up our own rights.

As a striking example of parental guilty good intentions, notice in community planning, how every adult requirement of quality, style, and efficiency, is sacrificed to suburban utilities of safety and playground.

BEING MASTER WITHOUT AUTHORITY

Contrast it—to make the point clear—with a master and his disciples, whether an artist or an artisan or a scholar: he uses the kids for his purposes, he says do and don't with a clear conscience, because his soul is fixed on the work; he teaches them out of his compassion to prevent error and advance the future. They, in turn, are neither humiliated nor browbeaten nor exploited. They are growing into the work through him because he is a master of the work; and the compelling proof of all this does not come from authority but from the work. Now regarding the Family as a school of growth in the art of personal life and of exploration and inspiration toward a career, what experienced mother, or father feels like a master of the subject and can command and forbid with conviction except in some elementary issues of health and safety and perhaps grammar and manners? (As Yeats said, "The best lack all conviction—the worst are full of passionate intensity.") We do not know the method to reach the goal we do not know. This is often expressed by the sentence, "I don't care what my children do or become, so long as they will be happy." An honest, humble, and sensible sentence, but it puts parents in the impossibly anxious position of trying to fulfill an indefinite responsibility. So instead of improvising with wit and love on a foundation of experience and unquestioned personal achievement, they necessarily rely on Psychology and Mental Hygiene.

Another cause of preoccupation with the children is that children have become the only colorable excuse for existence of the monogamous family. Economically, women make money and own most of it. As a way of life, with the general breakdown of the old sexual conventions and the weakening of the old inhibitions, monogamous marriage is felt as a trap and a frustration; people are exposed to, and allow themselves to feel, temptation but are not so able to take satisfaction, so there is plenty of resentment and guilt, projected resentment. Frankly, again, it is my observation that if many marriages (maybe most) could be simply dissolved after a few years, the partners would suddenly become brighter, rosier, and younger. And again I would therefore urge, Change the whole institution, except that the situation is not simple: we are still in the toils of jealousy of our Oedipus-complexes, and in the present social fragmentation the companionship of marriage, such as it is, is a safeguard against isolation and loneliness. (The Family was a bulwark of the private economy, and now it is a refuge against the collective economy.) But these grounds for the continued existence of the institution cannot stand much ethical scrutiny, considering the cost. It is the children that make the effort unquestionably worthwhile; and of course with the two or three children now standard, the burden of justification that must be borne by each little darling is great indeed.

SALVATION THROUGH SEX-TECHNIQUE

As a defense against all the repressed thoughts against it, it has become the highest aim in life of an entire generation to "achieve" a normal happy marriage and raise healthy (psychologically healthy) children. That is, what was always taken as a usual and advantageous background for work in the world and the service of God, is now regarded as an heroic goal to be striven for. This is preposterous. Yet, I should like to repeat it, the sentiment is deeply justified by the fact that at least this goal *can* be personally striven for; it is connected with real, not merely symbolic, satisfactions and responsibilities; and the same cannot be said for other goals for most people, which are either fictions of prestige and power, or are managed collectively. Consider, as a test, when the goal cannot be achieved or when the marriage cracks up: it is the exceptional case where the person's work or social role is important enough and real enough to occupy his thoughts and keep him going with manly fortitude. Viewed in this light, the thousand manuals of sex-technique and happy marriage have the touching dignity of evangelical tracts, as is indeed their tone; they teach how to be saved, and there is no other way to be saved.

The well-intentioned loving and resentful parents make a vocation of the children until finally they can send them off, at increasingly early times, to nursery-schools and schools. Perhaps the schools will provide "exploration and inspiration toward a career." But the situation of the teachers in the schools is fundamentally no different. For always the question is, What to teach? what is realistically *worth* teaching? The curriculum becomes poorer and poorer, because an honest educator cannot seriously believe that the solid sciences and humanities are life-relevant to the average of this mass of pupils. Nor is so-called "vocational" training the answer. (The name tends to be applied precisely in the absence of vocation.) Neither the jobs trained-for nor the kill-time training add up to what could enliven a human soul. The answer of the school is again Psychology; what the teacher has is not a subject-matter but a Method, and what he teaches is Interpersonal Relations. The only art that is essential is to read simple words, for production and distribution depend on reading. (So there has been universal free primary education for a hundred years, and the earmark of the delinquent who won't fit into the economy is that he won't or can't learn to read.) But the savage and intolerable irony is the current raving for more mathematics and physics, lest our bombs, radar, and rockets fall behind Russia's—these beautiful studies that have been transcendent goals for many of our best! now advocated so basely and the professors greedy for the subsidies and students on any conditions.

SUCCESS WITHOUT ACHIEVEMENT

Brought up in a world where they cannot see the relation between activity and achievement, adolescents believe that everything is done with mirrors, tests are passed by tricks, achievement is due to pull, goods are known by their packages, and a man is esteemed according to his front. The delinquents who cannot read and quit school, and thereby become still less able to take part in such regular activity as is available, show a lot of sense and life when they strike out directly for the *rewards* of activity, money, glamour, and notoriety, which will "prove" in one fell swoop that they are not impotent. And it is curious and profoundly instructive how they regress, politically, to a feudal and band-and-chieftain law that is more comprehensible to them. The code of a street-gang has many an article in common with the Code of Alfred the Great.

It is disheartening indeed to be with a group of young fellows who are in a sober mood and who simply do not know what they want to do with themselves in life. Doctor, lawyer, beggar-man, thief? rich man, poor man, Indian chief?—they simply do not know an ambition and cannot fantasize one. But it is not true that they don't care; their "so what?" is vulnerable, their eyes are terribly balked and imploring. (I say "it is disheartening," and I mean that the tears roll down my cheeks; and I who am an anarchist and a pacifist feel that they will be happier when they are all in the army.)

THE PSYCHOLOGY OF ABUNDANCE

This is a sad picture. Naturally; for it is always sad when you write about something, rather than do something. (Poetry is not sad, it is an action.) I do not think there is cause for indignation, nor for despair. Not for indignation, because so many people are doing their best and many of these difficulties that have arisen are surprising and must simply be addressed patiently. Not for despair, for my feeling is that we are in a stage of transition: to finding some kind of collective arrangements that will be rich with animal vitality and creative spontaneity and will be without Interpersonal Relations. Of course I cannot imagine such an apparently contradictory thing or I would be writing that instead of this. Meantime we psychologically-informed parents are doggedly (and out of our own hides) contributing to the explosion of it. By the millions—soon by the vast majority—we have let up on toilet-training, we have been liberating sexuality, we have honestly relinquished an old-fashioned authority because we do not know right principles. Then in the new generation there is more and more health and available energy, and less and less to do with it; more and more unprejudiced, not-class-ridden and good-humored kids who are, yet, more and more stupid. This is the psychology of abundance that goes with the economy of abundance.

With the alleviation of the anxieties of poverty, there naturally loom vaster and at first vaguer anxieties of destiny. Our present task, it seems to me, is just to get rid of a few more ideas, to get rid of *Life* so we can have a little life, and finally to get rid of Psychology so we can have a little contact and invention. As Laotse said, "Good government is to empty the people's minds and fill their bellies."

This was Goodman's first essay to appear in *Liberation* (September 1956), which had begun publication in March of that year.

Sex
and
Ethics

I suppose there will be general agreement that in this topic, sexual ethics, a chief chapter of it would be responsibility. Responsibility, for instance, to the other person, or responsibility of the consequences of one's acts. Responsibility to the other person not to exploit another person's feelings, for instance; responsibility for consequences—the typical case would be having an unwanted baby.

I think rather more important, perhaps even than those two—although these are very important—is responsibility on the part of young people especially, but on the part of everyone, to one's self and his or her feelings. A certain sincerity and courage with regard to his or her own feelings which, if it existed, if there were more self and more acceptance of the self, I think many of the awful hangups which produce situations which are seen in youthful sexual behavior would, in fact, not exist.

In America, as it is at present, most behavior—and this is not only in sexual matters—has nothing to do with what one is or would normally desire or naturally desire, but what is expected of one or in order to provide something which has got nothing to do with the functioning of it.

I will spell out very briefly just four items and then try to get behind it to trace a source. I think I am like Abbey [another panelist], all of our troubles are the troubles of society. We have no special duties, we are hung up, we live in a bad world, our main duty is to change that world.

Two people are attracted. I think normally the main source of attraction is the character on the face, a certain sweetness, strength, candor, attentiveness of the other person. Added to this, no doubt, are the remnants of very early images which make one person attractive sexually and another person not, and very likely—as the 18th Century used to say—there is some chemical affinity—but that is a very, very different thing from the conformity to movie types or to the President's wife, Jackie Kennedy, as being that which is supposed to be desirable that year.

It is very different from deciding on the part of the young man "I am going to go with that girl because all of the others will envy me, she is just so stunning," or the kind of mere ideas that kids have and unfortunately adults have (this is a brutal type)—or this one tends to run in the young men I meet mostly: "there is a girl who is obviously pre-psychotic, and this promises some endless wildness or other, and she is so interesting"—but it really has nothing to do with sexual attractiveness. In fact, normally we would be frightened by the very things that are made attractive because of a mixed up background situation.

That is the same thing with regard to the sexual act itself. I would say if two people kind of like one another, have a sexual bout and they enjoy themselves, then it is inevitable that the people will get to like one another and the boy will treat the girl kindly and as a friend, and with good luck the relationship will deepen.

St. Thomas, the moral philosopher of the Catholic Church, points out that the chief human use of sexuality is to get to know another person; by having sexual relations you get to know them, and he thinks that is the chief human use, as opposed to the natural-law use of sexuality. I am not sure the Catholics here are so happy about this interpretation but they would have a much better church if they would follow this doctrine.

Quite contrary, though, the use of the sexual act as we see in Yale or Princeton and among the Puerto Ricans gets to be conquests, something to boast about, with the sailor ethics to go ashore and not to get involved—it is bad to get involved. Now this is something that is wrong. They're not just letting the thing be.

And then it is the same thing where they say it is mere lust. It is St. Thomas again who says that the second chief use of sexuality is pleasure. He gives three uses: the natural law—procreation; getting to know another person; and pleasure. Those are the three uses of the sexual act, according to St. Thomas Aquinas. What is pleasure? St. Thomas, being an Aristotelian—Freud or Aristotle would say that pleasure is an organic sign. Other things being equal, if something gives you pleasure it is good for you, it is an organic sign of a very deep sort, going—as Freud says, the anaclitic is dependent on all kinds of important vital functions. This does not mean, however, that what you think will give you pleasure will give you pleasure, and an endless amount of sexual activity occurs because of people's notions that this is what you are supposed to do in order to have a good time, without any real desire operating altogether. In other words, they precisely leave their mere lust out; if there were a little more lust there might not be so many hang-ups.

Then an enormous amount of sexual activity among adolescents is not sexual altogether, it is a gang conformity. You go into a routine that the gang does—if the girl doesn't do it, she is out. Or it is a proving phenomenon: A kid, say a drop-out from school, feels utterly worthless. He has got to prove himself some way, so he proves he can get an erection. It is not the sex which is enjoyable, it is the fact that he is potent, which proves something. In other words, what I am saying by these introductory remarks is that if we would let the function be and the people be themselves, there would be rather less need—I don't mean no need but rather less need—for ethics and for conferences about such problems.

When Abbey pointed out at the beginning of her speech—she started out by saying "Why do we pay so much attention to youth?" I think the reason is quite simple—she didn't bother answering it—it is that we provided them with such a bad world at present that there is an enormous guiltiness.

Dr. Leveton [another panelist] points out that they will grow up into the world, that is right, but in more ordinary circumstances than ours they would simply grow up and we wouldn't have to pay so much attention to them, certainly not the way that this conference is about.

What is the actual situation in our society at present which causes this utter dislocation of natural function and letting the kids be?

My friend, Jim Coleman, the sociologist at Johns Hopkins, the author of *The Adolescent Society,* pointed out recently in a seminar that in our society with regard to our children we divide their behavior into two parts: the serious behavior and the other behavior.

The serious behavior is one thing and one thing only, it is that they are supposed to go to school and get good grades. This is middle class and also lower class, this is the one serious thing, everything else is either frivolous or cute or to be interrupted at the adults' will at any time. This includes the things which in other societies would be considered the most essential and serious parts of growing up. For instance, what music a child listens to. In any more organic society that would be a most crucial thing, but this is considered part of the triviality, the Elvis Presley thing mentioned as "an interesting one."

The kind of money they spend on teen junk and the fast cars and the fast driving—that is all part of the frivolous part of life, and you are afraid they will speed, but apart from that it makes no difference.

Any hobby or reading that a child does, any intellectual pursuit a child starts out on—and this is the thing, I think, that my friend Professor Friedenberg has quite beautifully studied—any real intellectual interest of the kid is regarded as though it is trivial. It is very nice he has it, but he has to do German 202, because that is the thing that is going to get him a National Merit Scholarship and that is all that counts.

Among the frivolous, cute, or interruptable things of a child's life are the dating—the mere fact that we call it dating means that it is trivial—and the fact that a child might want his own money, that he might want to leave school, get some money, maybe go back to school in order that he can have some independence—these are considered of no concern whatsoever.

Now it is in those circumstances that a child is apparently supposed to learn responsible habits with regard to important things like sexuality. Just consider it: he is under a tutelage in which he is forced to do these serious things, and in the case of a lower class child it takes at least 13 years, from kindergarten to high school, and it takes a middle class child from 16 to 17 to even 19 years in which he sits in a room and does somebody else's lessons. Just think of that, that you adults are forcing on a growing animal this inconquerable torture. The lessons being determined not in any way according to the child's real aptitude or interest. How would you like to be put in a jail for 14 years, let's say, and you are supposed to do somebody else's lessons, and at the end of that time when you graduate at 21, then you are supposed to vote, you are suddenly supposed to know how to vote when you have never made any decisions or free choices of your own! You are supposed to get married, you are supposed to find a job. As Dr. Leveton said, you are supposed to choose a career, suddenly at that. How? How, when at no time previously has any freedom been given?

Then it gets even worse from the teen-ager's point of view when he comes to realize that what is taken seriously and seriously imposed on him by his adults is largely not serious, it is frivolous. That is, the actual schooling is frivolous, because most of the teen-agers, the great, great majority are not going to get the jobs that they have been schooled for in any way. Those jobs are vanishing quickly.

In the first place, almost everybody who gets a job in our society—this is not true of top ranking scholastic types in the middle class—is more trained than the jobs warrant in our society and, in fact, most of the jobs that are gotten in our society have no connection with real productivity or any human worth of the job.

For instance, the factory worker whom Coffey has studied very well, the worker in the Ford line. Listening to the conversation of the Ford factory worker about the car he is making, he says "there are too many cars on the road, anyway, and there was no need for this new model." The workers then have a contempt for the job they are working on.

Likewise, take any middle class kid. He gets a job in which he will exercise no initiative whatever. What he has done is to replace the tutelage of papa and of the schoolteacher for the tutelage of the corporation boss—its rules—and at no point in his whole life span is he ever allowed to mature, to grow up to make decisions, to exercise initiative of any kind.

Now in such a case how will his wife respect him when he marries?

He is a person who cannot afford to talk out against the boss. There isn't any inner ambition of his own which he is ever really allowed to fulfill. It is under these circumstances that we get some rather peculiar sexual behavior, because the sexuality pattern has got something to do with what he can't do, it is supposed to make him manly. It isn't sexuality that is manliness to the man, it is a manly man that gets the manliness through sexuality. And a society which makes it impossible for a person to pattern self and to feel worthwhile is a society which makes it impossible to learn any responsibility, and certainly not sexual responsibility.

Let me get the pathos of these kids going out afterwards and saying, "Well, at least I will make an early marriage and this is one thing, I will get married and have normal, healthy children, and at least this is one part of life where I can exercise some initiative. There is no boss over my head there." That is true enough but this is putting a burden on a marriage which is quite impossible, and then very often in such cases the marriage becomes something which has tied them down: "I would have had a career as a pianist," the woman says, "if I had not married him. Somehow he prevented me from fulfilling myself."

Obviously the married state is not a goal in life, it is a supportive background for doing the work of the Lord. I mean it is one of those things, it is a splendid supportive background for worthwhile activity in the world. The upbringing of children is one of the worthwhile activities, of course.

Now I would like to rush on through just these last points I have here in order not to omit them completely.

Another thing which stands in the way of letting things be and letting responsibility mature is the ideas people have about sex in our society, and the contradictoriness of the ideas. For instance— sex is beautiful, sex is natural, ecstatic. Everybody in this room believes this and unfortunately most of this is true—in a sense that two generations ago when they were defiantly rebelling against Victorian repression it *was* true to say this, but in the form it is said by the middle class and the household magazines at present it is utterly false. Sex is not beautiful in that sense, sex is dirty. Of course it is, there is nothing wrong with that dirt, of course; it is not ecstatic, if it is good it is sleep-inducing. The idea of the apocalyptic orgasm is pure epilepsy. It is surely natural but it is not natural in the sense that things go on and nice and orderly. Quite the contrary, it can be extremely disruptive—it can make the kid quit school, and then he *should* quit school for a while, and society should have some way of letting him get some money meanwhile.

Then it gets to be a notion of what is the acceptable standard, and Dr. Leveton used the words "our behavior was getting beyond the acceptable standards."

Well, the acceptable standards tend to be gang worries of proving something, which is also conveyed by adults who are arrested adolescents (and by the commodity market which makes a lot of money out of this whole sexual teen-age sub-culture), in the following way: If the kid is sexual, let's say at age 12, he is punished—I know, I was punished a lot. If he is not sexual at age 13 then you take him to the psychiatrist.

There *is* a discontinuity of adolescent from pre-adolescent, but it is not nearly so great as Dr. Leveton was saying, because half of the discontinuities, like the pimples, are psychosomatic according to the theory I would follow. They are the result of not allowing freedom, play, etc. beforehand.

Consider this: when the progressive educators asked for the Junior High School to be established it was, as they said, a very important discontinuity—"At the sexual age we will put the children in a special place where there will be sexual training." Now I ask you in California, do any of the junior high schools mention the word sex? Do they give any sexual training? Pictures about childbirth or so forth?—it is a fantasy...well, in my city they don't.

Then when things get rough there gets to be a fantastic growing of horns on the part of the adults. There must be conformism to a standard which is quite fundamentally either an outmoded police code or a standard, really, of juvenile gangs, which the adults have adopted as proper behavior, or the standard of *Good Housekeeping Magazine* or something of this sort. It is remarkable, let's take a typical example, the pornography as mentioned say, by Abbey.

It is accepted everywhere now that masturbation, if done in the proper way, is not only good but healthy. The chief aim, I would say, in 99 cases out of 100, the point of pornography, is to have something to masturbate to. It is better than making up your own visual images, it gives you a social contact in a rather empty activity. That is what pornography is for and what on earth is wrong with it?

If, on the other hand, Dr. Spock and the Department of Labor Manual go on to say, if the child masturbates, that is fine, perfectly normal. Don't encourage it, don't discourage it, that is how it is. If it seems to be excessive, then there must be some demand for security which is not fulfilled.

On the other hand masturbation, I think most psychiatrists would say, can be harmful if it is done wrong physiologically; that is, if no noise is made, if the pelvis is held motionless, if you do not let your breath out, that is bad. It is harmful if the images are guilt-inducing.

Now the attitude toward the pornography is typical of the whole anti-sexual attitude which precisely creates sadistic pornography—because they are not, by making laws, going to get rid of sexual desires or of pornography, but what they are going to do is to combine sexuality and punishment. Therefore you begin to get sadistic or hard core pornography, which says that if you are punished, then you can have the bang. Precisely by our attitude toward this we create the very thing that is objected to, whereas the thing itself for some reason makes judges' hair curl.

Our kids are brought up in a situation where we have an unfinished sexual revolution. There has been a failure of repression in the Freudian sense; that is, things that used to be in the unconscious and kept down by every force of society are now unleashed by the entire advertising system, the movies, modern literature. There has been a sexual revolution; in modern psychiatry there has been a sexual revolution. Instead of letting the thing run its course in order that we can get back to some kind of normal behavior, we cannot stop the repressed contents from coming to the surface—but we then inhibit continually along the line, leading to distortion.

Now exactly the same is happening with our family pattern. We have a pattern of urbanization at present which has made the old farm family not very workable, and you can cry all you want, Abbey, about divorce, but it is not a very workable pattern, the old farm family, at present. What the pattern should be I don't know; I think we should all be discussing it. Instead we try to cling to something which is bygone, and impress it on forces of life which are not going to be so repressed, and then by this inhibiting of a natural force all we get is distortion. It is in these circumstances that we begin to have to worry a good deal about teen-age sexuality.

If we gave them a better economy, if we gave them years which were useful, if we gave them an educational system which instead of being a lock-step allowed for the finding of identity, then I don't think we would have sexual problems. Thank you.

In 1963 Goodman was part of a symposium held at the University of California Medical Center on "Sex and Ethics." Never before printed, this selection reproduces the tape-recording verbatim and is a good example of Goodman's speaking style, usually ad-libbed from a few notes on the backs of envelopes.

Designing
Pacifist
Films

I.

I am asked for my thoughts about the content and style of anti-war films, and how to make such a film.

First of all, such a film must at least not do positive harm by predisposing its audience toward war. The images of senseless violence, horror, and waste that are usually employed in the commercially successful "anti-war" films do have a titillating effect and remain in the soul as excitants and further incitements. Let me show how this works.

(1) In cinematic conditions of bright screen and dark theater, lasting for many minutes and tending to fascination and hypnosis, images of horror easily detach themselves from the kind of intellectual and ethical framework in which they are usually presented, and they attach themselves to quite different subliminal ideas. We must bear in mind how a child wakes up screaming with his nightmare of the animated cartoon he has seen, the nightmare now expressing a kind of wish.

(2) Also the response of a theatrical mass audience is different from the more intellectual and ethical response of a small company or an individual reading. (Perhaps TV is a special case.) What a theater audience experiences most vividly is how it has, anonymously, shared in breaking a taboo, in witnessing with accomplices

the forbidden and shocking. The "message" of the spectacle is then employed as a rationalization. Of course it is only the rationalization that is mentioned outside the theater or in the reviews, though the advertising hints at the shocking.

(3) This dual process is specific for the heightening of guilt: a forbidden stimulation with one's censorship lowered by crowd feeling, disapproved by one's ethical and social self. Now, the effect of guilt is not reform or, finally, deterrence; but inevitably resentment for having been made guilty, and perhaps then clandestinely or unconsciously choosing more congenial buddies. (Pacifist propaganda in general, let me say, is prone to arouse guilt just because it is irrefutable and on the side of the angels. This is an important reason why accompanying persuasion some immediate *action* must be available—just as a loving sexual seduction must lead to acts or it does harm.)

(4) The arousing of lust and self-disapproval leads to the specific pornographic effect of wished-for punishment (the hallmark of popular sexual art). The image of punishment is often provided in the film itself, as its poetic justice. Such self-punishment is evil in itself; but worse is that usually it is projected far and wide as vindictive hatred of scapegoats. And alternatively, it seeks for allies in mass suicide, as if to say, "*We* are not worthy to live."

(5) Especially in cinema, the conditions of fantasy and the habits of the audience are so discontinuous with behavior in the waking public world that the shock of strong images is sentimentalized: the rationalizing sorrow and regret is used to *insulate* the experience from any possible action. The energy of revulsion turns into pity, a pornographic emotion, rather than active compassion or political indignation—not otherwise than with Christians who exhaust their neighbor-love in the sentimentality of the Cross. The next step is for the sentimentalized horror to be taken as matter-of-course in the public world, just as for those Christians the poor *must* always be with us, so Christians can be charitable.

(6) Finally, bad audiences cannot be relied on to respond to a whole work of art; they will select from it what suits their own repressions, and interpret according to their own prejudices the very fact that they have been moved despite themselves. The lovely is taken as dirty, the horrible as sadistically thrilling. This

derogation is partly revenge against the artist. Bad audiences follow the plot as a story; they do not identify with the whole work as the soul of the poet, but they identify with the actors of the story and take sides. Given a film about capital punishment, for instance, a Camus will notice, and be steeled in revulsion by, the mechanism of execution: he will deny the whole thing the right to exist because it is not *like* us (this is the reaction-formation, denial, that is characteristic of active compassion); but a vulgar audience will identify with the victim, get involved in the suspense, thrill to the horror, and weep with pity. The effect is entertainment, not teaching or therapy; and to be entertained by such a theme is itself damaging.

II.

By a good audience, of course, a work of genuine art cannot be easily taken amiss and abused in this way. By definition, the images of genuine art do not allow themselves to be detached from its idea, for the whole is solidly fused in the artistic activity. But this standard of excellence is useless for our present purposes, since such works are not conveniently had for the asking. And when they do occur, they are just as likely to be embarrassing to our rhetorical purposes. For example—I choose classics of literature that are beyond debate—both Homer's *Iliad* and Tolstoy's *War and Peace* are infused by, and teach us, a profound pacifism, a lofty and compassionate dismay at the infatuated violence of men in their armies. Yet they certainly also express, and even celebrate, the demonic in war, the abysmal excitement of mankind gone mad. This was interesting to these artists and it *might* be to any contemporary artist—how could one know? The counter to such demonism in a great artist would have to be a kind of saintliness. We are here clearly outside the context of planning pacifist films.

Again by definition, in a work of genuine art the images of horror, etc., do not have a pornographic effect and do not incite to repetitions, for the experience is finished and cathartic: the fearful images are purged, transcended, interpreted, or otherwise integrated with the rest of life. An art work leaves its audience with a saner whole philosophy (more congenial to pacifism in so far as pacifism is truth); and it has taken some of the venom from the cruelty and arrogance in the soul. But such a re-creative "finished" experience is precisely not rhetoric; it does not lead directly to action or any *immediate* policy. The Athenians seeing Euripides' *Trojan Women* were no doubt wiser and sadder about the very course of folly that they continued plunging along. (I do believe, however, that great art, forcibly confronting us with a more meaningful universe, does *initiate* conversion, and pacifists do well to perform these achieved monuments of their tradition.)

My guess—I judge from my own art-working—is that a serious modern artist who happens to be a pacifist (and how could he not be, if he once attends to these matters?)—if such an artist begins to move artistically among the scenes of war, his art action will soon lead to the exploration and expression of his *own* horror, rage, pain, and devastation. The vegetarian will disclose his own cannibalism, the pacifist his murderousness. Such works, e.g., *Guernica,* are monuments of how it is with us; they have no leisure for a practical moral, nor even for the luxury of indignation. The eye lamp flamingly thrust forward over Guernica does not light up the deed of Nazi bombers, but the violent soul of Picasso, brought to a salutary pause.

If we consider spurious, *kitsch,* or propagandistic antiwar art, on the other hand, its actual pornographic and provocative effect is equally to be expected, for the fantasy and the art-working convey the disorder of the weak artist and speak to the underlying wishes of the bad audience.

We thus have, by and large, the ironical situation that precisely the best cause, which has irrefutable sense and common humanity, ought to avoid "psychological," "artistic," and mass-rhetorical effects.

III.

What, then, are the available resources of pacifist persuasion that can be used for a pacifist film? They can be roughly classified as:

(1) Factual education.

(2) Analyses of character-neurotic and social-neurotic war ideology, and the withdrawal of energy from the causes of war spirit.

(3) Opportunities for positive action, and pacifist history and exemplars.

1a. As a strictly prudential argument, pacifism has an easy case, perhaps too easy a case, so that people do not take it seriously, it is too obvious. People have always known that war is a poor expedient, inefficient for any plausible purpose. And "present-day war," not only *our* present-day war, has long been out of the question. It is best if the facts, of the senselessness of it, are allowed to speak for themselves, without admixture of moral or emotional appeal or any grandiose references to saving the human species. The matter is much simpler. War talkers are pretty close to fools or else not a little crazy; their postures and remarks are not proper to normal grown men. This can be simply demonstrated, relying on logic, statistics, and history. The framework must be an irrefragable and unmistakable structure of verbal propositions, even printed subtitles, however "uncinematic"; for we are dealing with a deeply neurotic and even schizophrenic phenomenon, and the *reality of ordinary reasoning, and ordinary dismissal of stupidity,* must be strongly affirmed.

1b. On the other hand, the dangers of pacifist action—e.g., the risks involved in unilateral disarmament—should also be dispassionately and *fully* presented, so far as they can be fairly estimated. *It is not necessary to have an answer for every argument,* even grave arguments, for we cannot do what is senseless and unworthy of men anyway. Pacifism is a decision. The "serious" position is not, as Niebuhr, for instance, seems to think, to choose a lesser evil; it is to realize that we cannot have been so wrong for so long without purgatorial suffering.

1c. The facts of war policy, war makers, and war economy ought to be exposed with unsparing honesty and detail, at the risk of inevitable censorship. E.g., delineating the personalities—a Teller, Kennedy, or J. Edgar Hoover—on whom so much is allowed to depend. But further, the immense network of the power structure must be made clear and diagrammed, so that a person comes to realize how nearly every job, profession, and status is indirectly and directly involved in making war.

2a. Psychologically, our "tough" warriors live by a conceit of themselves as strong, to ward off the anguish of their spirits broken by authorities they could not face up to; and a conceit of themselves as hard, to ward off loss of love and fear of impotence. A film might profitably analyze the military posture, pelvis retracted, belly kept hard, exhalation restricted; the military ethos of inhibited feeling; the conceit of superiority by slavish identification with authority symbols. For comparison, analyze the social and family genesis of an underprivileged gang tough. Explain the details of Marine discipline as a means of destroying manliness. The system of griping fostered in armies as a means of maintaining childish dependency and avoiding mutiny. But further, show how in our times the classical sociology of the armed services as a substitute for civilian responsibilities is combined with the use of the services as complements of, and training for, organizational civilian life. The soldier seeks for ratings like a junior executive, while the Organization Man has a tough as his secret ideal. A thorough social and psychological analysis of these types might immunize the young.

2b. Analyze the notion of the Enemy as a projection (scapegoat) and also as a political red herring. Show in detail how Enemies have been manufactured and miraculously reformed by techniques of press and promotion. Show also how foreign nations have thus manufactured the Americans as the Enemy and assigned to us Enemy traits and wishes.

2c. But probably the chief factor of war spirit that must be analyzed is not the military character nor the projection of the Enemy, but the paralysis with which the vast majority of people of all countries accept the war that they oppose both by conviction and feeling. This must betoken an inner, fatalistic attachment to the feared disaster, and it is best explained as "primary masochism" (Reich): the hypothesis that, because of their rigid characters, people are unable to feel their pent-up needs, especially of sexuality and creative growth, and therefore they dream up, seek out, and conspire in an external catastrophe to pierce their numbness and set them free. The prevalent conditions of civilian peace and meaningless jobs tend to heighten this lust for explosion. (My experience, however, is that in analyzing this factor of war, one is opposed precisely by the more moralistic pacifists themselves. Rather than condone normal homosexuality or encourage the sexuality of their children, they would, apparently, accept the brutality of armies and see people blown to bits. One is dubious about the sanity of their pacifism, which seems to be rather a defense against their own hostile fantasies.)

Social and psychological subject matter of this type is sufficiently interesting in itself and is only confused by attempts at drama or case history; a straight classroom approach, the illustrated lecture, is most quietly effective.

3a. Factual exposure of the political and corporate operations of war society, and psychological and social analysis of its war ideology and spirit ought to disattach and release the energy that had been bound up in conventional symbols and habits of life. We must then have uses for this energy and opportunities for pacifist action. In principle, any animal satisfaction, personal self-realization, community welfare, or humane culture will draw energy from the structure of conceit, projection, and fatalistic masochism of the war spirit. "Waging peace" is the best means of preventing war, and pacifists do well to invent and support programs for the use of our wealth and energy freed from the expense, fear, and senselessness of war. In my opinion, let me say, there is also natural violence that diminishes war, e.g., the explosion of passion, the fist fight that clears the air, the gentle forcing of the virginal, the quarrel that breaks down the barriers to interpersonal contact. War feeds on the inhibition of normal aggression. (Of course, many pacifists disagree with this point of view.)

3b. Specifically pacifist action—usually in the form of refusing—is called for when people are required to engage directly in war-making, e.g., by the conscription, the civil defense, working in war science or war factories. The defense of civil liberties, also, seems to be congenial to pacifists, because the libertarian attitude goes contrary to the power state.

3c. Finally, the preferred pacifist means of exerting social force has gotten to be nonviolent direct action, shared in by the group. Any instance of this, even if it fails, is proof of the feasibility of the pacifist position, for it shows that sensible and moral individual and small-group action is possible, and thereby it diminishes our masochistic paralysis in the face of an approaching doom "too big for men to cope with." (The history and the heroes of civil disobedience and nonviolent direct action, achieving or failing to achieve happiness, social welfare, or cultural progress, constitute the mythology of pacifism. They have the heartening exemplarity and the, perhaps, sentimental irrelevance of any mythology.) To my mind, pacifism is like Rilke's unicorn, it *"feeds on the possibility of existing."* For the resistance to modern warfare is natural and universal; the arguments against pacifism are weak; and the spirit of war is reducible by analysis; but what is needed is stories, examples, and opportunities for action concrete in the experience of the audience.

IV.

Factual and analytic handling of images of war can neutralize their pornographic effect. My bias is that even the exemplary images of pacifist action are best handled in a documentary fashion, avoiding audience identification with their heroes and keeping the real situation in the foreground. The purpose of the film is not so much inspiration as to point to opportunities in the audience's real environment. *It is better to err on the side of dryness. The heart is already enlisted.* Emphasis on the pacifist "movement" with its charismatic symbols and "leaders" betrays us into the field of public relations, where we are swamped. The charismatic excitement that gives courage and solidarity must emerge in each concrete occasion of pacifist action, and it will emerge, if it is really a man's own occasion. We are in the tradition of bearing witness. It was just the genius of Gandhi to notice faultless occasions.

The kinds of theme I have outlined could be the substance of a useful series of documentary pacifist films. Developed forthrightly and in particular detail, they would certainly prove offensive to many audiences, including some pacifist audiences, but they could hardly fail to hit home. They would rouse anxiety both by the character analysis of the audience and by the need for the audience to make decisions in their actions. The shared shock of the truth and of possibility is, in our society at present, equivalent to breaking a taboo. For most, I guess, the effect of such films would be uneasy silence, a dangerous but transitory state of feelings. The hope is that some of this feeling would be mobilized to decisive action, just as some would surely result in ugly reaction. Perhaps most persons would be made deeply thoughtful.

For its makers, such a document would certainly be a pacifist action, a commitment, and a bearing witness.

First appeared in *Liberation* (April 1961).

Reflections
on
Racism,
Spite,
Guilt
and
Non-violence

WHITE RACISM

*T*he premise of the Kerner report on civil disorders is, "Race prejudice has shaped our history decisively.... White racism is essentially responsible for the explosive mixture which has been accumulating in our cities since the end of World War II." Both parts of this are not true. Since the end of World War II it was a rapacious policy of rural enclosure and, in Puerto Rico, a rapacious mercantilism that drove unprepared colored peoples north in unassimilable quantities, whether their reception would be racist or not; and add the whites disemployed out of Appalachia. To account for the explosive mixture, one does not need fancy new concepts like white racism; the old story of criminal neglect of social costs for private gain is more to the point. Further, historically, with notable exceptions, the northern whites have not been racially prejudiced—though they have been something else, perhaps more disastrous. It is best to get rid of these clichés and call each thing by its right name.

In classical psychology, race prejudice is a projection onto others of one's own unacceptable traits. It is a species of paranoia, the repressed traits returning as floating threats. It is characteristic of the authoritarian personality, brought up with severe inhibition of the child's initiative and animal nature; and the paranoia is excited by economic or other insecurity that makes the adult ego labile. Typically, a failing petty bourgeoisie with puritanic upbringing will have racial prejudices. The Germans were classically racist, with a full-blown ideology of Aryan supremacy that made them feel grand, whereas the Jews poisoned the bloodstream and were responsible for the Versailles treaty. Degraded by the Civil War, Southern whites developed the full-blown racism of the Ku Klux Klan; they had to be better than somebody, and niggers were inferior, apelike, a threat to Southern womanhood.

In this classical sense, the northern white middle class has hardly been racist at all. Their upbringing, though not free, has been unrestrictive by European standards. They certainly have not failed economically. Where there *is* more authoritarianism and insecurity, as among newly prosperous blue-collar workers—e.g., Poles, Italians, Irish, or Appalachians in Chicago—there is more racial prejudice; the same holds for retired rentiers like the Californians threatened by inflation. But the usual majority objections to blacks that have caused the suburban flight have not been "prejudices" but a Gradgrind kind of facts, narrowly realistic. Blacks do downgrade the schools and make it hard for junior to compete for MIT; they make streets unsafe; they swell taxes by being on relief and not pulling their oar; they are not prepared for better jobs that have (irrelevant) mandarin requirements. By contrast, in the important area of discrimination in unionized semi-skilled jobs, there have been strong prejudices by blue-collar workers; and the most vehement opposition to open housing has come in·rentier neighborhoods.

In many cities the police are recruited from just the most prejudiced classes, and this has been calamitous. And everywhere, of course, police are subject to the factual prejudices of their dangerous craft; poor suspects of any color have never gotten loving care from cops. (It happens that hippies and vocal pacifists are the worst treated of all, but this is an effect of paranoiac prejudice, since these pose an inner threat to the policeman's manly perfection.) Schoolteachers are a striking example of a kind of factual prejudice produced by narrow craft idiocy: probably most of them start out with fairly innocent attitudes, but when little black children do not learn to read *Dick and Jane,* the teacher's annoyance and anxiety, fearful of the supervisor, can come close to hatred.

Historically, there has been, and persists, a northern middle-class exclusiveness, provincial and conformist, that could reasonably be called "racist." But let us look at this, too, accurately, for the remedy depends on the diagnosis. Blacks have always been strange. There were few in the eastern and middle-western country and towns from which many of the whites came. Their mores were not necessarily inferior, ludicrous, or bad, but unknown. When blacks were hired as domestics, for instance by New York Jews, they were not looked down on but treated like articles of furniture. Not in business, they did not belong to clubs. Living in their own neighborhoods, they did not belong to white churches. But to be socially excluded has been the common fate of immigrant poor. Color is not the decisive factor: black Puerto Ricans, even with their culture of poverty, now make an easier adjustment. But Negroes have been continually recruited from an entirely inappropriate slave and depressed-rural background, and their exclusion has been fatally cumulative. Then, with the recent overwhelming influx of new immigrants, and their teeming offspring, the familiar atmosphere of the northern cities has changed drastically; strangeness has become menace; panic flight has ensued.

What picture of the white middle class emerges from this analysis? It is not so much racist as narrow, self-righteous, and busy. But of course. This is the same tribe that, north and south, displaced the Indians, had Negro slaves in the first place, needlessly bombed Hiroshima, and destroys Vietnamese. Whether one calls it brash enterprise or imperialist arrogance, to these people their victims are not quite persons. If the deviants shape up, fine, one does business with them—and even extraordinary efforts are made to help them to shape up. But if they persist in being themselves, they are exterminable. "Essentially," as the Kerner report puts it, busy self-centered people do not want to be thwarted or bothered. This bleakly explains more than "racism" does.

On the other hand, the Americans have the virtues of their defects, and these are more promising. Being busy, self-interested, independent, and successful, they have also been spectacularly extroverted, pragmatic, and generous. They will pay enormous sums to convert the heathen, wash the unwashed, and teach the mentally retarded to spell. And there has been an absolute contradiction in their racial attitudes. For instance, on the one hand there was the smug silence about the Indians and Negroes in classical New England literature; on the other hand there was the pan-humanism of Cooper and Walt Whitman. The framers of the Declaration of Independence obviously meant it when they said all men were created equal; yet some of the same authors allowed the organic charter, the Constitution, to speak of "three-fifths of a person." (This was exactly the kind of detail on which Gandhi would have fasted to the death.) The bother with the premise of the Kerner report is that, if it were true, nothing less would avail than psychiatry for epidemic paranoia, probably including shock treatment—and this is, of course, the proposition of the black terrorists. A more *prima facie* diagnosis allows us to appeal to the outgoingness, the pragmatism, the enlightened self-interest of Americans.

Unfortunately, in modern conditions, we must notice the *increasing* anxiety and privatism of the middle class. As businesses become more centralized and the standard of living more demanding and complicated, independence and enterprise are severely constricted. And more and more we see that American horsesense and generosity, which have been saving graces, give way to a desperate need to keep things under control. Self-righteousness can then become "efficient," a cold violence that has no inner check. There is a fanaticism of business as usual, called Preserving Law and Order, manner of Mayor Daley. If citizens fail to socialengineer the deviant into conformity, they quickly resort to mechanical measures, police, tanks, marines, bombers. When the threatened victims respond with desperate counter-measures, it is necessary to up the ante and there can be a massacre. Yet in modern conditions, it is again not necessary to speak of "white racism"; what is evident is a *general* drive to dispossess, control, and ignore human beings who are useless and bothersome, whether small farmers, displaced coal-miners, the aged, the alienated young, the vastly increasing number of "insane." And unassimilable racial minorities.

But modern conditions also have advantages. The very centralization and affluence that dehumanize allow also for pragmatic remedies on a grand scale; an 800 billion Gross National Product and the mass media can mount "crash programs." Second is the remarkable moral development of the young, sophisticated and free of economic pressure. In their own way they are as ignorant and self-righteous as the day is long, but they are not narrow, mechanical, or privatist, and they disregard caste and color. Finally, there is evidence that there is still life in the American democratic process itself, that peculiar mixture of morality, civil liberties, self-interest, and sporadic violence, swelling to make institutional change. Led by the young, the blacks, and the increasingly impatient "new class" of intellectuals, there is a revival of populism. Even the mass media, which have done so much to brainwash us, now seem—sensationally and inaccurately—to be informing us, because the journalists are new intellectuals. It is an odd "System."

BLACK RACISM

In the nature of the case, blacks in the United States are, by and large, racist, from Uncle Toms to Black Muslims. Whites can disregard blacks, but blacks can hardly disregard the power that owns and runs everything. Whiteness, as Fanon points out, inevitably invades the unconscious. Frustrated and deprived, blacks project onto the whites the put-down and hostility that they themselves feel. It would be too bitter to see truly the indifference that is usually really there.

(It is hardly necessary to discuss racial relations in order to make a catalogue of human sadness. But on the black side, lack of acquaintance, the mutual misunderstanding of manners and signals, must be especially devastating. For instance, willing to be friendly but being suspicious and vulnerable, he may start out with testing, either boring politeness or probing insult. But if the white is a simple person, he will be bored or annoyed, and shrug and sign off, and the world is so much worse than it was. This can quickly spiral downward to general mutual avoidance and fear. Yet, given ghetto conditions, it would be unusual for a black child *not* to grow up with suspicion, if the only whites he is exposed to are police, schoolteachers, and bill-collectors.)

The sophisticated ideology of Racism itself has been picked up by intelligent blacks from white paranoids; it is a fairly recent invention of Germans, Boers, and the Ku Klux Klan. (Until the nineteenth century, race was not much used as a projection-screen, though religion, caste, and nationality were vastly overworked. Even anti-Semitism was mainly religious and could usually be alleviated by conversion.) And now we see that the artifact of a "racist society" is picked up from black militants by the Kerner report. Presumably the report's rhetorical purpose in this is to sting white guilt in order to get action, but, as we shall see, this is a slender reed to lean on.

At present, southern blacks are less racist than northern blacks. Being more acquainted with real white madmen, they themselves have less paranoia and more sense of plain injustice; whereas northern blacks have to cope with bland unconcern or downgrading by neutral rules, at the same time as they are suffering. A case in point is "Law and Order." A Jim Crow law is mad on the face of it; but to northern middle-class whites, due process is only reasonable, it provides a neutral forum for discussion and legislation. They cannot see that to dispossessed people due process is precisely the usual run-around that they have been getting. Besides, northern blacks are now a more failing class than southern. The excessive urbanization is fiscally and physically unworkable, and is unlivable. Religion and family are shattered. There is more anomie. The great bloc of immigrants and estranged youth may have a little more money but they are much worse off than they were in the rural areas from which they were driven.

A poignant example of the clash of black racism and white lack of empathy was the expulsion of white students from the civil rights and Black Power movements, e.g., from SNCC. Innocently righteous and confident in themselves, the white students took too much initiative and too much for granted. This made it hard for the blacks to run their own show, which was indispensable if they were to regain their own confidence. If the blacks had responded with fraternal, even if angry, competition, it might have cemented a deeper friendship. Instead they responded with jealousy, including sexual jealousy, and expulsion. The possibility of free cooperation has been foreclosed. Yet, since the blacks still need help, for instance funds and facilities and to swell a demonstration, there now develops the ugly situation that sympathetic whites are manipulated, hustled, or lied to; and it must be a further humiliation for blacks to do this.

During the recent fracas at Columbia, the blacks invited their SDS allies out of a joint action because, a leader said, "They were shaky and would vacillate and panic and could not be depended on. With black kids the issue is clear, to fight racism." (One is struck by the testimonial to Socrates' definition of courage, to have an idea.) My guess is that the whites had a more complicated idea; but in fact the more structural issue of the action, to fight military infiltration of the university, did get lost in the shuffle, so the blacks were proved correct.

Generally speaking, it has been a mistake, in my opinion, for black militants to try to make "integration" and "black power" absolute and incompatible. The basic theory behind it is nonsense, to lay stress on the color of civilization as the Germans laid stress on its nationhood: and, practically, too much science and wisdom, as well as wealth, resides in the dominant community to try to dissociate from it without being continually phony. It is stupid to regard Galileo or Faraday as "white" rather than as human—and to be saying it into a microphone. And negatively, it would be stupid to have a black and white committee against nuclear fallout or cancer. (By contrast, draft resistance warrants separate committees, since those with and those without student deferments have different problems.) I doubt that, outside the South, there are many middle-class whites who have any feelings at all about being "white" as such. To the extent that to belong to a racial or national group is indeed a cause of pride—frankly, as a child of the Enlightenment, I think this is thin gruel—the minority group will thrive best in a mixed society where it has influential soul-brothers or *Landsmänner*. And politically, the majority of blacks and the best of the whites in fact want "integration" and will insist on it.

Nevertheless, illogic has its place. *Le coeur a ses raisons que la raison ne connait pas.* It is now thinkable that there *could* be a black committee against nuclear fallout, whereas ten years ago it was impossible to mount a protest in Harlem on this issue at all. People have to humanize themselves in their own way. It produces a curious dillemma. For example, at the Conference for New Politics, just the most energetic of the blacks insist on the official recognition of their caucus; whereas just those whites who are most thoughtful and most deeply committed to social justice are embarrassed and do not know what to do with this demand, because in fact the unity of mankind is the truth.

SPITE

The actual situation, without fancy constructs, is that some are hurting and the others don't care. Starting from this obvious premise, for the oppressed a primitive method of coping is spite. Spite probably played a part in the expulsion from SNCC—"you aren't invited": it is the chief ingredient in the black theater of insult, genre of LeRoi Jones; and I think it has been an important factor in the riots—"burn, baby, burn." Spite is the vitality of the powerless; it is a way of not being resigned, of keeping a lost fight alive by preventing the dominator from enjoying his domination.

(Needless to say, let me say at once, there are other factors in the riots. In some cities there has been evidence of a political plan for insurrection, part of a plan for world insurrection. The looting speaks for itself as reasonable free appropriation by people who are hopelessly poor. Burning white businesses in the ghetto makes a rational, though desperate, political point. There is a spontaneous explosion of frustration. In any culture of poverty there is a carelessness about one's own possessions and life, just as the homicide rate is high. On the part of the intelligent and energetic young, who have played a big role, rioting is exactly equivalent to white youth uprisings on campuses and streets around the world, in fascist, corporate liberal, and communist countries: it is an *acte gratuit* of freedom in the face of irrational authority; the youth component is more important than the racial or ideological component.)

Commentators seem to be unwilling to say the word spite; yet it is not an ugly or useless passion. It is a means of preserving or even of finding identity. Saul Alinsky especially has often tried to use it for community development, e.g., by organizing dispossessed and fragmented people simply to take revenge on shortweight grocers. But the trouble with spite, of course, as Alinsky also knows, is that its victories do not add up, and the letdown can lead to worse despair.

Spite is often self-destructive, "biting off one's nose to spite one's face"; one burns down one's own neighborhood partly because one cannot burn down theirs, but also to make them feel bad. This purpose usually fails; to "natural calamities" the affluent Americans promptly respond with clothing and canned goods, and do not feel bad but good. To hit home, it is necessary to produce an apocalypse as when Malcolm X, during his fanatical period, prayed for an atom bomb to destroy New York, Allah's revenge. But I have heard, too, of a "political" purpose of self-destruction, to make precisely the unengaged blacks worse off and so swell the Cadres of revolt. This motive, if it exists, is evil.

Somewhat more practical is spitework as blackmail. It is possible that some riot areas, like Watts or Newark, have received a tangible pay-off, as well as sociology. C.V. Hamilton puts it formally when, in a recent essay, he speaks of a *quid pro quo*: "Blacks receive economic support and political power; whites receive a chance to live in a healthy, developing, equitable society." But the results have been meager, and, as a political proposition, shakedown must finally produce a devastating backlash. Nevertheless, the same substance can be put in a theoretical form that is quite acceptable political science and hopefully workable: "For the commonweal of a pluralistic society, it is necessary for every group to flourish, and every group has the duty to throw its weight around to get justice for itself and the whole." It is not newsy in American history that this might involve some violence; consider, for instance, the burned barns and derailed trains of 1885 agrarianism, or the defiance of court and police in the labor movement, with many killed. Hamilton has to use the language of blackmail because he cannot speak of commonweal; he seems to need the ideology of race war in order to organize a following.

In my opinion, we would be much further along if Black Power had long ago presented its concrete political program, e.g., local control of police, schools, and other services; the underwriting of local small businesses and cooperative housing. Such things are perfectly plausible and, if fought for, would by now have been won. (I have been plugging them for twenty years, but I have no troops.) If a decade ago, as we urged, the integrationists had asked for the guaranteed income for all Americans instead of welfare, we would now have it; liberals get used to anything, once they hear the words. Five years ago, the March on Washington should have highlighted the Vietnam War, as some of us again urged. But moderate black leaders insisted that these things were too far out. And militant black leaders insisted on the spiteful recourse of sulking and putting on the whites the burden of guessing what is needed and coming across to prove their good will. Blacks shouted "Black Power!" and puzzled sympathetic whites asked, "What is Black Power?" A painful example has been James Baldwin's gambit: he forces the white interlocutor to ask, "But what do you want?" "You know what we want." "No, I really don't." "We want just what you want." Perhaps Baldwin says this ingenuously, but he is in error; for usually the white man does not think of himself as a "white man," but just as an individual in his own state of confusion and misery, in which being white does not help at all. Unless he is very empathetic, he does not see the disadvantage of being *not* white. If Baldwin would say, "We need thus and so to live better. How can *you* be of use in *our* getting it?" then the white man will either help according to his abilities or confess that he doesn't care enough to put himself out. Of course, a psychological use of the spiteful gambit is to avoid the risk of rejection.

But this is water under the bridge. Concrete programs for local control *are* emerging, there is certainly more acquaintance, and despite spectacular militant tactics there seems to be diminishing backlash. One has the impression that, in the white community, private groups small and large are far ahead of the political officials and Congress. These include, let me say wryly, big business corporations which have a natural self-interest in fire-prevention and will even make an extra buck out of racial harmony—you'll see.

But to account for the slow emergence of concrete demands, we must bear in mind, too, that dispossessed and dependent people are disoriented and do not themselves know what they want. If something positive is given, it is suspected as second-rate or a trap or a token never adequate to need. If something is taken or achieved by one's own effort, it thereby becomes degraded, or is a cause of envy among one's fellows and proves that one has been "co-opted." This is the neurosis of the victimized that Robert Jay Lifton has been studying.

Sensitive minds, like James Baldwin again, understand perfectly that just to get into the middle-class American mainstream is not humanly good enough; but then it is hard for him to explain to poor people what, these days, would be humanly good enough. Consider the current social imputation of many jobs as "menial." When I was young, driving a bus or trailer-truck was manly, difficult, and responsible; now when there are many black drivers, it is ordinary. Construction work used to be skilled; but a black or Spanish bricklayer or mason tends to be considered unskilled. White road-workers in Vermont have a decent job; black road-workers with the same equipment have a menial job. Postman, a job requiring unusual tact and judgment, has always been a dignified occupation; now that, like other Federal employment, it is open to many blacks, my guess is that it will be considered drab. A German or Jewish waiter is a mentor or kibitzer; a black waiter has a servile job. This social imputation of worth is made, of course, by both whites and blacks. Whites, however, usually do not give it a second thought, as their young move into other jobs. The question is why the blacks go along with the same imputation. The dismaying thing is that objective criteria like the kind of work, the worth of the product or service, and often even the wages count for very little. In this frame of mind, it is impossible to be free and independent.

But this subjective evaluation by the standards of public relations is endemic in American society. Nothing is regarded as itself, on its own merits. Thus, in the present essay which ought to be on politics and ends and means, I find myself discussing emotions and unconscious emotions, like racism, spite, revenge, and guilt. I find this pretty sickening. Perhaps the chief hope in the young, with their flesh-and-blood interests, simplifications of the standard of living, casteless friendships, and direct action, is that they will bring us back to objective reality, however crude.

GUILT

A chief use of spite is to make the others feel guilty; this not only prevents their enjoying their domination but may result in tangible "amends." It is clear that with many middle-class whites, this ruse has disastrously succeeded. Disastrously, because no good has ever come from feeling guilty, neither intelligence, policy, nor compassion. The guilty do not pay attention to the object but only to themselves, and not even to their own interests, which might make sense, but to their anxieties.

Psychoanalytically, guilt is repressed resentment and this is latent dynamite. For a time the guilty may forbear retaliation for annoyance or insult and may pay token amends, but soon they turn a deaf ear and then resentfully get even.

The dilemma is that blacks are indeed victims, of a system of property relations and policing, but the present-day northern whites, as persons, are not consciously nor importantly victimizers. There is exploitation of black people in their own neighborhoods, which can be helped by phasing out of their neighborhoods; but such exploitation is trivial in the Gross National Product and is overwhelmingly outweighed by the general tax-cost in black social services, special services, special policing, etc. Since they are not economically necessary, blacks cannot get redress by striking and bargaining. Since most whites are not exploiting them, they cannot give them redress by stopping their exploitation. When there is disorder and the cops crack down, the whites feel that *they* were aggressed on, and this is technically true. The black demand "Just get off our backs" makes sense in asking whites to stop running the ghettos through the school bureaucracy, the welfare bureaucracy, the police, and slumlords; but it is a poor slogan since, in the inflationary urbanism and high technology, blacks simply must have white subsidy, professional help, and jobs in the only economy that there is.

Almost all whites now agree blacks ought to get preferential treatment and there are stirrings in this direction. But this cannot come to much if it is done by guilt, to make amends; it must be done for political motives, self-interest, decency, commonweal, and justice. Unhappily, the Americans, who neglect other public works, whose rivers stink, whose towns are hideous, whose country-side is despoiled, and whose children are mis-educated, neglect this public good too. My guess is that, just beneath the surface, it is they who have the slogan, "Get off our backs."

Really to remedy our domestic colonialism (and our foreign colonialism) requires profound institutional changes and structural changes in the economy. We would have to divert the military technology to useful production; control the inflation that makes poor people poorer; reverse the policy of rural enclosures that swells the cities; manage the advertising, design, and pricing of consumer goods so that people can live decently without being in the rat race; get rid of the irrelevant mandarin diplomas for licensing and hiring. To stop being exclusive, American society would have to be about human beings rather than the Gross National Product, and the privatist competition for a cut. It would have to give up its delusion of social-engineering everybody, and tailor its help to local needs and local social organization. But all this amounts to a religious conversion and seems hopeless. It is possible that we cannot have such a conversion without convulsions; unfortunately I do not hear of any convulsions that would lead to the relevant conversion. The violent champions of Che or Lenin rarely say anything relevant to the real problems of a country like ours. It is understandable that blacks are hung up on their gut issues of being hemmed in and pushed around, but it is distressing that the Peace and Freedom Party or Students for a Democratic Society cannot get beyond gut issues. Radical liberals, like Harrington, Keyserling, or Rustin, propose New Dealish remedies like more public housing, schooling, and transit, that would recreate the same problems bigger and worse. Liberals feel guilty. "Conservatives" arm the police.

NON-VIOLENCE

Meantime we must live with the immediate problem: what to *do* when some are hurting and others, who have power, don't care? *How* to make narrow, busy, and self-righteous people understand that other people exist?

It was exactly for this problem that Gandhi, A.J. Muste, and Martin Luther King devised and experimented the strategy of active massive non-violent confrontation, both non-violent resistance and aggressive non-violence. In my opinion, this is the only strategy that addresses all aspects of the situation. It challenges unconcern. It attacks institutions and confronts people as well. It personalizes the conflict so that habitual and mechanical responses are not easy. It diminishes strangeness. It opens possibilities for the narrow to grow and come across, instead of shutting them out. It interrupts the downward spiral of the oppressed into despair, fanaticism, and brutality. Most important, it is the only realistic strategy, for it leads to, rather than prevents, the achievement of a future community among the combatants. We will have to live together in some community or other. How? In what community? We really do not know, but non-violent conflict is the way to discover and invent it.

Non-violence is aggressive. Since the injustices in society reside mainly in the institutional system, though the personal agents may be innocent or even quite sympathetic, it is necessary to prevent the unjust institutions from grinding on as usual. It is necessary not to shun conflict but to seek it out. So Gandhi, Muste, and King were continually inventing campaigns to foment apparent disorder where things apparently had been orderly.

Naturally, aggressive massive non-violence is not safe. (Gandhi lost thousands.) If only mathematically, when there is a big crowd, some will be hurt—sometimes because of one's own young hotheads, more usually because the police panic and try to enforce impossible Byzantine restrictions, Law and Order. On the other hand, actions of this kind are far less likely to lead to a shambles. In the present climate of cold violence armed with a lethal technology, this is a major concern.

I do not think that non-violence is incompatible with fringes of violence or flare-ups of violence, so long as its own course is steadily political, appealing to justice, self-interest, and commonweal, and if the political object of the campaign speaks for itself. Gandhi, of course, was a purist about avoiding violence, though he said that it was better to be violent against injustice than to do nothing; both Muste and King were willing to cooperate with violent groups, if they did not try to take over. Psychologically, indeed, it is probably an advantage for a non-violent movement to have a group like the Black Panthers in the wings, committed to violent self-defense, for this quiets down the more rabid opposition and makes a calmer zone for real political and economic confrontation. (Sometimes it doesn't work out so smoothly.)

Non-violence, and King's own campaigns, do not necessarily pre-judge the issue between "integration" and "black power." Separatism is ruled out, however, since the point of confrontation is to come to mutual recognition and commonweal. It is not necessary to "love" one's enemies, but there must be a belief that common humanity is more basic than racial difference; and this belief must be *bona fide* or non-violence becomes a mere tactic and has no energy. Certainly King's followers took his universalist Christian rhetoric at face value. (So did I.) As I have said, it is the only realistic position; it is the tendency of history. In the world, we cannot continue to have "peaceful" co-existence, which is really cold war; we will come to community or perish. In this country, it is not the case that there could be two societies, as the Kerner report threatens. Either the dominant group will hem in the blacks in *apartheid* reservations, which is unthinkably abhorrent, or there will be a democratic pluralism or general miscegenation, each of which has attractions.

In the northern cities, however—and this is a grim complication—there are two distinct problems which somehow have to be solved at the same time. The first is the one we have been discussing, how to get whites to pay attention to blacks as existing, and for this, aggressive non-violence makes the most sense. But the second problem is that we have allowed, in the ghettos, the formation of what Oscar Lewis calls a Culture of Poverty, insulated, ingrown, dependent; and how can such a culture become free and independent? I don't know; but it is possible that rioting, burning, hurling insults, apparently stupid militancy, and an extravagant black racist ideology are indeed means of regaining confidence at this level of dispiritment. King, as he came to deal with northern problems, had begun to take this factor into account, though it clearly pained his heart and mind. And it is encouraging that whites, and white officials like Lindsay, may be finding the compassion that is here the only relevant thing we have to give.

The violent who are interested in insurrection and "revolutionary" overturn inevitably consider non-violence as "reformist." According to their theory, since it is piecemeal and does not aim to demolish the System and replace it (with what?), it cannot change anything. In my view, especially in complicated and highly organized societies, it is only by opening areas of freedom piecemeal that we will transform our lives. "Seizing power" in such societies is precisely counter-revolution and stops the social revolution short. But the human contact of aggressive non-violence is exquisitely relevant to the deepest danger of modern times, the mechanical violence of 1984. Because of it and the new spirit of the young, we will not have 1984.

Finally, it is said that non-violence might suit the Hindus but it is contrary to American spirit and tradition. Quite the contrary. It seems to me to be simply an extension of traditional American populism, the democratic process as conceived by Jefferson, that has always revived in times of great crisis: acting "illegally" and "petitioning," rousing the general will, protected by the Bill of Rights, with fringes of violence, and ending up with important institutional change. In every major country in the world, power is terribly deeply entrenched; but America is the most likely place for a non-violent movement toward freedom to succeed.

Since I have this occasion, let me say a word about the death of Martin King. He was a stubborn, reasonable man, and political without being a fink. I do not know any other national leader for whose death I would have wept.

In my opinion, the extraordinary general grief of the Americans was not, as has been charged, hypocritical or empty. The grief for death and sympathy for survivors is one of the few emotions that bring all people, even divided families, together. I think that whites now recognize blacks a little more as persons than they did before, and this should have consequences.

This essay appeared in *The New York Review of Books* (May 23, 1968).

The
Psychology
of
Being
Powerless

I.

*P*eople believe that the great background conditions of modern life are beyond our power to influence. The proliferation of technology is autonomous and cannot be checked. The galloping urbanization is going to gallop on. Our overcentralized administration, both of things and men, is impossibly cumbersome and costly, but we cannot cut it down to size. These are inevitable tendencies of history. More dramatic inevitabilities are the explosions, the scientific explosion and the population explosion. And there are more literal explosions, the dynamite accumulating in the slums of a thousand cities and the accumulating stockpiles of nuclear bombs in nations great and small. Our psychology, in brief, is that history is out of control. It is no longer something that we make but something that happens to us. Politics is not prudent steering in difficult terrain, but it is—and this is the subject of current political science—how to get power and keep power, even though the sphere of effective power is extremely limited and it makes little difference who is in power. The psychology of historical powerlessness is evident in the reporting in and the reading of newspapers: there is little analysis of how events are building up, but we read—with excitement, spite, or fatalism, depending on our characters—the headlines of crises for which we are unprepared. Statesmen cope with emergencies, and the climate of emergency is chronic.

I have been trying to show that some of these historical conditions are not inevitable at all but are the working-out of willful policies that aggrandize certain interests and exclude others, that subsidize certain styles and prohibit others. But of course *historically*, if almost everybody believes the conditions are inevitable, including the policy makers who produce them, then they are inevitable. For to cope with emergencies does not mean, then, to support alternative conditions, but further to support and institutionalize the same conditions. Thus, if there are too many cars, we build new highways; if administration is too cumbersome, we build in new levels of administration; if there is a nuclear threat, we develop anti-missile missiles; if there is urban crowding and anomie, we step up urban renewal and social work; if there are ecological disasters because of imprudent use of technology, we subsidize research and development by the same scientific corporations working for the same ecologically irrelevant motives; if there is youth alienation, we extend and intensify processing in schools; if the nation-state is outmoded as a political form, we make ourselves into a mightier nation-state.

In the self-proving round the otherwise innocent style of input-output economies, games-theory strategy, and computerized social science becomes a trap. For the style dumbly accepts the self-proving program and cannot compute what is not mentioned. Then the solutions that emerge ride even more roughshod over what has been left out. Indeed, at least in the social sciences, the more variables one can technically compute, the less likely it is that there will be prior thinking about their relevance rather than interpretation of their combination. Our classic example—assuming that there will be a future period for which we provide classic examples—is Herman Kahn on Thermonuclear War.

In this lecture, therefore, I will no longer talk about the error of believing that our evils are necessary, but stick to the more interesting historical fact of that belief. What is the psychology of feeling that one is powerless to alter basic conditions? What is it as a way of being in the world? Let me list half a dozen kinds of responses to being in a chronic emergency, which, unfortunately, in America are exhibited in rather pure form. I say unfortunately, because a pure response to a chronic emergency is a neurotic one; healthy human beings are more experimental or at least muddling. Instead of politics, we now have to talk psychotherapy.

II.

By definition, governors cannot forfeit the thesis that everything is under control, though they may not think so. During President Kennedy's Administration, Arthur Schlesinger expressed the problem poignantly by saying, "One simply *must* govern." The theme of that Administration was to be "pragmatic"; but by this they did not mean a philosophical pragmatism, going toward an end in view from where one in fact is and with the means one has; they meant turning busily to each crisis as it arose, so that it was clear that one was not inactive. The criticism of Eisenhower's Administration was that it was stagnant. The new slogan was "get America moving."

This was rather pathetic; but as the crises have become deeper, the response of the present Administration is not pathetic but, frankly, delusional and dangerous. It is to *will* to be in control, without adjusting to the realities. They seem to imagine that they will in fact buy up every economy, police the world, social engineer the cities, school the young. In this fantasy they employ a rhetoric of astonishing dissociation between idea and reality, far beyond customary campaign oratory. For example, they proclaim that they are depolluting streams, but they allot no money; forty "demonstration cities" are to be made livable and show the way, but the total sum available is $1.5 billion; the depressed area of Appalachia has been reclaimed, but the method is an old highway bill under another name; poor people will run their own programs, but any administrator is fired if he tries to let them; they are suing for peace, but they despatch more troops and bombers. This seems to be just lying, but to my ear it is nearer to magic thinking. The magic buoys up the self-image; the activity is either nothing at all or brute force to make the problem vanish.

In between the ideality and the brutality there occurs a lot of

obsessional warding off of confusion by methodical calcula-
tions that solve problems in the abstract, in high modern style. A
precise decimal is set, beyond which the economy will be inflationary, but nobody pays it any mind. We know at what average
annual income how many peoples cause what percentage of dis-
turbances. A precise kill-ratio is established beyond which the Viet
Cong will fold up, but they don't. Polls are consulted for the
consensus, like the liver of sheep, without notice of signs of unrest
and even though the Administration keeps committing itself to an
irreversible course that allows for no choice. And they are ever-
lastingly righteous.

In more insane moments, however, they manufacture history
out of the whole cloth, so there is no way of checking up at all.
They create incidents in order to exact reprisals; they invent (and
legislate about) agitators for demonstrations and riots that are
spontaneous; they project bogeymen in order to arm to the teeth.
Some of this, to be sure, is cynical, but that does not make it less
mad; for, clever or not, they still avoid the glaring realities of world
poverty, American isolation, mounting urban costs, increasing
anomie, and so forth. I do not think the slogan "The Great
Society" is cynical; it is delusional.

Perhaps the epitome of will operating in panic—like a case
from a textbook in abnormal psychology—has been the government's handling of the assassination of John Kennedy. The Warren
Commission attempted to "close" the case, to make it not exist in
the public mind. Thus it hastily drew firm conclusions from
dubious evidence, disregarded counter-evidence, defied physical
probabilities, and perhaps even accepted manufactured evidence.
For a temporary lull it has run the risk of a total collapse of public
trust that may end up in a Dreyfus case.

III.

Common people, who do not have to govern, can let themselves feel powerless and resign themselves. They respond with the
familiar combination of not caring and, as a substitute, identifying
with those whom they fancy to be powerful. This occurs dif-

ferently, however, among the poor and the middle class.

The poor simply stop trying, become dependent, drop out of school, drop out of sight, become addicts, become lawless. It seems to be a matter of temperature or a small incident whether or not they riot. As I have said before, in anomic circumstances it is hard to tell when riot or other lawlessness is a political act toward a new setup and when it is a social pathology. Being powerless as citizens, poor people have little meaningful structure in which to express, or know, what they are after. The concrete objects of their anger make no political sense: they are angry at themselves or their own neighborhoods, at white people passing by, at Jewish landlords and shopkeepers. More symbolic scapegoats, like either "the capitalist system" or "communism," do not evoke much interest. One has to feel part of a system to share its bogeymen or have a counter-ideology, and by and large the present-day poor are not so much exploited as excluded.

But to fill the void, they admire, and identify with, what is strong and successful, even if—perhaps especially if—it is strong and successful at their own expense. Poor Spanish youth are enthusiastic about our mighty bombs and bombers, though of course they have no interest in the foreign policy that uses them. (If anything, poor people tend to be for de-escalation and peace rather than war.) Readers of the *Daily News* are excited by the dramatic confrontation of statesmen wagging fingers at each other. Negroes in Harlem admire the Cadillacs of their own corrupt politicians and racketeers. Currently there is excitement about the words "Black Power," but the confusion about the meaning is telling: in the South, where there is little Negro anomie, Black Power has considerable political meaning; in the Northern cities it is a frantic abstraction. Similarly, the contrary word "Integration" makes economic and pedagogic sense if interpreted by people who have some feeling of freedom and power, but if it is interpreted by hopeless resentment, it turns into a fight for petty victories or spite, which are not political propositions though they may be good for the soul.

The anomie of the middle-class people, on the other hand, appears rather as their privatism; they retreat to their families and to the consumer goods—areas in which they still have some power and choice. It is always necessary to explain to non-Americans that middle-class Americans are not so foolish and piggish about their standard of living as it seems; it is that the standard of living has to provide all the achievement and value that are open to them. But it is a strange thing for a society to be proud of its standard of living, rather than taking it for granted as a background for worthwhile action.

Privacy is purchased at a terrible price of anxiety, excluding, and pettiness, the need to delete anything different from oneself and to protect things that are not worth protecting. Nor can they be protected; few of the suburban homes down the road, that look so trim, do not have cases of alcoholism, ulcers, insanity, youngsters on drugs or in jail for good or bad reasons, and so forth. In my opinion, middle-class squeamishness and anxiety, a kind of obsessional neurosis, are a much more important cause of segregation than classical race prejudice which is a kind of paranoia that shows up most among failing classes, bankrupt small-property owners, and proletarians under competitive pressure. The squeamishness is worse, for it takes people out of humanity, whereas prejudice is at least passionate. Squeamishness finally undercuts even the fairness and decency that we expect from the middle class. Paranoiac prejudice has resulted in hot murder and setting on police dogs, but squeamishness has resulted in the cold murder of disregard and proposals to put poor people away in Vietnam.

The identification with power of the powerless middle class is also characteristic. They identify not with brutality, big men, or wealth, but with the efficient system itself, which is what renders *them* powerless. And here again we can see the sharp polarity between those who are not politically resigned and those who are. Take the different effects of what is called education. On the one hand, the universities, excellent students and distinguished professors, are the nucleus of opposition to our war policy. On the other hand, in general polls there is always a dismaying correlation between years of schooling and the "hard line" of bombing China during the Korean War or bombing Hanoi now. But this is not because the educated middle class is rabidly anti-communist, and certainly it is not because it is ferocious; rather, it is precisely because it is rational that it approves the technically efficient solution that does not notice flesh-and-blood suffering. In this style the middle class feels it has status, though no more power than anybody else. No doubt these middle-class people are influenced by the magazines they read, which explain what *is* efficient; but they are influenced because they are "thinking" types, for whom reality is what they read.

The bathos of the irresponsible middle class is the nightly TV newscast on our national networks. This combines commercials for the high standard of living, scenes of war and riot, and judicious pro-and-con commentary on what it all means. The scenes arouse feeling, the commentary provokes thought, the commercials lead to action. It is a total experience.

IV.

Let me illustrate the anomic psychology with another example, for it has come to be accepted as the normal state of feeling rather than as pathological. (I apologize to the Canadian audience for choosing my example again from the Vietnam war. But my country is bombing and burning those people, and my friends and I are unable to prevent it.)

During the hearings on Vietnam before the Senate Foreign Relations Committee, Senator Thomas Dodd of Connecticut— who had been mentioned as Lyndon Johnson's choice for Vice-President in 1964—was asked what he thought of the sharp criticism of the government. "It is the price that we pay," he said, "for living in a free country." This answer was routine and nobody questioned it. Yet what an astonishing evaluation of the democratic process it is, that free discussion is a weakness we must put up with in order to avoid the evils of another system! To Milton, Spinoza, or Jefferson free discussion was the strength of a society. Their theory was that truth had power, often weak at first but steady and cumulative, and in free debate the right course would emerge and prevail. Nor was there any other method to arrive at truth, since there was no other authority to pronounce it than all the people. Thus, to arrive at wise policy, it was essential that everybody say his say, and the more disparate the views and searching the criticism, the better.

Instead, Senator Dodd seems to have the following epistemology of democracy. We elect an administration and it, through the Intelligence service, secret diplomacy, briefings by the Department of Defense and other agencies, comes into inside information that enables it alone to understand the situation. In principle we can repudiate its decisions at the next election, but usually they have led to commitments and actions that are hard to repudiate. Implicit is that there is a permanent group of selfless and wise public servants, experts, and impartial reporters who understand the technology, strategy, and diplomacy that we cannot understand; therefore we must perforce do what they advise. To be sure, they continually make bad predictions and, on the evidence, they are not selfish but partial or at least narrow in their commercial interests and political outlook. Yet this does not alter the picture, for if the President goes along with them, outside criticism is irrelevant anyway and no doubt misses the point, which, it happens, cannot be disclosed for reasons of national security. And surely irrelevant discussion is harmful because it is divisive. But it is the price we pay for living in a free country.

What can be the attraction of such a diluted faith in democracy? It is what is appropriate in a chronic low-grade emergency. In an emergency it is rational, and indeed natural, to concentrate temporary power in a small center, as the ancient Romans appointed dictators, to decide and act, and for the rest of us to support the *faits accomplis* for better or worse. But since we face a low-grade emergency—nobody is about to invade San Francisco—we like to go on as usual, including sounding-off and criticizing, so long as it does not affect policy.

Unfortunately, this psychology keeps the low-grade emergency chronic. There is no way to get back to normal, no check on *faits accomplis,* no accountability of the decision-makers till so much damage has been done that there is a public revulsion (as after a few years of Korea), or, as seems inevitable, one day a catastrophe. Worst of all, there is no way for a philosophic view to emerge that might become effectual. Who would present such a view? In the classical theory of democracy, the electorate is educated by the clashing debate, and the best men come forward and gain a following. But in Senator Dodd's free country acute men are likely to fall silent, for what is the use of talk that is irrelevant and divisive?

The discussion in the Foreign Relations Committee, excellent as it was, was itself typical of a timid democracy. Not a single Senator was able to insist on basic realities that could put the Vietnam war in a philosophic light and perhaps work out of its dilemmas. (Since then, Senator Fulbright has become more outspoken.) In this context, here are some of the basic realities. In a period of worldwide communications and spread of technology, and therefore of "rising aspirations," nevertheless a majority of mankind is fast becoming poorer. For our own country, is it really in our national interest to come on as a Great Power, touchy about saving face and telling other peoples how to act or else? In the era of One World and the atom bomb, is there not something baroque in the sovereignty of nation-states and legalisms about who aggressed on whom?

It will be objected that such anti-national issues can hardly be raised by Senators, even in a free debate. But the same limitation exists outside of government. In the scores of pretentious TV debates and panel discussions on Vietnam during the past two years, I doubt that there have been half a dozen—and these not on national networks—in which a speaker was invited who might conceivably go outside the official parameters and raise the real questions. Almost always the extreme opposition is himself a proponent of power politics, like Hans Morgenthau (it usually *is* Hans Morgenthau). Why not A.J. Muste, for instance? Naturally the big networks would say that there is no use in presenting quixotic opinions that are irrelevant. (The word "quixotic" was used by David Sarnoff of the National Broadcasting Company in his successful bid to Congress to deny to third-party candidates equal free time.) By this response, the broadcasters guarantee that the opinions will remain irrelevant, until history, "out of control," makes them relevant because they were true.

V.

This brings me back to my subject—how people are in the world when history is "out of control." So far I have noticed those who unhistorically will to be in control and those who accept their powerlessness and withdraw. But there is another possibility, apocalypse, not only to accept being powerless but to expect, or perhaps wish and hasten, the inevitable historical explosion. Again there are two variants, for it is usually a different psychology, entailing different behavior, to expect a catastrophe and beat around for what to do for oneself, or to wish for the catastrophe and identify with it.

To expect disaster and desert the sinking ship is not a political act, but it is often a profoundly creative one, both personally and socially. To do it, one must have vitality of one's own that is not entirely structured and warped by the suicidal system. Going it alone may allow for new development. For instance, when the youth of the Beat movement cut loose from the organized system, opted for voluntary poverty, and invented a morals and culture out of their own guts and some confused literary memories, they exerted a big, and on the whole good, influence. Also, the disposition of the powers-that-be to treat gross realities as irrelevant has driven many intellectual and spirited persons into deviant paths just to make sense of their own experience; thus, at present, perhaps most of the best artists and writers in America are unusually far out of line, even for creative people. They hardly seem to share the common culture, yet they are what culture we have. (According to himself, Dr. Timothy Leary, the psychedelics man, espouses the extreme of this philosophy: "Turn on, tune in, drop out"; but I doubt that relying on chemicals is really a way of dropping out of our drug-ridden and technological society.)

We must remember that with the atom bombs there is a literal meaning to deserting the ship. This factor is always present in the background of the young. Those who disregard it will never understand their skepticism or their courage. For instance, during the Cuban missile crisis I kept getting phone calls from college students asking if they should fly at once to New Zealand. I tried to calm their anxiety by opining that the crisis was only diplomatic maneuvering, but I now think that I was wrong, for eyewitnesses to behavior in Washington at the time tell me that there *was* a danger of nuclear war.

More generally, the psychology of apocalypse and the decision to go it alone are characteristic of waves of populism such as we are now surprisingly witnessing in the United States. The rhetoric of the agrarian populism of the eighties and nineties was vividly apocalyptic, and that movement brought forth remarkable feats of cooperation and social invention. The current urban and student populism, as I have pointed out in these lectures, has begun to produce its own para-institutional enterprises, some of which are viable.

The practice of civil disobedience also must often be interpreted in terms of the psychology of apocalypse, but even sympathetic legal analysts of civil disobedience fail to take this into account. It is one thing to disobey a law because the authorities are in moral error on some point, in order to force a test case and to rally opposition and change the law. It is another thing to disobey authorities who are the Whore of Babylon and the Devil's thrones and dominions. In such a case the conscientious attitude may be not respect but disregard and disgust, and it may be more moral for God's creatures to go underground rather than to confront, especially if their theology does not include an article on paradise for martyrs. As a citizen of the uncorrupted polity in exile, it might be one's civic duty to be apparently lawless. There is a fairly clear-cut distinction between civil disobedience in a legitimate order and revolution that may or may not prove its own legitimacy; but the politics and morality of apocalypse fall in between and are ambiguous.

VI.

Quite different, finally, is the psychology of those who unconsciously or consciously wish for catastrophe and work to bring it about. (Of course, for the best youth to desert the sinking ship also brings about disaster, by default.) The wish for a blow-up occurs in people who are so enmeshed in a frustrating system that they have no vitality apart from it; and their vitality in it is explosive rage.

Very poor people, who have "the culture of poverty," as Oscar Lewis calls it, are rarely so psychologically committed to a dominant social system that they need its total destruction. They have dreams of heaven but not of hellfire. A few exemplary burnings and beheadings mollify their vengeance. Their intellectual leaders, however, who are verbal and willy-nilly psychologically enmeshed in the hated system might be more apocalyptic. For instance, Malcolm X once told me—it was before his last period which was more rational and political—that he would welcome the atom bombing of New York to vindicate Allah, even though it would destroy his own community. James Baldwin is full of hellfire, but I have never heard much of it in popular religion.

On the whole, at present in the United States the psychology of explosive apocalypse is not to be found among rioting Negroes crying "Burn, baby, burn," nor among utopian Beatniks on hallucinogens; it is to be found among people who believe in the system but cannot tolerate the anxiety of its not working out for them. Unfortunately, it is a pretty empty system and anxiety is widespread.

Most obviously there is the large group of people who have been demoted or are threatened with demotion: businessmen and small-property owners who feel they have been pushed around; victims of inflation; displaced farmers; dissatisfied ex-soldiers; proletarians who have become petty bourgeois but are now threatened by automation or by Negroes invading their neighborhoods. Consciously these people do not want a blowup but power to restore the good old days; but when they keep losing out, they manifest an astounding violence and vigilantism and could become the usual mass base for fascism. In foreign policy, where imagination has freer rein, they are for pre-emptive first strikes, bombing China, and so forth. I do not think this group is dangerous in itself—I do not think there is an important Radical Right in the United States—but it is a sounding board to propagate catastrophic ideas to more important groups.

My guess is that, under our bad urban conditions, a more dangerous group is the uncountable number of the mentally ill and psychopathic hoodlums from all kinds of backgrounds. Given the rate of mental disease and the arming and training in violence of hundreds of thousands of young men, there is sure to be an increase of berserk acts that might sometimes amount to a reign of terror and could create a climate for political enormities. Not to speak of organized Storm Trooping.

The most dangerous group of all, however, is the established but anomic middle class that I described previously. Exclusive, conformist, squeamish, and methodical, it is terribly vulnerable to anxiety. When none of its rational solutions work out at home or abroad, its patience will wear thin, and then it could coldly support a policy of doom, just to have the problems over with, the way a man counts to three and blows his brains out. But this coldly conscious acceptance of a "rational solution" would not be possible if unconsciously there were not a lust for destruction of the constraining system, as sober citizens excitedly watch a house burn down.

The conditions of middle-class life are exquisitely calculated to increase tension and heighten anxiety. It is not so much that the pace is fast—often it consists of waiting around and is slow and boring—but that it is somebody else's pace or schedule. One is continually interrupted. And the tension cannot be normally discharged by decisive action and doing things one's own way. There is competitive pressure to act a role, yet paradoxically one is rarely allowed to do one's best or use one's best judgment. Proofs of success or failure are not tangibly given in the task, but always in some superior's judgment. Spontaneity and instinct are likely to be gravely penalized, yet one is supposed to be creative and sexual on demand. All this is what Freud called civilization and its discontents. Wilhelm Reich showed that this kind of anxiety led to dreams of destruction, self-destruction, and explosion, in order to release tension, feel something, and feel free.

A chronic low-grade emergency is not psychologically static. It builds up to and invites a critical emergency.

But just as we are able to overlook glaring economic and ecological realities, so in our social engineering and system of education glaring psychological realities like anomie and anxiety are regarded almost as if they did not exist.

The psychological climate explains, I think, the peculiar attitude of the Americans toward the escalation of the Vietnam war. (At the time I am writing this, more bombs are being rained on that little country than on Germany at the peak of World War II, and there is talk of sending nearly a million men.) The government's statements of purpose are inconsistent week by week and are belied by its actions. Its predictions are ludicrously falsified by what happens. Field commanders lie and are contradicted by the next day's news. Yet a good majority continues to acquiesce with a paralyzed fascination. This paralysis is not indifference, for finally people talk about nothing else—as I in these lectures. One has the impression that it is an exciting attraction of a policy that is doomed.

This essay first appeared under the title "The Psychology of Powerlessness" in *The New York Review of Books* (November 3, 1966). The version reprinted here is the one Goodman gave as part of the Massey Lectures on the Canadian Broadcasting Corporation, and then revised as Chapter 5 of *Like a Conquered Province*.

The
Anti-Social
and
Aggression

I. SOCIAL AND ANTI-SOCIAL

*T*he underlying social nature of the organism and the forming personality—fostering and dependency, communication, imitation and learning, love-choices and companionship, passions of sympathy and antipathy, mutual aid and certain rivalries—all this is extremely conservative, repressible but ineradicable. And it is meaningless to think of an organism possessing drives which are "anti-social" in this sense, opposed to his social nature, for this would be a conserved inner contradiction; it would not be conserved. But there are, rather, difficulties of individual development, of growing-up, of realizing all of one's nature.

The society of persons, however, is largely an artifact, like the verbal personalities themselves. It is continually being changed in every detail; indeed, to initiate social changes, to create institutional artifacts, is probably part of the underlying conservative social nature, repressed in any society one chooses to consider. In this sense, a personal behavior is meaningfully "anti-social" if it tends to destroy something of the mores, institutions, or personality current at the time and place. In therapy we must assume that a

delinquent behavior that contradicts a person's social nature is alterable, and the delinquent aspects of it will vanish with further integration. But with a delinquent behavior that is merely anti-social, contradicts the social artifact, it is always a question whether with further integration it may not become more pronounced and the person try harder not to adjust himself to society but to adjust society to himself.

II. CHANGES IN THE ANTI-SOCIAL

In considering the anti-social, let us first distinguish what the neurotic considers anti-social from what is anti-social.

Any drive or aim that we have but will not accept as our own, that we keep unaware or project onto others, we fear to be anti-social. Obviously, for we inhibited it and drove it from awareness because it did not cohere with an acceptable picture of ourselves, and this picture of ourselves was an identification with, an imitation of, those authoritative persons who constituted our first society. But of course when the drive is released and accepted as part of ourselves, it turns out to be much less anti-social; we suddenly see that it is not unusual, is more or less accepted, in our adult society—and the destructive intensity that we attributed to it is less than we feared. An impulse that was vaguely felt to be hellish or murderous turns out to be a simple desire to avoid or reject something, and no-one cares whether we do or not. But it was the repression itself that (a) made the idea a persistent threat, (b) obscured its limited intent and made us not see the social actuality, (c) painted on the lurid colors of the forbidden, and (d) itself created the idea of destructiveness, for the repression is an aggression against the self and this aggression was attributed to the drive. (To cite the classic instance: in 1895 Freud thought that masturbation caused neurasthenia; later he found that it was guilty masturbation, the attempt to repress masturbation and the inhibition of orgastic pleasure, that caused neurasthenia. Thus it was the very fear of the damage, mistaken medicine abetting the sexual taboo, that caused the damage.) Since Freud first wrote, the "contents of the id" have become less hellish, more tractable. Likely he would not now have felt called on to use that vaunting motto,

Flectere si nequeo superos, Acheronta movebo

—which would have been a pity.

Yet the neurotic estimate is also in the right. Theorists have gone too far in showing that the underlying drives are "good" and "social"; they have tried too hard to be on the side of the angels. What has in fact happened is that in the past fifty years there has been an extraordinary revolution in social mores and evaluation, so that much that was considered wicked is not now considered wicked. It is not that certain behavior is now acceptable because it is seen to be good or social or harmless, but that it is considered good, etc. because it is now an accepted part of the picture of humanity. Man does not strive to be good; the good is what it is human to strive for. To put this another way, certain "contents of the id" were hellish not only because the repression made them so in the four ways mentioned above, but because also (e) they contained a residue that was really destructive of the then social norms, it was real temptation or vice—and it was real social pressure, passed through the early authorities, that led to the neurotic repression.

Where the repressed temptation was fairly universally present, however, when once it was revealed as common and somewhat accepted, it made its way in the open with astonishing rapidity; becoming public and more or less satisfied, it lost its hellish aspects; and in a generation the social norm has changed. Indeed it is remarkable with what unanimity society comes to a new picture of itself as a whole; one would have expected parts of the moral code to be more tenaciously conservative (but of course there has been the cooperation of every kind of social factor: changed economy, urbanism, international communication, increased standard of living, etc.). It is only by visiting a very provincial community, or by picking up an 1890 manual of child-care or an essay on "Christianity and the Theater," that one realizes the sharpness of the change. And what is capital is this: the older attitude is not necessarily lurid, exaggerated, nor especially ignorant; rather it is often a sober well-considered judgment that something is inadvisable or destructive that we now hold to be useful or salutary. For instance, it used to be seen with perfect clarity that strict toilet-training is useful to form ruly character; this is by no means ignorant, it is probably true. But they said, therefore *do* it; and we say, therefore *don't* do it. One reason for the change, for example, is that in our present economy and technology, the old standard of closeness, laboriousness, and duty would be socially injurious.

Freud took seriously this hostile residue, that which was in fact socially destructive. He kept warning of the social resistance to psychoanalysis. If our modern mental-hygienists find that what they release is invariably good and not anti-social, and that therefore they need not encounter resistance among the liberal and tolerant, it is simply that they are fighting battles already mainly won and are engaging in, no doubt necessary, mopping up. But aggressive psychotherapy is inevitably a social risk. This ought to be obvious, for social pressures do not deform organismic-self-regulation that is "good" and "not anti-social" when it is properly understood and said with the acceptable words; society forbids what is destructive of society. There is not a semantical mistake but a genuine conflict.

III. UNEQUAL PROGRESS AND SOCIAL REACTION

Let us consider two quite spectacular recent changes in mores in which psychoanalysis has played a leading role: the affirmative attitude toward sexual pleasure and the permissive attitude in child-care. These changes are now so widespread that they should be cumulative; that is, there should be enough actual satisfaction and self-regulation (in certain spheres) quite generally to diminish public resentment and that projection of bogey-men; therefore the taboos should become still less enforced, and there should be still more satisfaction and self-regulation, and so forth. Especially in the case of children, the permission of thumbsucking, the more self-regulating standards of nourishment, the permission of masturbation, the relaxation of toilet-training, the recognition of the need for body-contact and suckling, the omission of corporal punishment, all these ought to show fruit in the happiness of the rising generation. But let us scrutinize the case more closely.

We have here an interesting example of unequal development, the advance in some respects toward self-regulation while maintaining, and even increasing, a neurotic deliberateness in other respects. How does society adjust itself to attain a new equilibrium in the unequal development, to prevent the revolutionary dynamism latent in any new freedom—for any freedom would be expected to release energy and lead to a heightened struggle. The effort of society is to isolate, compartment, and draw the teeth of the "threat from below."

Thus, the increase in the quantity of fairly unrestrained sexuality has been accompanied by a decrease in the excitement and depth of the pleasure. What does this mean? It has been argued that deprivation as such is necessary for the accumulation of tension; but organismic-self-regulation ought to suffice to measure the times of appetite and discharge without external interventions. It is said that faddish imitation and "over-indulgence" cheapen sexual pleasure; this is true, but if there were more satisfactions, more contact and love, there would be less compulsive and automatic indulgence; and the question we are asking is, *why* is there less satisfaction, etc.? It is wiser to consider this particular de-sensitizing as similar in kind to the rest of the desensitizing, contactlessness, and affectlessness now epidemic. They are the result of anxiety and shock. In the unequal development, the release of sexuality has come up against a block of what is not released; anxiety is aroused; the acts are performed, but the meaning and the feeling is withdrawn. Not fully completed, the acts are repeated. Guiltiness is generated by anxiety and lack of satisfaction. And so forth.

A chief block, we are shortly going to argue, is the inhibition of aggression. And this is obvious anyway from the fact that the commercial exploitation of sexuality, in the movies, novels, comic-strips, etc. (as Legman-Keith has demonstrated), concentrates on sadism and murder. (The style of this kind of commercialized dream is always an unerring index of what goes on, for it has no other criterion but to meet the demand and sell.)

A chief social device for isolating sexuality is, paradoxically, the healthful, sane scientific attitude of sex-education on the part of educators and progressive parents. This attitude sterilizes sexuality and makes official, authoritative, and almost mandatory what by its nature is capricious, non-rational, and psychologically explosive (though organically self-limiting). Sexuality is organically periodical, no doubt, but it is not by prescription that one loves. It was against this isolation that Rank warned when he said that the place to learn the facts of life was in the gutter, where their mystery was respected, and blasphemed—as only true believers blaspheme. It is now taught that sexuality is beautiful and ecstatic and not "dirty"; but of course it is, literally, dirty, *inter urinas et faeces*; and to *teach* that it is ecstatic (rather than to let this be the surprise of an occasion) must, in the vast majority of persons whose aggressions are blocked and who therefore cannot give in themselves nor destroy resistance in others, only cause disappointment and make them ask, "What, is it only this?" It is far better, permitting everything, to say nothing at all. But the so-called wholesome attitude, that turns an act of life into a practice of hygiene, is a means of control and compartmenting.

Of course the pioneer sex-educators were revolutionaries; they were bent on undoing the contemporary repression and unmasking the hypocrisy; therefore, they shrewdly seized on all the good and angelic words. But these same words are now a new taboo—"sex is beautiful, keep it clean"—they are a social defense-in-depth. This is why deprivation and the forbidden seem to lead to more intense sexual excitement; it is not that the organism needs these extrinsic aids, but that, in the blocked organism, they prevent compartmenting, they keep open the connections to resentment and rage and the unaware aggression against authority and, at a very deep level, to the desperate risking of the self. For at the moment that one is defying the taboo and running the fatal danger, one is likely to have a flash of spontaneous joy.

The permissive attitude in child-care, again, is a delicious study in unequal development and the social counter-defenses; only a comic genius like Aristophanes could really do it justice. Consider simply that, on the one hand, our generation has learned to unblock much of the noisy savagery of children; and on the other we have tightened the regimental order of all our physical and social environment. We have minimum housing in big cities—and neat playgrounds that no self-respecting boy would be seen dead in.

Naturally the parents are flattened in-between. The astonishing overestimation of children in our culture, that would have baffled the Greeks or the gentry of the Renaissance, is nothing but the reaction to the repression of the spontaneity of the adults (including the spontaneous urge to slaughter their children). Also, we are overcome with our own inferiority, and identify with the children and try to protect their native vigor. Then as the children grow up, they have to make a more and more deliberate and complicated adjustment to the civilization of science, technique, and super-government. Thus the period of dependency is necessarily longer and longer. The children are allowed every freedom except the essential one of being allowed to grow up and exercise economic and domestic initiative. They do not finish going to school.

The contradictory compartments are apparent: in progressive homes and schools we encourage self-regulation, lively curiosity, learning by doing, democratic freedom. And all this is carefully impossible in the city-plan, in making a living, in having a family, in running the state. By the time the lengthy adjustment has been made, there has been no sharp frustration that could rouse a deep-seated rebelliousness, but only a steady molding pressure that forms good healthy citizens, who have early nervous breakdowns and complain that "life has passed me by." Or another outcome, as we shall see, is to wage a good, well-behaved, orderly, and infinitely destructive war.

The history of psychoanalysis itself is a study of how teeth are drawn by respectability. It is a perfect illustration of Max Weber's law of the Bureaucratization of the Prophetic. But this law is not inevitable; it is a consequence of unequal development and consequent anxiety, the need of the whole to adjust itself to the new force and to adjust the new force to itself. What must psychotherapy do to prevent this bureaucratizing respectability? Simply, *press on to the next resistance.*

IV. THE ANTI-SOCIAL IS PRESENTLY THE AGGRESSIVE

The most salient passional characteristics of our epoch are violence and tameness. There are public enemies and public wars unbelievable in scope, intensity, and atmosphere of terror; and at the same time, unexampled civil peace and the almost total suppression of personal outbreaks, with the corresponding neurotic loss of contact, hostility turned against the self, and the somatic symptoms of repressed anger (ulcers, tooth-decay, etc.) In Freud's time and place the passional climate seems to have been much more marked by deprivation and resentment as regards both pleasure and sustenance. At present in America, there is a general high standard of living and the sexuality is not so much frustrated as it is unsatisfactory. On a more superficial level, the neurosis has to do with isolation and inferiority; but these are generally felt and therefore less serious; the mores are increasingly emulative and eager for sociability. Underlying is the inhibited hatred and self-hatred. The deep-going neurosis, which appears masked in such dreams as comic-books and foreign-policy, is retroflected and projected aggression.

The cluster of drives and perversions that are called aggressive—annihilating, destroying, killing, combativeness, initiative, hunting, sado-masochism, conquest and domination—these are now felt to be the anti-social *par excellence*. "But!" one can hear the spluttering objection, "these are *obviously* anti-social, destructive of the order of society!" The fact of the immediate unquestioning social rejection of various aggressions can be taken as *prima facie* evidence that it is in the analysis and release of aggressions that we must look for the next progress of society toward happier norms.[1]

---

[1] The change in the anti-social since Freud's time is also indicated by the change in the method of psychotherapy from symptom-analysis to character-analysis and further. This is partly an improvement in technique, but partly it meets a different run of cases. The symptoms were originally "neurasthenic"; they were, as Freud said (circa 1895), the direct result of sexual frustration; the psychogenic symptoms were transparently sexual acts. (Medical men mention the disappearance of cases of grand hysteria.) Now, it seems, this direct sexual poisoning is less common; for instance, there is obviously much more masturbation without overwhelming guilt. In the character-neuroses the sexual block is related not to the discharge, but somewhat to the act, and largely to the contact and feeling. The therapeutic attitude is likewise altered: the older orthodoxy was a kind of seduction (with disapproval), and the character-analysis is combative.

V. ANNIHILATING AND DESTROYING

The attitude and acts called "aggressive" comprise a cluster of essentially different contact-functions that are usually dynamically interconnected in action and thereby get a common name. We shall try to show that at least annihilating, destroying, initiative, and anger are essential to growth in the organism/environment field; given rational objects, they are always "healthy," and in any case they are irreducible without loss of valuable parts of the personality, especially self-confidence, feeling, and creativity. Other aggressions, like sado-masochism, conquest and domination, and suicide, we shall interpret as neurotic derivatives. Most often, however, the total mixture is not accurately analyzed and is "reduced" too much *en bloc*. (The ineradicable factors are in turn repressed.)

Let us begin by distinguishing annihilating from destroying. Annihilating is making into nothing, rejecting the object and blotting it from existence. The gestalt completes itself without that object. Destroying (de-structuring) is the demolition of a whole into fragments in order to assimilate them as parts in a new whole. Primarily, annihilation is a defensive response to pain, bodily invasion, or danger. In avoidance and flight, the animal takes himself out of the painful field; in killing, he "coldly" removes the offending object from the field. Behaviorally, shutting the mouth tight and averting the head, and smashing and kicking. The defensive response is "cold" because no appetite is involved (the threat is external). The existence of the object is painful, but its non-existence is not enjoyed, it is not felt in completing the field; the enjoyment sometimes apparent is the flooding back at relaxing one's shrinking: sigh of relief, beads of sweat, etc.

When neither flight nor removal is possible, the organism has recourse to blotting out its own awareness, shrinking from contact, averting the eyes, clamping the teeth. These mechanisms become very important when circumstances require opposite responses to the "same" object (really to different properties bound together in one thing): especially when need or desire makes necessary the presence of an object that is also painful and dangerous. One then is obliged to possess without spontaneously enjoying, to hold without contact. This is the usual inevitable plight of children and often the inevitable plight of adults. The analysis must make clear just what property in the object is needed and what is rejected, so the conflict may come into the open and be decided or suffered.

Destroying, on the contrary, is a function of appetite. Every organism in a field grows by incorporating, digesting, and assimilating new matter, and this requires destroying the existing form to its assimilable elements, whether it be food, a lecture, a father's influence, the difference between a mate's domestic habits and one's own. The new matter must be accepted only according to its place in a new spontaneous functioning. If the previous form is not totally destroyed and digested, there occurs, instead of assimilation, either introjection or areas of no contact. The introject may have two fates: either it is a painful foreign matter in the body and it is vomited forth (a kind of annihilation); or the self partially identifies with the introject, represses the pain, seeks to annihilate part of the self—but since the rejection is ineradicable, there is a permanent clinch, a neurotic splitting.

The destructive appetite is warm and pleasurable. It approaches, reaching out to seize, with teeth bared, and it slavers in chewing. Such an attitude, especially if literally or figuratively there is killing, is of course deemed ruthless. Declining to commit the destruction, the self can either introject, or else inhibit the appetite altogether (renounce certain areas of experience). The first is the response especially to the inheritance of the family and social past; forcibly fed, not at one's own time and need, the self introjects parents and culture and can neither destroy nor assimilate them. There are multiple partial-identifications; these destroy self-confidence, and in the end the past destroys the present. If the appetite is inhibited, through nausea or fear of biting and chewing, there is loss of affect.

On the other hand, the warm pleasurable (and angry) destroying of existing forms in personal relations often leads to mutual advantage and love, as in the seduction and defloration of a shy virgin, or in the breaking down of prejudices between friends. For consider that if the association of two persons will in fact be deeply profitable to them, then the destruction of the incompatible existing forms they have come with is a motion toward their more intrinsic selves—that will be actualized in the coming new figure; in this release of the more intrinsic, bound energy is liberated and this will transfer to the liberating agent as love. The process of mutual destruction is probably the chief proving ground of profound compatibility. Our unwillingness to risk it is obviously a fear that if we lose this we shall have nothing; we prefer poor food to none; we have become habituated to scarcity and starvation.

VI. INITIATIVE AND ANGER

Aggression is the "step toward" the object of appetite or hostility. The passing of the impulse into the step is initiative: accepting the impulse as one's own and accepting the motor execution as one's own. Obviously initiative can be stifled by the repression of the appetite altogether, as described above. But more common in modern times, it is likely, is the dissociation of the appetite from the motor behavior, so that it becomes manifest only as garrulous planning or dreamy prospects. One has the impression that with the giving up of hunting and fighting, people cease to move altogether; the motions of athletic games are not related to organic needs, the motions of industry are not one's own motions.

A child's statement, "When I grow up, I'll do so and so," indicates his initiative, the imitative assumption of behavior that will realize the desire still obscure in him till it is acted. When it is repeated by the adult, the unfinished desire persists but the initiative is gone. What has occurred in between? It is that, in our economy, politics, and education, the so-called goals are too alien and the ways of reaching them therefore too complicated, not enough to hand. Everything is preparation, nothing realization and satisfaction. The result is that the problems cannot be worked through and assimilated. The system of education results in a number of unassimilated introjects. After a while the self loses confidence in its own appetites. There is a lack of faith, for faith is knowing, beyond awareness, that if one takes a step there will be ground underfoot: one gives oneself unhesitatingly to the act, one has faith that the background will produce the means. Finally, the attempt to assimilate is given up and there is bafflement and nausea.

At the same time as the initiative is being lost in bewilderment, in pursuing too difficult ends, it is being directly discouraged in the pursuit of simple ends, as a child is slapped for being "forward." Fear results in giving up the appetite. On the whole, there is the reduction to a simpler order of appetite and non-initiative or dependency: to be fed and cared for, not understanding how, and this leads to a persistent insecurity and inferiority.

Let us suppose, however, that an appetite is strong and is under way toward its goal, and it then meets an obstacle and the appetite is frustrated: the tension flares and this is hot anger.

Anger contains the three aggressive components, destroying and annihilating and initiative. The warmth of anger is that of the appetite and initiative themselves. At first the obstacle is regarded simply as part of the existing form to be destroyed, and it is itself attacked with pleasurable heat. But as the frustrating nature of the obstacle becomes manifest, the on-going tension of the engaged self becomes painful, and there is added to the warm destructive appetite the cold need of annihilating. In extreme cases the appetite (the motion toward the goal) is quite transcended and there is fierce white fury. The difference of white fury (murderousness) from simple annihilating (need for the thing not to exist in the field) is the outgoing engagement of the self; one is already committed to the situation, is not just brushing it off; murderousness is not simply a defense, for oneself is engaged and therefore cannot merely avoid. Thus a man who is slapped becomes furious.

In general, anger is a sympathetic passion; it unites persons because it is admixed with desire. (So hatred is notoriously ambivalent with love. When the transcendence of desire toward "pure" anger is based on a repression of desire, then the self is wholly engaged in the hostile attack, and if the repression suddenly dissolves—for instance by finding that one is stronger and is safe—the desire has suddenly crystallized into love.)

It will be seen that the usual formula, "Frustration leads to hostility," is true but too simple, for it omits mentioning the warm appetite in the angry aggression. Then it becomes difficult to understand why anger, an angry disposition, persists when annihilation of the obstacle has been effectively achieved by death or distance (e.g., the parents are dead, yet the child is still angry with them), or again, why in revenge and hatred the annihilation of the enemy gives satisfaction, his non-existence is *not* indifferent but is fed on: he is not only annihilated but destroyed and assimilated. But this is because the frustrating obstacle is first taken as part of the desired goal; the child is angry with dead parents because they are still part of the unfinished need—it is not enough for him to understand that, as obstacles, they are out of the way. And the victim of revenge and hatred is part of oneself, is loved, unaware.

On the other hand, it is the admixture of annihilating within anger that rouses such intense guilt with regard to difficult loved objects; for we cannot afford to annihilate, make nothing of, what we need, even when it frustrates us. Thus it is that persistent anger, uniting appetite and annihilating, leads to the inhibition of appetite altogether and is a common cause of impotence, inversion, etc.

In red anger, awareness is somewhat confused. In white fury it is often very sharp, when, stifling all bodily appetite, it yet draws on the vividness of imagery that belongs to delayed appetite, as the self confronts its object to annihilate it. In purple or congested rage the self is bursting with its frustrated impulses and is confused indeed. In black wrath, or hatred, the self has begun to destroy itself in the interests of its hostile aim; it no longer sees the reality but only its own idea.

VII. FIXATIONS OF THE ABOVE, AND SADO-MASOCHISM

Annihilating, destroying, initiative, and anger are functions of good contact, necessary for the livelihood, pleasure, and protection of any organism in a difficult field. We have seen that they occur in various combinations and are likely to be pleasurable. Acting the aggressions, the organism fills out its skin, so to speak, and touches the environment, without damage to the self; inhibiting the aggressions does not eradicate them but turns them against the self (as we shall discuss in the next chapter). Without aggression, love stagnates and becomes contactless, for destroying is the means of renewal. Further, a hostile aggression is often rational precisely where it is considered neurotic: e.g., hostility may be turned toward a therapist not because he is "father" but because he is again some one who is forcing unassimilable interpretations and putting one in the wrong.

The fixations of these functions, however—hatred, vengeance, and premeditated murder, ambitiousness and compulsive love-hunting, habitual combativeness—these are not so amiable. To these settled passions other functions of the self are sacrificed; they are self-destructive. To hate a thing involves binding energy to what is by definition painful or frustrating, and usually with diminished contact with the changing actual situations. One clings to the hateful and holds it close. In revenge and premeditated murder, there is a burning settled need to annihilate a "person" whose existence insults one's concept of oneself; but if this concept is analyzed, it is found that the drama is internal. So most righteous indignation is directed against one's own temptation. The cold killer, again, is trying systematically to annihilate his environment, which is tantamount to committing suicide: "I don't care for them" means "I don't care for myself," and this is an identification with the terrible judgment, "We don't care for you." The combative man strikes one as a man with appetite who initiates an approach and then suddenly frustrates himself, because he feels inadequate, disapproved, or so; his anger flares against the frustrator; and he projects the "obstacle" into any likely or unlikely object; such a man clearly wants to be beaten.

In general (we shall consider it more in detail in the next chapter) when an appetite is repressed, habitually kept unaware, the self is exercising a fixed hostility against itself. To the extent that this aggression is kept inward, there is a well-behaved masochism; to the extent that it finds some environmental image of itself, there is a fixed sadism. The pleasure in the sadism is the increment of appetite released by letting up on the self; to strike, stab, etc. is the form in which the sadist desiringly touches the object. And the object is loved because it is like one's own dominated self.

In primary masochism (Wilhelm Reich) it is not the pain that is wanted but the release of the dammed-up instincts. The pain is a "fore-pain," a sensation in one habitually desensitized, that then allows much more feeling to be recovered.[2] The more the instinctual excitement is increased without a corresponding increase of awareness that it is one's own excitement and also one's own deliberateness in restricting it, the more the masochistic longing. (It would seem, by the way, that this situation would be experimentally induced by a physiological therapy like Reich's.) In masochism, the appetites become more expansive and increase the tension, and the restriction is correspondingly tightened; the longing for release is neurotically interpreted as the wish to have it done to one, to be forced, broken, punctured, to let loose the inward pressures. The masochist loves the brutal lover who both gives the underlying release and yet is identified with his own self-punishing self.

VIII. MODERN WAR IS MASS-SUICIDE WITHOUT GUILTINESS

Let us now return to the more broadly social context and say something further about the kind of violence that characterizes our epoch.

We have at present in America a combination of unexampled general wealth and unexampled civil peace. Economically and sociologically these are beneficent causes of each other: the more civil order the more productivity, and the more wealth the less incentive to destroy the civil order. By civil order we mean not the absence of crimes of violence, but the pervasive safety of both city and country. Compared with all other ages and places, travel is without danger anywhere by day or night. There are almost no brawls, riots or armed bands. Madmen do not roam the streets; there is no plague. Disease is quickly isolated in hospitals; death is never seen, childbirth rarely. Meat is eaten, but no urban person

---

[2] We should like to substitute the concept of "fore-feeling," as the small element releasing a large flow of feeling, for the Freudian concept of "fore-pleasure." For obviously fore-pain operates in the same way; a man stubs his toe and his cosmic rage and grief well forth. Or a fore-pleasure may bring on a deep feeling that would not be called pleasure; as a lover touches one with a consoling hand and, as D.W. Griffith said, "all the tears of the world wash over our hearts."

ever sees an animal slaughtered. Never before has there existed such a state of non-violence, safety, and sterility. Concerning our wealth, again, we need only point out that none of the debated economic issues has to do with subsistence. Unions demand not bread but better wages and hours and more security; capitalists demand fewer controls and better conditions for reinvestment. A single case of starvation is a scandal in the press. Less than ten per cent of the economy is devoted to elementary subsistence. More than ever in history there are comforts, luxuries, entertainments.

Psychologically the picture is more dubious. There is little physical survival frustration but little satisfaction, and there are signs of acute anxiety. The general bewilderment and insecurity of isolated individuals in a too-big society destroy self-confidence and initiative, and without these there cannot be active enjoyment. Sports and entertainments are passive and symbolic; the choices on the market are passive and symbolic; people make and do nothing for themselves, except symbolically. The quantity of sexuality is great, the de-sensitizing is extreme. It used to be felt that science, technology, and the new mores would bring on an age of happiness. This hope has been disappointed. Everywhere people are disappointed.

Even on the surface, then, there is reason to smash things up, to destroy not this or that part of the system (e.g., the upper class), but the whole system *en bloc,* for it has no further promise, it has proved unassimilable in its existing form. This sentiment is even in awareness with varying degrees of clarity.

But considering more deeply, in the terms we have been developing, we see that these conditions are almost specific for the excitement of primary masochism. There is continual stimulation and only partial release of tension, an unbearable heightening of the unaware tensions—unaware because people do not know what they want, nor how to get it, and the available means are too big and unmanageable. The desire for final satisfaction, for orgasm, is interpreted as the wish for total self-destruction. It is inevitable, then, that there should be a public dream of universal disaster, with vast explosions, fires, and electric shocks; and people pool their efforts to bring this apocalypse to an actuality.

At the same time, however, all overt expression of destructiveness, annihilation, anger, combativeness, is suppressed in the interests of the civil order. Also the feeling of anger is inhibited and even repressed. People are sensible, tolerant, polite, and cooperative in being pushed around. But the occasions of anger are by no means minimized. On the contrary, when the larger movements of initiative are circumscribed in the competitive routines of offices, bureaucracies, and factories, there is petty friction, hurt feelings, being crossed. Small anger is continually generated, never discharged; big anger, that goes with big initiative, is repressed.

Therefore the angry situation is projected afar. People must find big distant causes adequate to explain the pressure of anger that is certainly not explicable by petty frustrations. It is necessary to have something worthy of the hatred that is unaware felt for oneself. In brief, one is angry with the Enemy.

This Enemy is, needless to say, cruel and hardly human; there is no use in treating with him as if he were human. For we must remember, as is shown by the content of all popular cinema and literature, that the dream of American love is sado-masochistic, but the behavior of love-making is not sado-masochistic, for that would be anti-social and indecent. It is "someone else" that is sadistic; and surely "someone else" that is masochistic.

Now in civil life, we have been saying, the cluster of aggressions is anti-social. But fortunately in war it is good and social. So people, longing for universal explosion and disaster, wage war against enemies who indeed enrage and fascinate them by their cruelty and subhuman strength.

The mass-democratic army is excellently apt for the popular needs. It gives the personal security that is lacking in civil life; it imposes a personal authority without making any demand on the secret self, for after all one is only a unit in the mass. It takes one from jobs and homes where one is inadequate and gets no great pleasure; and it organizes one's efforts much more effectively toward sadistic practices and a masochistic débacle.

People observe the débacle approach. They listen to rational warnings and make all kinds of sensible policies. But the energy to flee or resist is paralyzed, or the danger is fascinating. People are eager to finish the unfinished situation. They are bent on mass-suicide, an outcome that solves all problems without personal guiltiness. The counter-propaganda of pacifists is worse than useless, for it solves no problems and it increases personal guiltiness.

IX. CRITIQUE OF FREUD'S THANATOS

It was in similar circumstances that Freud dreamed up his theory of the death-instinct. But the circumstances were less extreme than now, for he could still at that time, in the flush of the theory of the libido, speak of a conflict between Thanatos and Eros and look to Eros for a counter-weight to Thanatos. The new mores had not yet had a trial.

Freud seems to have based his theory on three evidences. (a) The kind of social violence we have been describing: the World War I that went apparently counter to any principle of vitality and culture. (b) The neurotic compulsion to repeat or fixate, that he attributed to the attraction of the trauma. We have seen, however, that the repetition-compulsion is more simply explicable as the effort of the organism to complete with archaic means its *present* unfinished situation, each time enough organic tension accumulates to make the difficult attempt. Yet in an important sense this repetition and circling round the trauma may correctly be called a death-wish; but it is precisely the death of the more deliberate inhibiting self that is wished for (with its apparent present needs and means), in the interests of the more vital underlying situation. What is necessarily neurotically interpreted as a wish for death is a wish for a fuller life. (c) But Freud's most important evidence was probably the apparent irreducibility of primary masochism. For he found that, far from being reduced, precisely as patients began to function more, their dreams (and no doubt Freud's own dreams) became more catastrophic; the theorist was then forced by the evidence to extrapolate to a condition of perfect functioning and total masochism: i.e., to die is an instinctual craving. But on the theory of masochism we have been advancing, this evidence is better explained as follows: the more the instinctual release without the corresponding strengthening of the self's ability to create something with the new energy, the more disruptive and violent the tensions in the field. And just as the physiological method of Reich experimentally induces this condition, so the anamnestic free association of Freud: there is release without integration. But Reich's better control of the situation enabled him to find a simpler explanation.

Yet as a biological speculation, Freud's theory is by no means negligible, and must itself be met speculatively. Let us cast it in the following schematic form: every organism, says the theory, seeks to diminish tension and reach equilibrium; but by reverting to a lower order of structure it can reach a still more stable equilibrium; so ultimately every organism seeks to be inanimate. This is its death-instinct and is a case of the universal tendency toward entropy. Opposed to it are the appetites (eros) that tend to the ever more complex structures of evolution.

This is a powerful speculation. If we accept the presuppositions and mystique of Nineteenth Century science, it is hard to refute. Its rejection by most theorists, including many of the orthodox, is largely, one feels, because it is offensive, anti-social, rather than because it is seen to be erroneous.

But to think, as Freud does, of a *chain* of causes, consisting of connected elementary links back to the beginning, is a misreading of the history of evolution; it is to make actual and concrete what is an abstraction, namely some line of evidence (e.g., the fossils in the strata of rocks) by which we learn the history. He speaks as if the successive complexities were "added on" to a single operating force, of "life," isolatable from its concrete situations; as if onto a protozoon were added the soul of a metazoon, etc.; or conversely, as if within a vertebrate were introjected an annelid, etc.—so that falling asleep as a vertebrate, the animal then addresses itself to falling asleep as an annelid, then as a platyhelminth, and finally to becoming inanimate. But in fact every successive stage is a new whole, operating as a whole, with its own mode of life; it is *its* mode of life, as a concrete whole, that it wants to complete; it is not concerned with seeking "equilibrium in general." The condition of a molecule or of an amoeba is not an unfinished situation for a mammal because the existing organic parts tending to completeness are quite different in the separate cases. Nothing would be solved for an organism by solving the problem of some other kinds of parts.

(It is useful to consider Freud's theory as a psychological symptom: if a man resigns the possibility of present solutions, he must blot out the present needs; and thereby he brings to the fore some other needs of a lower order of structure. The lower order of structure is then given a kind of existence by the act of present resignation.)

Freud seems to misunderstand the nature of a "cause." A "cause" is not itself an existing thing but a principle of explanation for some present problem. Therefore a *chain* of causes—proceeding in either direction, as a final teleological goal or as a primitive genetic origin—the longer such a chain gets, the more it becomes nothing at all, for we seek a cause in order to orient ourselves in a specific individual problem, for the purpose of changing the situation or accepting it. A good cause solves the problem (of specific orientation) and then ceases to occupy us. We set down the causes in a chain, as in a textbook, not when we are handling the actual material, but when we are teaching it.

Lastly, Freud's theory systematically isolates the organism from the on-going organism/environment field; and he isolates an abstract "time" as another factor. But this field is existing; its presentness, its on-going time, with the continual event of novelties, is essential to its definition and to the definition of "organism." It is as part of this ever-novel field that one must think of an organism as growing, and of the species as changing. The passage of time, the change in time, is not something that is added onto a primal animal that has an internal principle of growth isolated from the time of the field, and that somehow adjusts to ever-new situations. But it is the adjustment of ever-new situations, changing both the organism and the environment, that is growth and the kind of time that organisms have—for every scientific subject has its own kind of time. To a history novelty and irreversibility are essential. An animal trying to complete its life is necessarily seeking its growth. Eventually the animal fails and dies, not because *it* is seeking a lower order of structure, but because the field as a whole can no longer organize itself with that part in that form. We are destroyed just as, growing, we destroy.

The aggressive drives are not essentially distinct from the erotic drives; they are different stages of growth, either as selecting, destroying, and assimilating, or as enjoying, absorbing, and reaching equilibrium. And thus, to return to our starting point, when the aggressive drives are anti-social, it is that the society is opposed to life and change (and love); then it will either be destroyed by life or it will involve life in a common ruin, make human life destroy society and itself.

This essay first appeared as Part 2, Chapter VIII of Volume Two of *Gestalt Therapy* (1951). Volume Two, called "Novelty, Excitement and Growth," was the theoretical part of the book, written entirely by Goodman, who collaborated with Fritz Perls in developing the theory, but not in its final formulation.

Novices of art
understate
    what has them by the throat
    the climax; You speak out

for me, spirit who affright
me in the lonely night,
    nor do I know till I express it
    the message boiling in my breast.

IV

WRITERS
AND
WRITING

The
Psychological
Revolution
and
the
Writer's
Life-View

I am a writer, and certainly the writer must present his own life-view, his own hypothesis of what the world is, rather than explore or impose a psychologist's theory. But it happens that my life-view, the way I do see things, and therefore the way I write, has been immensely qualified by Freud, Sullivan, Wilhelm Reich, Karl Abraham, Rank, and Groddeck. Presumably these irrelevant theories have become second nature to me; they are not theories but part of my growth in experience. So I *see* the psychosomatic, the fantasy, the unexpressed interpersonal act or avoidance, almost as I see red and blue. This must be not uncommon among modern writers, and my main point in this talk is to show some obvious effects on how they write.

I.

Our general theme is the relation of psychoanalysis and literature and three kinds of relation occur to me: the exploration of the "psychological meaning" of works and authors; psychologizing itself as a literary genre; and the effect of psychological learning on texture and style. The last is my theme, but let me speak a moment to the other two.

The first, usually in the form or revealing the unconscious motives of works and authors, tends to leave me, as a lover of literature, right where it found me; whether the revealing is the often charming detective work of Theodor Reik or the rediscovery of archetypes by Jungians. No doubt a literary work exists in the world in non-literary ways, but a successful literary work reveals its meaning directly on its literary surface, and that meaning is most efficiently and concretely explored by literary-critical methods: structural analysis, history, and linguistics. This was certainly Freud's doctrine in *Leonardo*; he intended to explain not how Leonardo painted but why he ceased to paint. This is an interesting biographical question, but it has only a tangential relation to the art of Leonardo. With regard to successful works, however, my bias is that critics in even the *Kenyon Review* tell us more than psychoanalysts.

There is a small but interesting category of literature, however, where psychologizing is useful. This is when the work is puzzling, leaves us restive and uneasy, like *Hamlet*. When there is a certain skewness and apparent failure, and yet the whole exerts a fascination, an attraction. Then psychology can powerfully help by disclosing the avoidance in both the writer and the audience.

Such are not the usual cases of literary study. Most generally, the questions "Who was Sophocles?" "What does *Oedipus* mean?" are answered by analyzing the surface of the works. History and text-criticism are indispensable, to make us know exactly what the surface is; structural and textural analysis will then bring the work home to us. The "meaning," of course, is our own re-experiencing of it.

II.

The second possible relation of psychology and literature is more interesting (though it does not much interest me personally as an artist). This is to make psychological investigation itself the substantive literary plot. And I do not think we properly estimate the literary value of truly Freudian case-histories, which are moving stories, as contrasted with the pseudo-case-histories of, e.g., the so-called existentialist psychoanalysts who impose a theory on the plot. A Freudian case-history is a real novel, a real adventure-story, for it shows a particular man, Freud, asking a patient a question, and the patient responds so-and-so, and Freud thinks *aha!* Then the next time the patient appears, there is a quite different situation; the plot has moved; and Freud asks a different kind of question. This gradual unfolding of the depth of meaning by the on-going asking of questions meeting new situations, is one kind of good novel.

But of course an immense amount of classical literature has had this exact structure, or has had it as a major element in a larger structure. It must be so, for a chief use of the art-act for the artist is to probe in the dark until he knows at the end what he did not know in the beginning. He gets deeper into the characters (they begin to "live" in a way he had not planned), and his work grips *him*, until it finally lets him go. And this can be seen in the work.

Put formally, we could say that traditionally all plays and stories in which there is a hidden plot—something unknown to the protagonist, something he has avoided, some mistake he has unwittingly made, but which will be revealed and lead to his downfall (or sometimes salvation)—are in principle psychological investigations. And in fact they have used psychological methods, dream interpretation and Socratic techniques not too dissimilar from psychoanalytic techniques, often better than professionals, for artists are spontaneous and stick close to the concrete.

(Let me say, by the way, that both artists and psychoanalysts and patients invent as well as discover both their process and their endings. A "cure" that consists merely in uncovering some trauma or complex from the past is like the "solution" of a pulp detective-novel, and has about as much cathartic effect.)

In general there is something in common between the action of psychoanalyzing and the act of literary or artistic exploration, and the formal case history itself, in the hands of a master like Freud, is a considerable new genre of literature. It has of course been much imitated by novelists, playwrights, and movie-makers.

III.

My own interest in psychology, as a writer, is rather different. It is that the psychological tradition of the past sixty years has given an important extension, and refinement, to naturalism as a literary style. There are certain things which we now include as a matter of course in our naturalistic depiction which previously were done with difficulty and sporadically. I shall mention half a dozen items. They are obvious and matter-of-fact; I do not think that anybody would seriously deny that their *commonplaceness* is an effect of psychological revolution. On the other hand, there are few if any such matters which cannot be shown here or there in previous literary work; and of course Freud and his fellows themselves grew and worked in an intellectual and literary climate that had important proto-psychoanalytic elements: romantic fantasy, positivistic behaviorism, and genetic evolutionism.

An important psychological premise that has become commonplace in modern literature is the continuity of the life experience, what Wordsworth meant when he said the child is father of the man. The modern writer takes it for granted that his adult characters have been children and adolescents, whether or not he explicitly depicts their growth. Samuel Butler's *The Way of All Flesh* explicitly depicts the powerful effect of the family-constellation—which the hero escapes by what Rank would call "counter-willing," after a catastrophe; this novel was conceived just in the period of the first psychoanalysts and was therefore not "influenced" by them. Dreiser's *An American Tragedy* gives similar attention to the family-constellation, the hyper-religious background of the little boy playing the tambourine on the street, and was probably influenced by psychoanalysis. In this case the youth, making a series of compromises and reaction-formations, cannot free himself to cope with society and is destroyed. More generally, in one form or another, the *Erziehungsroman*, the educational romance, has been continually written for two centuries. *Wilhelm Meister* and *Emile* are great early examples. Flaubert's *Sentimental Education* actually uses its spiral plot, broadening experience but circling about its problem, and its parallel ambivalent characters, in order to psychoanalyze and broadly hint at an Oedipus-complex.

Ibsen is said to have written little life-histories of his characters before composing a play. Now all this, life history, childhood reminiscence, family-constellation, circling back, have become the implicit or explicit fabric of contemporary story-telling.

The representation of the unconscious, what is unknown or only vaguely known to the persons but is operative in their behavior, is also now standard procedure. An interesting gambit is narration by avoidance—circumlocution—as in Henry James, to mention an author uninfluenced by Freud. The characters seem continually to be engaged in small talk and in petty conventional behavior; meantime their underlying passions, which are socially unacceptable, are working themselves out. In this respect James' technique is powerfully naturalistic: it depicts a society in which passionate adventure may occur but must never be mentioned; the woman must never be "compromised." In Flaubert (as in *Hamlet*) the meanings are avoided by the subjects themselves, so that not doing is sometimes the most important action. There is then a strong tendency for the persons to rationalize with a persistent tone of mocking irony on the part of the more knowing author.

More tragic is the explosion of the pent-up avoided and unknown; what psychologists would call the return of the repressed. Traditionally, in tragic plots where there is an overt conflict, the repressed returns as a kind of identification of the protagonist with his antagonist; he betrays himself in dreams and hallucinations, sudden weaknesses, unrealistic battle-plans. In a more "modern" writer like Dostoievski, the explosive return of the repressed becomes more or less the expected way of the world and the characters are all "mad Russians." Our contemporary writers—perhaps unfortunately—have all this at their fingertips; they know the score about their characters so well that the telling allows no surprise for themselves or their readers, and there is no tension.

Another property of contemporary writing is the continuity of the dream life, the day-dream life, the waking life, the slips and tendentious errors, the fantasy, the wishful thinking. Thus the incursion of the manic and fantastic—which was a lurid light in the late Romantics like Hoffman, Poe, or Baudelaire—becomes a domesticated part of naturalistic portrayal. Thomas Mann writes even programmatically in this manner; he was of course directly influenced by the psychologists, as well as springing from the tradition in which psychoanalysis arose. E.M. Forster more subtilely and surprisingly weaves together the rational and irrational, the controlled and the uncontrollable; because he surprises more, he catches more closely, in my opinion, the factual feel of the "psychopathology of everyday life."

In my opinion, an important advantage of our grasp of the continuity of the night life and the day life is the diminishing of "symbolism" and "levels of meaning" in form. Instead of allegories and "symbols" there is the denser texture of causal relations plus a certain amount of "over-determination." Everything is all-of-a-piece.

An obvious literary area in which psychology has diminished superstitiousness and prejudice is the depiction of the sexual part of life. Psychological naturalism here has certainly helped us avoid confusing the ethical and the existential. Ethical problems are solved in the narrative, just as in psychoanalysis itself, not by prejudging the data but by the on-going work itself. It is a great advantage, it seems to me, that we have gotten beyond the icy naturalism of the nineteenth century in which the warmth of Eros is lost and also beyond the religious erotization of sexuality, as in D.H. Lawrence. The contemporary tendency, like the ancient, is to portray the sexual scene just as it is whatever it is, and in the good writers, to go on from there. What is is often very problematic and difficult, but it does not help to have romantic conventions or anti-romantic conventions, nor again moral prejudices, nor anatomizing indifference. Because of the psychological revolution, it is easier for the contemporary writer (and reader) to accept sexual behavior as it is and to proceed to cope with the problematic.

Let me mention one final literary resource that some of us have gained from the psychological revolution, a keener and more persistent attention to the psychosomatic and the character-analytic, in gesture, posture, facial expression; and the corresponding interpersonal expression in tone of voice, and speech and body attitude. The kind of handling of the psychosomatic and characteristic which is so remarkable in Dickens, we try to approximate with less caricature and exaggeration. We depict the hoodlum strut or the pompous corporation chest not merely as local-color and stereotype, but trying also to relate it to what the person is doing to his own body and feelings, what he is perhaps unaware trying to do to the others, and how he is himself in the world.

To illustrate this post-psychological naturalism, let me quote a few random passages from my own prose. It is likely that any particular device in my writing could be illustrated in narratives written long before psychoanalysis was invented-and-discovered, but in my own case I know pretty well where I learned to write this way. Since my adolescence, Freud, Abraham, Groddeck, among others, have been important writers for me, and there is no doubt that my own way of looking at things and describing them has come to be in their terms. That is to say, as a writer I do not "apply" the findings of psychology; but I write as I experience, and I have been brought up to experience "psychologically."

Here is a paragraph from a story, "Our Visit to Niagara":

> ...Returning, I was holding my boy by the hand and we watched the Horseshoe Falls. Refreshed by my shower in the waters of Lake Erie, I was no longer perplexed by the notoriety and venality of Niagara Falls. The coloration of Niagara Falls did not oscillate into a chromolithograph of Niagara Falls; but the fact persisted as it was continuously coming and becoming: that the ragged water rounding the deep bend under the cloudy sky was falling into the Gorge whence rose a strong voice, and mist.

Thus far there is nothing which is post-psychological. But now—

> For his part, the small boy had played enough at throwing himself into the water in sticks and riding the current; he was content to stand still and watch like a grown person, but smirking none the less and bobbing his head in excited appreciation.

This sentence became possible after the development of Child Psychology.

> At a certain moment—I could tell by the tingling in his hand—his excitement gave way to orgastic wonder. He was very still and then he said, "It keeps coming."

This sentence was certainly more likely after learning to pay attention to Psychosomatic Medicine.

Here are a few other sentences from the same story:

Isobel had, quietly, become frantic. Always looking for the whirl-pool. As we rolled northward along the Gorge—she was driving—sudden-ly she would pull over to the side of the road and jam the brakes. We would get out of the car to look at the Gorge, but this was not, apparently, the place; and we went on. I assumed for a while that there really was a particular place she was looking for, that embodied her Niagara Falls. . . She kept looking away to the other side of the road, where their house had been if indeed it had been, if this was this road. . . Or, simply the headache in her temples made her whimper, a headache not to be alleviated by weep-ing, for it was the stretching of wide eyes of fright—near-sighted eyes behind horn-rimmed spectacles that she would not take off.

Here again, is the beginning of a story called "Jeremy Owen." It is very unlikely that this collection of sentences would have been written before the last fifty years:

"Hey, Jeremy, when do we eat?" hinted O'Donell loudly. He was the Chevrolet agent and he had recently gotten Jeremy an honest buy, so he felt at home in his little restaurant. But Jeremy was looking blankly at the meat on the grill that he had mechanically turned off. He did not start as if his thoughts had been elsewhere. They were nowhere. He made the sandwich and brought the dish. Astoundingly he did not bring the coffee.

The auto salesman *was* astounded. He looked up with sudden eyes, like a small boy who knows that something is wrong if the routine is interrupted. But he was not a sharp observer and he imagined that Jeremy was preoccupied; he did not see that he was ceasing to be occupied at all. Perhaps he did see it, but he could not accept the terrible fact that "Mama isn't going to feed me any more." Their eyes met. O'Donell was abashed to ask for his coffee. But he had to have coffee. "Hey, Jeremy, do you still make that good coffee?" he called pleasantly.

That is, there is depersonalization, lapse of memory, continuity of the life history, neurotic denial, rationalization. A little further:

"You in love, Jeremy?" said O'Donell pleasantly. But the perplexity on his forehead said, "Is something wrong, Jeremy?" Jeremy responded to his forehead and not to his words. His impulse was simply to take off his apron and walk out; he instead dutifully spelled it out and said, "I don't seem to want to serve you any more, do I? I don't mean you, Red Hugh—" As soon as he had said the words he realized that he had indeed withdrawn from these people and was in a crisis. The sweat stood on his face.

We have the emphasis on a psychosomatic expression; and the moment of insight brought on by overt expression of the underlying situation. Once he says it, he knows it and is changed.

This is an edited version of Goodman's part in a symposium for Members in Training of the National Psychological Association for Psychoanalysis, first published in the *Psychoanalytic Review* (Fall 1963).

On the Intellectual Inhibition of Explosive Grief and Anger

I.

*F*or the explosive release of strong feelings, such as anger and grief, a person must have the object of passion concretely present, even tangibly present in some way. The object of one kind of anger is a present obstacle; grief is for an object present by its felt absence. To blaze with anger and be ready to strike, a person must first be approaching what he desires, he must be actively committed to the approach; and he must believe that the obstacle in his way is the real cause of his frustration. To bawl for loss, he must first have been attached to something, and then he must believe that its absence is the real cause of the misery he feels.

We see that children easily have these beliefs and often flare up and often cry. Faced with even a temporary delay or absence, children pound and scream and bawl; but as soon as the situation changes, they are bafflingly sunny, and take their gratification with relish, or feel secure again when mother returns. It is said that "children cannot wait," but just the contrary is true. It is children who *can* wait, by making dramatic scenes (not otherwise than religious people get through hours of stress by singing hymns). They have a spontaneous mechanism to cushion even minor troubles. Rather it is the adults who have inhibited their spontaneous expression, who cannot wait; we swallow our disappointment and always taste what we have swallowed. For where the occasions of passion occur, where there is actual frustration and misery, and yet anger and grief are not explosively released, then the disposition itself is soured, and such happiness as follows is never full and unclouded.

Especially among intellectual and sensitive persons, there is an inevitable abuse of intelligence and understanding that keeps them from the conviction that there is a real, present object of anger and grief; and thus they cannot purge these passions. This is their philosophic or scientific insight that the tangible obstacles or losses are not the "real" ones; for the "real" causes of trouble are seen to be remote, general, intangible; they may be social, technological, even cosmological. Behind the immediate frustration or loss, is the understood cause of it. But the thought of such general or distant causes is not able to bring on an explosive release in the physical particular person. There is no doubt that such a flight to the abstract—and indeed, most "thinking" altogether—is a neurotic method of avoiding strong feelings, of substituting "knowing about" for awareness; yet it seems to me that this use of intelligence is inevitable, because indeed such insights are true. The dilemma is this: that desire aims at something tangible, at a present change in ourselves and our physical environment; but when desire is thwarted or love lost, the passional feelings that have been physically roused find no tangible object on which to be vented.

The classical solution of this dilemma has been to equalize matters by turning desire itself toward what is theoretical or ideal: "intellectual love." This has several immensely important variants. One is to achieve stoical *apatheia*, the dissociation of emotion altogether. Another is to achieve Buddhist compassion, the secure response to inevitable misery (in psychoanalysis, this great and constructive frame of mind is a reaction-formation). Neither of these—*apatheia* or compassion—has any relation to animal happiness, so we need not discuss them here. But Intellectual Love can be embarked on also with full risk and, soon enough, somatic commitment; and there then emerge the following interesting possibilities. Suppose intellectual love is frustrated—e.g., by the problem of evil or the problem of infinity—then one comes to a kind of anguish or terror that marks precisely the "return" of the alienated tangible world, perhaps fraught with menace. The particulars of the world will then be regarded not as indifferent to the intellect, but as symbols. A more amiable possibility is that intellectual love is gratified, e.g., by finding proofs of grace and cosmos; then there is said to be a kind of serene ecstasy in which precisely the tangible world is recreated in love; the saint returns to us and performs miracles, the scientist orgastically achieves his theory, and so forth.

Let us ask, however, what occurs with the intellectual and sensitive person who does not leave behind the tangible objects of desire to devote himself to ideal objects. Superficially considered, such a man has a good thing: he enjoys, or at least tries for, animal satisfaction, yet he avoids the worst pains of frustration and failure. It is only when the going gets rough, when he meets too much opposition, that he finds that he cannot take the tangible obstacles seriously, he knows better. Nevertheless, as every intellectual knows, this hedging bet is a desperate disease. He would give anything, he says, to experience frank bawling and hot wrath.

We are not speaking of those who repress grief and anger altogether—as when a child is made to fear the consequences of his anger and is shamed out of crying, and grows into a smiling insensitive adult. This is the inhibition of appetite itself, and must be treated by character analysis. In this essay I want to speak of a well-defined group: persons who have appetites, who show initiative in approaching and possessing their objects and are therefore subject to frustration and loss, but who cannot give way to anger and grief because they know too much. The character neurotics who repress appetite and passion altogether, before they arise, seem to have been intimidated, for example, by harsh parents. Our sensitive intelligent persons, on the contrary, seem to be anxious about blind passion itself: when things do not work out, the self is threatened with confusion, and so the intensity of appetite, grief, anger is controlled and made to *dribble away,* partly in reasoning. The mechanism of dribbling away makes us think of the last-minute inhibition of orgastic surrender and ejaculation. Correspondingly, at the last minute he withdraws from contact. Contrast him as a child with a less intelligent child forced to repress. If a child is intelligent and intuitive, he can avoid dire consequences so long as he takes care of himself; he learns to keep within his safety zone. Here is he lonely but he is also protected from terrible disappointments and punishments. He feels, too, that if he ventured outside his zone, his anger might become uncontrollable and he might murder somebody. He does not repress but he learns to "know better."

In this essay my interest is not in interpreting these misfortunes of the past, but in the problem of coping with this tried and proved defense in the present.

II. GRIEF AND WEEPING

The intellectual person feels his deprivation but he does not weep because, as he says, "My feelings are not hurt, *I* am not hurt." Since he sees that the causes of his loss are objective and general, he knows that they are not aimed especially at him. He is not insulted. (If he were insulted, his ego-protecting anger would flare and this would bring on grief.) Quite the contrary, by his intelligent understanding of causes, he is able to identify himself with the depriving power, he is even somewhat magnified.

Suppose he is in love. So long as pleasure is forthcoming, he cautiously but progressively opens out to it and enjoys his beloved. But as soon as there is threat of loss, he rises above the situation. He at once sees that the loss is inevitable: it is inevitable in the character of the beloved and in his own character, and these cannot be changed; indeed, he might understand that the very increase of their pleasure has created their anxiety, for they have begun to risk confusion, so they withdraw. All this is because of something that happened long ago; it is in the nature of our institutions; it is objective, he himself being one of the objects. It does not touch him at present; he does not feel himself, subjectively, as lost. So he is not softened to bawl.

Nevertheless he feels he is deprived and he is miserable. Being miserable, he characteristically draws back from the feeling of loss and explains it, and he lets his grief dribble away. He is ennobled by understanding. He is now wiser still. The experience was worth it. But he is not purged, and he is henceforth less open to love. He has not mourned enough to be able to live again.

We could say that what is lacking is *surprise*. If he were surprised, he would not have the opportunity to rise above the situation and survey it and let his feeling dribble away. But he is intelligent and foreseeing, not easily surprisable. He is quick to judge by portentous signs and he is always ready. (When such a person becomes more cynical and callous, he even begins to rehearse the outcome beforehand, the more efficiently to prevent any anxiety—or novelty—from occurring.)

Of course he is perfectly right. His lost love is not for him a real object of grief, for, protecting himself, he did not spontaneously engage himself, but only deliberately and cautiously. It is certainly his own character that is the real object at least of anger, for it is a frustrating obstacle to him. If he could feel this, he would weep in pity for himself hemmed in by his character. But it is just one's own character that one does not feel. It is the character of an intelligent sensitive person to understand itself in principle, but not to feel engaged in the struggle between happiness and character, and break down. As an object of observation, a man's character is no surprise to him; he has long known its ways. Does he ask himself the question, "Have I been happy for thirty-forty-fifty years?"

Nevertheless, it is not the case that an intelligent sensitive man who cannot weep for his misery cannot weep at all. We find, to our surprise, that he weeps in two interesting situations, and these give us useful clues how to help him.

First, he weeps when he attends to something of pure and simple beauty that suddenly surprises him. It may be a phrase of melody or words, a flower, a graceful or noble gesture or behavior. Such things, when they occur surprisingly, bring tears to his eyes, and he may even softly weep. The sequence is as follows: because the object is beautiful, promissory of pleasure and giving pleasure, he allows it to come close to himself and then, at the surprising turn to something still simpler and more resolving, he has had neither the time nor the inclination to guard against it; he *is* surprised and touched. Feeling rises, and the feeling that rises is—unexpectedly—weeping. Why is this?

Such beauties are the signs of paradise; experiencing them is an activity of paradise. But paradise is lost. So the tears are, after all, tears not of joy but of loss. It is his own hurt self that he is weeping for, because now, in these special circumstances, *his persistent misery is confronted with an actual loss that he believes in.* On reflection, we can understand why it is precisely an object of beauty that can get behind, or under, the habitual defenses of intelligence. The experience of beauty is preconceptual; it moves between sensory presentness and a meaning coming into being, not yet rigidly defined. Experience of beauty is prior to the separation that a man makes between his present pleasure—which is meaningless, because he does not fully give himself to it—and his general conception of what would "really" satisfy him, which he does not believe, because it is merely a thought. But the tangible present object stands, as part for whole, for a tangible lost object, and he weeps. But it is only an object of beauty, whose meaning he again gathers and interprets, and his soft weeping dries before it deepens to orgastic sobbing.

It is not by accident that the intelligent sensitive person often turns out to be an artist, to create this experience that is alone meaningful to him.

The social situation that brings our man to tears is still more curious; it is relenting, the relaxation of unnecessary torture. Note that, again, it is precisely not a deprivation but a kind of gift that is the prelude to weeping. Thus, suppose a judge sympathizes with a condemned man and says he is sorry. He holds out his relenting hand to shake yours, perhaps remarking that justice is not perfect. He expresses his relenting in order to save your feelings, not, of course, to suspend the sentence. And so, because your feelings *are* saved, you take the reptilian hand and choke up. One's intellectual defenses were strongly marshaled against the oppressor, but now the tension is relaxed. The tears are for oneself, but not because the self has been saved but because, in so far saved, it can afford to feel what it has lost. The relenting is a sign that the oppression, with which one identified in part simply by standing trial, has not after all been inevitable; one *could have been* happy, but it is lost. In this soft mood one then accedes to the present unhappiness. Naturally one does not frankly bawl for it, but chokes back the crying and dries the eyes.

Tragic poets relent and win the audience's tears at just the worst moment, as when Mrs. Alving in *Ghosts* suddenly recognizes that her husband had perhaps had a hard time of it himself, and was somewhat justified. In tragedies, the pity is for the protagonist as he approaches his catastrophe; the fear is for him and oneself at the catastrophe; but the tears are for oneself when, after the catastrophe, there is a relenting of the judgment. The poet sympathizes—I quote from Genet's *Les Pompes Funèbres*—*"T'as été malheureux, hein?"* *T'as été malheureux, hein?*

That is, identifying with the depriving and condemning causes that now relent, our man allows himself a certain self-pity. This is already a great step, for especially the intelligent sensitive man is likely to be harsh and implacable toward himself, to make the highest demands on himself. Often, because he understands, he is kindly to others and makes no demands on them. For others he is kindly and he feels sorry, but he does not love them; himself he loves, but he is not kindly to himself. He knows enough to regard his hurt self as a small insignificant object; he has grown beyond identifying with himself, he understands the causes. But in the special case of relenting, he can pity his small self.

Nevertheless, the small self is not the whole self. The one who is pitying is not himself suffering a present loss.

So we see that our man weeps—and therefore provides us with clues—for beauty and the remnants of self-security. Both are present gifts that revive the memory of old losses, but it is only present losing that one can frankly bawl for.

III. SOLUTION

The intellectual sensitive man does not presently lose because he does not presently stake himself. Our clues make us see that two things are necessary for frank bawling. First, instead of looking for reminders of paradise, which lead to weeping softly, *he must engage in the present hope and effort for paradise.* In such a pursuit he cannot passively identify with the existing causes of things, for paradise does not exist. So, second, he must identify with paradise by actively *making* the causes of his reality. Then, instead of relenting pity for himself, which leads to choking up, he will be vulnerable to present tangible loss. For in the pursuit and creation of paradise, a man is surprisingly confronted with obstacles and present loss, and he is angry and bawls.

Usually, a man plays it safe by engaging only in what he knows he is more than adequate to. For an intelligent man this is not a small area, and he can respectably exist in it a long time. But if he wants to be surprisingly miserable, he need only raise the stakes, move where it is no longer safe for him, and aim at what he might or might not be adequate to. Precisely because one is able to cope with what is usual, one must therefore hunger also for paradise. Such an aim cannot be evaluated by a psychologist, for he is a man in the same situation and knows no more about it than his patient. We may now define "paradise" relative to the working of intelligence adequate to the usual. Paradise is practical activity among improbabilities, it is what is "foolishly hoped for." Engaged there in a struggle for life—for such activity is not safe—a man will have plenty of occasion for explosive passion.

Let us pause a moment and consider the usual existing condition of our intellectual sensitive man. He is likely tired, and he is too intelligent to hope and try foolishly. Assume that he has made an adequate adjustment in personal and social life; even his painful reactions are not unbearable; his personality does not break down. This is probable if he is intelligent and sensitive, can learn the maze, and intuit when to let his strong feelings dribble away. (An insensitive man runs more risk of breaking down.) He sees that the life that is practical is not paradisal. He feels the persistent misery involved in the loss of paradise, but he does not confront this as his present loss, because he is not turned to it practically. Where he happens to be practically engaged, he is not unsuccessful; he is perhaps more than adequate to such problems as arise; and just understanding his own and the world's troubles is a steady comfort. As the *New York Times* explained in a recent advertisement for itself, "You'll be delighted at the satisfaction you get every morning by knowing what's going on in the world." And what is the use of arguing? One protested enough as a child. The man employs his intelligence to protect himself from his misery, and this is as it should be. He uses his intelligence to calculate what is feasible and to understand what is lost. For intelligence has these two functions: to help complete unfinished situations by solving problems and coming to practical responses; or, where problems are insoluble, to circle and dissipate energy in fantasy and idea.

Why would such a man want to be surprisingly miserable? He is tired, miserable but not dissatisfied, enjoying the satisfactions of the usual standards. Why should he willfully encourage the hunger that will recreate his, and our, misery, when we have "gotten over" our misery, and things are well enough? In brief, what is his symptom?

He is unused and bored. Being intellectual and sensitive, he has grown to a considerable size and, unawares, continues to grow, but his pattern of "adequate" activity does not realize his powers, and this restiveness is interpreted by him as boredom.

Let us distinguish acute and chronic boredom. In general, boredom is fixing the present attention on what cannot be interesting because eros is attached to something outside of attention. In acute boredom, the unconscious attraction is definite, claims attention, and must be actively repressed—e.g., being somewhere and really wishing to be elsewhere. But habitual or chronic boredom is boredom with the pattern of activity as a whole, with oneself. It is being adequate where in fact one is more than adequate; failing to exercise powers, because they are dangerous or destructive; failing to hunger after impossibilities, because one will be disappointed; failing to deepen misery, until one is surprisingly miserable.

It is not with impunity that one exists with impunity.

In boredom one senses a constraining force that fixes the attention on what cannot be interesting enough. In acute boredom this is some present duty, for instance, that could, with more courage, be abrogated; it is often the reactive opposite of a guilty attraction actively repressed. The condition is therefore one of lively pain. But chronic boredom is spiritless. The constraint is both peculiarly relentless and peculiarly anonymous. There is nothing to oppose and it is omnipresent.

It is the self that must relent. The self, its theory and picture of itself and its habitual reasonableness, is the chief constraining force. As we say, "It takes two people to make a bore," and oneself is always one of them. Typical standards of the relentless self are: the need to be always right; to be consistent; unwillingness to be a fool; satisfaction with the situation as it is when it is well enough. The bother is that these standards are irrefutable. Our rationalizations are usually true.

So long as paradise is regarded as "lost" or again as "not yet," we are not able to cry, for our losing is not tangibly present. In the present it is not possible to know the laws of paradise, but only to make them.

IV. ANGER

Let us treat the men and women well, treat
them as if they were real—perhaps they are.

EMERSON

We may sketch more briefly the plight of the intellectual sensitive person who cannot give way to anger and strike a blow. His case is more familiar.

Self-pity and utopianism are disesteemed among us—they are, for instance, damning criticisms of novels and poetry; but the capacity for wrath and indignation is valued precisely among intellectuals; it is considered strong, manly, and serious; its lack is strongly felt.

But what to be angry with, and where to strike? Every man feels frustrated; a man is, for instance, frustrated by poverty that uses his time and hampers his enterprise; but the intelligent man understands that the obstacle is not really the employer or non-employer in front of him, but it is the economic institutions. Sexually frustrated, he realizes that the obstacle is not his tangible partner but the moral code, religion, upbringing, working in himself and his partner. How to strike at these? They are not things.

An expedient that used to be much recommended was to identify oneself with a group or movement dedicated to striking at the real obstacles; because of its size and power, the group is more commensurate with the vast obstacles. This is perhaps a practical mode of action but I doubt that it solves our dilemma. Instead of bringing oneself into the tangible presence of the frustrating obstacles, it confronts one with symbols or agents of the obstacles, e.g., the policeman or the school board; and if one is sensitive, his feeling toward these mere agents cannot be anger. But suppose that a man hardens his sensitivity and learns to feel and act as if these symbols and agents were his tangible enemies; then he even rather easily works himself into habitual wrath, a condition that we used to observe in many Communists, when there were Communists around. But it is not *oneself* that is wrathful, so the discharge is not deep-going. Rather, one strikes at an agent, using oneself as an agent. One is not angry, but has worked oneself into the role of being angry.

Let us again seek for clues in the opposite direction, in situations that are not particularly frustrating in any way but make our man flare up. First, let me mention a curious reaction that I should not believe if I had not observed it in myself and others. Someone is displaying, perhaps in a parlor conversation, a bumptious overbearing stupidity. Suddenly, quite beyond any expectation of his own behavior, the intelligent man strikes the stupid one in the face. He was not being immediately frustrated at all, but it is as if his frustration of all the hope of the world has arisen and caught him by the throat. If *this* object exists, he feels himself frustrated of everything, of paradise, of any possibility of making sense. The stupidity before him makes him feel that he is in a morass; his nausea rises; he blindly strikes. But of course the blow is itself senseless and the next moment he is apologetic and tries to make amends. The blow has no direction—"I didn't mean *you*"; it is blind, has no relation to one's practical concern—"I don't know what got into *me*."

A second occasion for flaring up is extremely familiar to myself. The intelligent man is earnestly giving his best opinion or advice, without trying to persuade, for he is disinterested in the affair and is just trying to be helpful; but the other smiles smugly and says, "Hm." The intelligent man then flares in anger and shouts, "Who do you think you are!" His affect is strong, but he does not strike. The affect is strong because his best "whole" self has been actively committed to its best activity, of earnest intelligent opinion. So committed, he ventures outside his safety zone toward a tangible contact. But he has been betrayed, not so much by the other's indifference as by his own engagement.

Let us look more deeply at this same occasion and mention a

usual sequence of which it is a part. The intellectual sensitive man makes a sexual advance and is rebuffed; but he does not yet feel the anger of frustration, for he understands that it is in the nature of things, etc. Instead, he is merely sad. Retreating to the security of his own best strength, he then begins to offer good general advice, friendly, but tinged with an hostility unknown only to himself. The other, noticing the hostility, withdraws into indifference. Now I flare in anger. For it is just in acting among generalities that, having given up the tangible, I am really trying to appropriate the world. I was not committed to the tangible sexual advance, but to the good advice I am deeply committed. Now I am really frustrated. My anger is strong, but I cannot discharge it by striking the tangible person before me—for I *am* disinterested, I have not been trying to persuade.

Just as he is always on the brink of tears, so our intellectual sensitive man is always on the verge of anger. He is angry with himself, with precisely his intelligence and its abuse in generalities, rather than its achieving tangible goods. The stupidity that enrages him is his own stupidity, for he is shrewd everywhere but in getting what he wants. There he is disarmed and stupid. He is angry with the world because it does not allow his earnest intellectual concern to become concrete in tangible effects; and he is angry with himself because his tangible desires do not really enlist his intellectual concern.

What he lacks is patience. Just as he is chronically bored because unused, so he is chronically impatient because greedy. This is why his aggressive initiative does not meet with a tangible object.

Impatience in general is desire without its object, going forward with desire to meet an object that is not tangible through properties of time, appropriateness, availability. Let us distinguish acute and chronic impatience. Acute impatience is the interruption or delay of a particular desire that is already on its way. But chronic impatience desires to desire, it abstractly anticipates its object, it exhausts itself in an idea, whereas desire would normally rise in the actual or imminent presence of its object. Inevitably the premature desire of chronic impatience is a cause of present frustration; it takes the object not as it is but as it is imagined—and also as it is feared, for to fail, except within one's own narrow conditions is an important purpose of chronic impatience. The frustrated intelligent man is especially prone to anticipate in this way. He gathers his unfinished desires in one perfect bundle of satisfaction that he desires, and the coming object must, somehow, be such as to fulfill all this recipe. He makes a demand on it according to his preconception. And meantime *he disregards the new possibilities in the actual object.* The presence of the object is necessarily disappointing to him; it is unworthy to enlist his intellectual concern. Also, the way he takes it does not fit it, so he acts, with regard to it, like a fool.

Chronically impatient, the intellectual sensitive man does not regard what is present as possibly interesting as it is, and as it is available; thus he is chronically bored.

V. SOLUTION

But supposing he waits patiently for the object before him to rouse his desire; and patiently uses his best intelligence on it as a possible object and exercises his best discrimination and other powers. Then, as the world goes, he will usually find himself really frustrated anyway, and, without reproaching himself for his stupidity, he will have occasion to flame with anger.

For let us bring together our two prescriptions: (1) to cease longing for lost paradise and to make a present effort for paradise; and (2) to cease aggressively anticipating the paradise not yet, but to wait patiently for felt desire. These are the present: the present effort, the felt desire. It is necessary for a person to have a sphere in which he can, actually, in the present, exercise his best powers. This he will not easily find. In the kinds of occasions that generally offer, he will have plenty of tangible objects that are the real causes of his grief and anger.

We have thus characterized the intellectual sensitive person nowadays as letting his passions dribble away; his grief dribbles away in consoling explanations; his anger dribbles away in impatient approaches. He is always sad and on the verge of anger. He is chronically bored and chronically impatient; unrelenting toward himself; stupid with regard to the others. If he would relent and pity himself, he would bring himself near to tears; and if he would then aim at a conditon worthy of a man, he would come to orgastic sobbing. If he would be patient and let his concern rise in the presence of desirable objects, he would use his intelligence incisively and objectively, and would soon flame with anger and—probably not strike—but *shake* the object in rage.

But he lets his feelings dribble away in order to avoid the excitement of explosive release that is too strong for him to bear. It is to avoid a terrible darkness, whether black or red, that he becomes wary and characteristically intellectual and sensitive. The available world being what it is—for he is not, for the most part, in error—he marshals his energy against these mounting excitements, and therefore in the present he is tired, impatient, bored.

This essay was published in the first issue of *Complex* (Spring 1950). The revised version printed here was included in Goodman's *Utopian Essays and Practical Proposals* (1962).

On
a
Writer's
Block

I.

*T*here are productive authors who cannot imagine a story to tell. This is not an inhibition of writing as such. They may be productive, able to finish whole works that have a beginning, middle, and end. By writing, they can disengage themselves from "inner problems" and get them outside, in public. They can act through a lyrical work that includes conflict, surprise, climax (ambivalences, ironies, resolutions); or again they can carry through a dialectical argument and write criticism, sociology, and so forth. But the inhibition sets in when they try to invent a dramatic plot with characters. Nothing seems interesting enough to engage them in beginning; or they cannot make the action move, or the action loses its direction and dwindles away. Such writers "resign themselves" to being lyric poets and theorists, but they feel unfulfilled as authors. What is the block?

The specific property of dramatic stories seems to be the imitating of interpersonal contacts and conflicts. We may then say right off: (1) *our authors are inhibited from freely imagining interpersonal relations.* Now, if we go deeper into this difficulty, we come on material of more genera¹ interest.

In the first place, we see that most persons, not authors at all, are able to tell stories of the contact and conflict of persons. People are continually daydreaming them, remembering them, telling them as gossip, retelling the stories of plays and movies. The daily newspapers are full of stories. The bother with most such primitive dreaming, recollection, repetition, or reportage is that it is not dramatically interesting, it is not "probable or necessary," as Aristotle would have said. The account of the interpersonal action does not penetrate the personalities of the actors, the story does not spring from their characters, thoughts, and passions. We are presented with nothing but "people" in different situations. Unless we fill out the internal relations from our own experience, the account does not move us and certainly it cannot instruct us. The dramatic author, on the contrary, draws out the internal relations of the characters for us and so unifies and explains the external situation; and he presents this internal-external complex as a work of the imagination.

In my opinion, it is at this last point, in projecting the inter-personal conflict as *imagined,* that our inhibited authors bog down. Like anyone else, they can tell a straight story, or daydream, or report an incident. And being sensitive, intelligent, and experienced, they can at once internalize the story, find its meanings, relate it to their own feelings and ideas. But then they find it to be too close to their own reality; they are frozen in the actuality of the story; they are unable to project it as a fiction. That is, (2) *their difficulty is in dissociating the events from their own actuality, in imagining that the events might be otherwise or that there might be others.* Then they cannot use their technique of authorship, of handling the medium and ordering the incidents, to disengage themselves.

II.

Let us briefly consider just the opposite condition: great ease in imagining interesting dramatic fictions. Two contrary exemplary types at once suggest themselves.

First, there is the person who has a lively interest in actual personal relations and feels them deeply, but is prevented from following them through to their conclusions because of situation, status, disease, or some such reason. Then, if he is a productive author, he can complete his arrested real impulses in fictions, and so work out the various alternatives. The actuality is imagined to be otherwise. This is classically the type of the "lady novelist" in a man's world; her fictions are the continuation of the actual gossip of letter writing. In the history of the modern novel, we can easily trace this series, from the dramatized actual letter to the fictional letter to the imagined story. The author starts with her actuality and completes it in a fiction.

On the other hand, there is the person who seems to live out his contacts as they exist, but on close inspection it is found that he is always experimenting with abstract possibilities. In his relations, the other people are always playing roles, they "stand for" something; and he himself is playing a role, trying it out. He does not have a very definite grasp of his own actuality; his desires are not *his*. They occur, for instance, in incompatible directions that force him eventually to disengage himself altogether; or he is suggestible to random forces. In a warring family he might consciously identify now with mama, now with papa, now with sister. Such a person, if he is a productive artist, might employ fictions as a means of discovering, fixing, and structuring his own actuality; or perhaps of identifying in all directions at once. This is, I think, the "novelist" par excellence. He can imagine other actualities; his problem is to bring them home to his own actuality.

In both these types it is clear where the need is: thwarted in life, fulfilled in fiction as a technique of life. On the one hand, the "lady novelist" does not *live* her life; on the other, the life that the "novelist" lives is not *his*. And from these different needs, there follow different problems of the art. The first must try more for the realism of the scene; the direction of the plot is given to begin with. The second must study the theme and construction; the experiences are real to begin with.

III.

But our author, inhibited in imagining stories, cannot imagine other actualities than his own, nor can he imagine his own actuality to be otherwise. What occurs is that his need seems to him to be so rigidly bound with his actual interpersonal situation that he feels himself existentially at stake; then he cannot play in the medium.

Consider, if he starts to write the story, he finds himself at once confronted with autobiography or case history, and these are socially taboo. One may not present the conflicts of actual persons, or attribute motives to them. Nor is this a merely external difficulty, avoidable by not publishing, for we must bear in mind that an author will regard his central act, authorship, as central in his interpersonal relations: to him, to write is to betray, to confess, to deal a blow, to woo. Further, if he presses on anyway, he soon finds it impossible to limit the plot and characters in order to tell a definite story, for in the actuality every detail is relevant; it is only the perspective of imagination that enables one to abstract and simplify. Then his story becomes inextricably complicated and wanders into a morass.

In the anxiety of confronting his actual interpersonal situation and still trying to complete his act of authorship, he may do one of two things (or, alternately, both of them). He may shut his eyes and give in to less externally defined feelings: so he carries through the action as a lyric poem. Or he may open his eyes and coldly scrutinize the external situation, dissociating it from himself; then he will theorize it.

The bother is that he cannot tell a lie. I mean, of course, a literal lie, the statement of a nonactuality. (I do not mean an artistic lie, an omission or inclusion for some nonartistic purpose, for no artist can lie in this sense.) Among poets, the inability to lie is far more common than is realized. Since they themselves rely largely on unsought feelings, they superstitiously regard every factual association as necessary for the effect. In a love poem, it is the beloved's factual name that must be employed, later to be replaced by some metrical equivalent that always jars on the poet himself as a lie. Thus, many of the obscurities of Mallarmé are simply due to his need to copy off the precise actuality—and the effect of such precise naturalism is, wonderfully, the *un*reality of an unexpected snapshot. Unable to falsify, poets avoid the embarrassments of the interpersonal story by telling only their feelings, without the events: the one who knows them personally reads between the lines, the public cannot guess. Yet we notice that poets are concrete and discursive in writing about the weather, landscape, plants, and animals.

Or, suppose the author opens his eyes and becomes a theorist: then he cannot lie because he has a noble superstition of objective truth. He avoids his interpersonal story by speaking in generalities. A celebrated instance of such avoidance is Kierkegaard. Or again, at a further remove from the personal, but recapturing some of the urgency of practical contact, the theorist may turn to sociology, politics, or psychiatry.

IV.

Let us compare and contrast our author who cannot imagine away from his own life story with an important type of novelist. This is the "first novelist," the young writer whose book is about a young writer with family and sexual problems remarkably similar to the author's, who expresses the thoughts of the author, and who is writing a first novel on a subject not much delineated for us. Obviously such a "first novel" plays in its artist's life a unique role. It is his act of rebellion against his family, and his act of self-appointment as an independent author. It is a kind of revenge against his past personal relations and it is a turning toward quite a new life with new relations. For instance, the completion of the story may inaugurate a change in the author's loves. The "first novel" is not embarrassed by the difficulties of telling the actual story. Rather it makes capital of them: it *means* to strike a blow. Afterward—the writer, assuming he is a productive artist, is either freed in imagination and becomes some other type of novelist; or often enough, he turns out to be just the poet, critic, or theorist that we are here talking about. According to the critics, he "does not fulfill his promise."

(However, we must distinguish between this "first novelist" and the "man with one book," for these are frequently confused. The "one book" is not a work of art at all; for, in general, the artistic strategy of living is ineradicably deep, and the one who has it will produce numerous works. The one book is rather a confession or exposition of the man's life as a whole: it is in principle a biography; it is to be correlated with his other nonliterary expressions, like the memoirs or apologiae of statesmen. It may be, of course, that the one book is written in youth, and is then mistaken by the writer and others as the beginning of an authorship. It is confused with a "first novel.")

V.

So far we have been raising a problem of art. But unfortunately the inability to imagine away from the actual interpersonal situation is calamitous also to personal happiness; it is an effect of unhappiness and a cause of unhappiness.

All creative adjustment requires the flexible interplay of imagination, perception, and proprioception. (I have discussed these ongoing relations—of hallucinations, sensation, and appetite—in *Gestalt Therapy*, Vol. II, ch. 12, iii-v.) Now suppose a man's imagination tenaciously clings to the actuality. The actuality will be overdramatized and overinterpreted: and finally sensation itself is obscured, because it is too fixedly and narrowly selective. On the other hand, bound down to dogged hour-by-hour commentary of the actual, the imagination loses the free flight that is its glory; and then it cannot make the great over-all interpretations— of hope and despair, anticipation of pleasure and loss, making plans—that give salt to actuality by touching off deeper eros or dread. A man who cannot imagine away from the actual soon cannot move, because he is like Zeno's arrow, which cannot move where it is and cannot move where it is not. He is doomed to boredom. He is doomed also to loneliness, for he cannot dissociate himself enough from his own plight to take an interest in the stories of others. The situation has a sad irony: for just because he takes his relation to others too seriously and dramatically, he soon ceases to know the others at all, and his own action is therefore sure to be stupid and unsuccessful.

When the imagination is free, even a constricted world affords scope and opportunity. But conversely, where the imagination is bound to the actuality, the world is a prison even without bars. It seems to our man that he is not imagining at all, he is seeing things as they are, and what he sees is dull and hopeless; but largely what he sees is what he is imagining.

To dare to feel, he shuts his eyes. To dare to see, he withdraws his feelings. He cannot imagine that the actual situation were different,. because that would arouse an unbearable excitement of unknown grief, anger, or even pleasure; but he cannot learn to tolerate those excitements because he will not imagine them. So the imagination is hobbled to the banal sequence of fact.

His productive art is also infected. We saw that he can invent poems or theories, or both, because these avoid the one possible dramatic story. Yet these are likely to be clouded, burdened, over-particularized by details of the oppressive actuality. The lyric song is marred by prosy fragments of story. (Indeed, it is good advice for poets to write prose stories, to keep their poems from incorporating the stories.) The theory, on the other hand, tends to rationalize only his personal situation.

VI.

In this impasse, for the purpose of therapy of this writer's block, we must return to the possibility that we previously brushed aside. (3) *Since the imagination cannot take wing away from the actual interpersonal events, the author must deliberately experiment telling the actuality as a story.* (Let me emphasize that this is a recourse of therapy, not of art.)

Surprisingly, the experiment turns out to require two separate decisions. The first decision is hard but rational. To tell the true story, to forgo publication, to hurt the others and oneself, to embark on an inartistically detailed and perhaps endless enterprise. These difficulties we have mentioned above.

Very soon, however, there arises a quite different decision that takes one by the throat, namely to dare to tell the story *as it comes up,* without withholding. This might occur as a series of decisions, but likely it is one terrible decision, to be taken once for all, at one moment, and that moment is the following: The author is embarked on telling the actual story, when suddenly he says to himself, "Oh, but—I see, I remember—if I tell *this* and try to unify it dramatically, I shall have to mention—*that*. But I didn't foresee that!" For obviously it is *not* the actuality that takes one by the throat! We do not observe that people ordinarily act as though they were in such extremity. It is something *unnoticed* in the actuality, that has been brushed aside, avoided.

(4) *The imagination is inhibited, and fixed to the actuality, because something is avoided in the actuality.* It is fixed to the *actuality* because the something is present there; but it is *fixed and cannot play* because the something is avoided.

It is my experience that once this decision to be frank is made, the other difficulties vanish. And it can be made unhesitatingly, though with suffering: for once they are handling their medium, free artists are characterized by reckless courage. The author is now on his mettle; he is freely engaged in his central act of authorship, to formulate what would otherwise escape. And at once the social taboo against disclosure and the fear of hurting are seen as usual things, for every author is long accustomed to saying precisely what no one, including himself, wishes to hear. It is on this edge, indeed, that he habitually moves. But further, he soon discovers that the actuality has been not the ongoing reality at all, but his fixed image of it. It is truly *only* a story that he is telling. The great hurt that he does is not to the others at all; it is a hurt done to himself, and done to him by others, namely his embarrassment and shame.

He is now interested in the story as a story; and once he is interested in it, it does not disperse indefinitely like the banal actuality; rather it organizes itself. *The principle of organization is the something that was secret in the actuality.* Previously the actuality was indefinite and wandering because the organizing figure was unnoticed; now that it is allowed to claim attention, the rest falls into place. Here then is the difference between the actual story and the first novel. The first novel is made definite mainly by the paucity of experience of the author, marshaled to the non-artistic purpose of rebelling against the past and affirming his authorship. The actual story is made definite by some hidden but now accepted need that appears in the foreground. Traditionally, such "actual stories" are finally published as "educational romances." By telling the story, the author frees himself from a certain phase of his life.

The inhibition of imagining stories is now freed. The apparent actuality is seen to be nothing but a set of stories; the overdramatizing that hampered an ongoing creative adjustment now serves as the drama of story. As a structure of actuality, the "educational romance" tends to have the following form: the "I" character of the novel maintains a certain identity with the author, but the "others" are found to bear only a superficial resemblance to actual persons; the "others" were formed in accordance with the plot, and the plot was formed in the author's imagination. This is a difference from the so-called *roman à clef*, for in the *roman à clef* the superficial resemblances and the actual situation are avoided, but the actual persons are reported; whereas in the educational romance the actual situations are often reported, but the internal plot is imagined, and the characters are imagos.

The obstacles to the activity vanish. But the activity itself is carried on in shame, recognition of error, retroflected anger or outward indignation, and grief. The art need that becomes evident is not so much a thwarted life that the work fulfills, nor a scattered self that the work reintegrates, but a phase of life wrecked that the work mourns for and memorializes.

So, in following the therapy of a literary inhibition of telling stories, we have become aware of four stages:

(1) The inhibition of freely imagining interpersonal relations.
(2) The fixing of the imagination on the actuality.
(3) Experimenting in making the actuality into a story.
(4) Finding something avoided in the actuality, to which the imagination has been fixed.

Obviously the malfunction of the flexible interplay of imagination and actuality has a general importance far beyond cases of a specific inhibition of writing. Conversely, the analysis of this specific problem casts light, in literature, on the production of several major genres of novels.

This essay first appeared in *Complex* (Winter 1952)—an issue not edited by Goodman. The version printed here was revised for *Utopian Essays*.

There was about my soul a space
intangible, untouched, I fell with horror there
and tirelessly like a pioneer
picked with my axe until I broke this wall—

and now I am trapped & cannot get away
and the panic is rising in my breast & throat:
in the dark the doorknob emptily
turns in my hand without a click.

V

NOTES
OF
SELF-ANALYSIS

On
Being
a
Writer:
An
Essay
for
My
Fortieth
Birthday

I.

Of many hundred pieces of literature that I have written in twenty years, there are almost none that I deliberately chose to write, wanted to write because I felt that it was useful to achieve some definite effect in the community or in the art, or to say something that I at the moment especially wanted to say, or to enhance some experience at the moment most important to me. By and large I did not need to write any of these particular works (except a few public refutations or exculpations, certain love poems, etc., but all of these small things). Obviously I had the need to write something or other, and this was the energy I in fact mustered, writing something or other. The problem of the particular work seems to me to have been as follows: not, I want to say this and so embark on writing it; but rather, this is something, perhaps the only thing at this time, that does not prevent my embarking on writing something or other.

The result is that so far as developing my independence and power in the world, the growth of myself as a free agent—having a goal, using my strength and tools, achieving the goal and enjoying its satisfactions—most of this work has been entirely wasted. Naturally, my literary work has been no different in this respect from my other chief activities: for in family, sexuality, money, friends, prestige, I have likewise achieved "something or other," but not the particular goods I ever wanted at the time. My commitments have been such as to ensure that I got not what I wanted but not nothing.

By "wanting something" as a writer, I mean an awares judgment either of some social end-in-view: how I want to be taken, whom I want to influence, what reward I hope for, what benefit or damage I can do; or again an awares judgment of my relation to the art and its tradition: what kind of poem do I want to write, what at this time is my best genre and theme, how can I advance the art technically, what present concern needs expression and therefore will mobilize my imagination and technique. In neither of these contexts have I usually been able to enlist my awares judgment of the goal; but "wanting to write" has sprung from a physical and emotional discomfort, a vague excitement, the pressure of the accumulation of random thoughts and images, and the command of some unknown speaker.

Indeed, rather than tending toward a goal, my work has rather contradicted, or. at best wandered from, my better judgment of what I wanted. I have done work that made me be taken as I did not want to be taken, that could not be rewarded, that did not enlist my sharpest abilities, that was indifferent to the present state of the art or my felt concerns. The fact that I wanted something definite at some time was a block to my doing anything intelligent or imaginative toward its achievement. Instead, I would embark on something irrelevant that nullified the possibility of achievement.

There have been a number of exceptions. These have occurred when, instead of my initiating the goal, the command to performance, some demand has been made on me, e.g., to do something for money immediately needed, to collaborate on developing an idea, to answer an opponent, to placate a lover. In such cases, authorized not by myself but by somebody else, I have sometimes been able to enlist my better judgment in doing the wanted job.

My habitual method of composition has made possible this persistent waste of effort. I do not make a plan, but set going at once on some thought or rhythm that is not impossible, not too irrelevant, not out of the question. This at once proceeds to "write itself," I do not write it; and the end of the opening paragraphs leads to something else that "comes up," I do not bring it up; and so on to the end. Whenever I made a plan for the "not impossible" project, it was obvious to me that this was not what I wanted to achieve at the time, and therefore I could not proceed with it. On the other hand, to make a plan toward what I in fact wanted seems to have been impossible to me—unless, as I have said, the want was externally authorized.

Now by my proceeding planlessly in this way, without an awares aim, much work has gotten itself done. This work probably has considerable value—so I am sometimes told and so, as a critic, I myself judge. (I have been one to boast of these works and glorify myself a good deal.) Certainly my method of composition is not uncommon among artists. But the point is that the work has been valueless to me, it is not what I want, it is wasted effort.

To be sure, it has not even been much effort, for the strenuous effort would have been to do the work that would satisfy my wants; but I have lolled, with a deliberate relaxation, most often with pleasure and sometimes finally with intense excitement, in "actions" that progressively presented themselves. My method of composition of particular works has been, thus, the same as my way of embarking on the works themselves: the abrogation of my own purpose, the embarking on the irrelevant. And here too the exception noted above has operated; for sometimes the particular work itself has generated an authoritative strenuous task: for instance, if I had already invested many pages of work in a long book and was suddenly stopped, nothing "came up": then to face this objective challenge, I have been able to mobilize more strenuous powers, with suffering, perhaps headache. Consequently, too, there is a sense of victory and of not having wasted myself. Or to give another kind of instance, if the automatically progressing work came to generate a moral problem, touched something I disliked or feared to say, then, in this externally authorized context of the social mores, I could gird my loins and make a strenuous effort, of defiance and having it out, in defense of "my" work, that was not indeed mine at all. Such exceptions as these have been frequent, for a prolific writer is often faced with problems of composition and of morals. Thus there are numerous local areas of effort and satisfaction in my authorship (and these have made me grow as a person);

so, less frequently, there have been in other parts of my life. But it is the main lines of my activity, the enterprises undertaken, the chief commitments I have made, that have been purposeless, effortless, and accomplishing nothing for myself.

In its inception much of my work has been a kind of journalism. In order to be authorized to begin writing—as if I were not precisely the author—I have often chosen an item of current interest or something usually treated and therefore acceptable. I myself had little strong concern for the issue—it did not present itself to me in dramatic form as an interpersonal relationship of my own (therefore if a story line would develop it would not be the story springing from this current item); but "it is the kind of thing people and other writers are busy about," and I too wanted to be busy. Very soon, however, the work wandered from the issue interesting or comprehensible to the others, without of course coming directly to what I myself wanted to be saying. Indirectly it would be saying what I wanted, especially by distorting the theme that I had apparently contracted to deal with. So critics have often taken me to be earnest just where I am playful and playful just where I am most in earnest.

Such work "wrote itself" unsatisfactory to me from the beginning. But others, to whom I had made an apparent contract, could have also the sense of being let down and disappointed. Having promised to treat something of interest to them, I perversely went off "on my own track," except that it was not even my own, for my own personal concerns would have been also theirs (tho not the item I started from). This disappointment that I likely caused may explain the usual reception of my works: silence, neither praise nor blame, and then disregard of the next work, no matter how I made it clamor for attention. If indeed I had followed my own bent, my own dreams, without journalistic corruption, I should have enjoyed, no doubt, a *"sucess d'estime,"* and by now have a respectable position thru mere persistence in sticking to my guns, as a man wins a favorable obituary by living long. But the one who stimulates and then is not attentive is worse than nothing, he is an annoyance, a tease.

A few small works that have remained more faithfully with the issues people are interested in, have not gone disregarded, have been moderately rewarded and talked about, have won me a social audience rather than the intimate audience I shall mention below. But even as I wrote them, I felt these pieces to be second-rate, for I inhibited the inventive ideas that came to me that would at once have gone beyond those issues. Thus, where I wrote more freely I spited the audience; where I did not I spited myself.

I do not disappoint in competitive tests, I confidently do my best. For instance I was an outstanding student when the task was assigned by the teachers and the curriculum.

But I have been disappointed that the others have ceased to assign me my task.

The group-problems that seem to set a task for others, are not spontaneously my problems.

I do not venture to assign the task to myself. I disregard myself.

Disappointed by the disregard of others, I spite them. Then I am further disregarded, unassigned, and so forth. And so with myself.

II.

I think often and with increasing conviction of giving up this way of writing. But the alternative is not to write otherwise, namely as I want to—I do not know how I would do that, nor if I could: the thought is blank.

Rather I have the sense, more and more actual, of resting on my laurels as a writer, altho there are no such laurels. The compulsion to continue writing just in order to be writing something or other, is diminishing. This is because I have been achieving certain simple goals, not of course by doing what I did not want, writing those particular works, but by persisting in doing what I did want, writing freely, however wrongheadedly. I shall speak of achieving occupation, money, friends, prestige, justification. Thru fear of lacking these I have been compelled to write at all costs; when these pressures are allayed, I can rest on my laurels. This does not mean giving up the practice of writing, for without doubt I can write any-thing, just as I can talk or reason, as occasion arises; but it means that I give up being a writer.

Let me try to recall the transition from writing to being a writer. I remember when I was fifteen, twenty-five years ago, writing certain compositions with fluency and excitement; there was no issue then of writing what I wanted or avoiding to write that, nor again of waiting for criticism, whether praise or blame. I recall, for instance, an adverse criticism by an inept teacher; my response was to look at him with simple unbelief, for I wrote as I played Chinese handball, just fine. I do not mean I had merely a technical ability, but the total art: to find a subject and grow warm with it, to use my habitual means and improvise new means.

During the next years, however, it was necessary for me to choose a career. I was not ready, did not want, to make any such choice, so I slipped into being a writer, for this was something or other and involved no special effort. It was just like that, there was no want or need, external or internal appointment. That is, I made of writing a particular career with the same unwanting passivity that, in writing, I have made particular works. In fact, I wanted (liked) to write just as I wanted to play ball, make love, learn sciences; but in the social, family, and psychosexual situation I was in, such an attitude did not constitute having a career. Then as later, and also much earlier, I did not venture to do what I wanted. Nevertheless I was careful to slip into a something or other that did not prevent a flow of excitement.

I never said, as I have heard so many young men say, "I should like to be a writer," for I already did write; and I did not like to be a writer, but it became assumed by the others and myself that I was one. Therefore there was not in my case, as in the others, a struggle and resolution, for instance a family conflict and a break for independence.

By the age of twenty, what I wrote were the works of a writer, they were corrupted. The unwantedness of the career as a whole infected every particular work written under pressure of that career. And the pressure—fears of isolation, poverty, dependency—could only increase, for what was unwanted could not succeed but rather alienated the chance of success. So I was compelled to undertake ever new unwanted works (I do not mean, of course, commercial or pot-boiling works, for those would at least have satisfied a definite want). A sign of my difficulty was that I wrote hardly a single work but at some moment I lost contact with what I was doing and exclaimed with desperate self-consciousness, "Look how well it is put together! where else do you find such a writer?"

Nevertheless I saw to it that, in spite of myself, the stream of writing wrote itself spontaneously and uncorrupted, tho it did not come to anything (just as, in defiance of my happiness, a stream of living has lived itself purely thru me, and does not come to anything). And now, as an inevitable social and personal effect, that only seems to be paradoxical, this excitement has in fact alleviated the compulsive pressures of my career and brought me to the prospect of retiring from that unwanted career and resting on my laurels. (And perhaps I shall be able freely to choose a career, perhaps of being a writer.)

Writing satisfied the demand of having an occupation. Since I did not want to satisfy it, I nullified it by wasting my efforts. This increased the demand to prove that I was occupied with something or other. But I met this demand, without pause, lavishly, in every genre, rarely at a loss for a subject, never repeating myself. This required little effort, the works wrote themselves, for I avoided the hard task of trying to realize my intention (a task normally resolved by bursting the bonds of the original intention and growing thru handling the medium; but I had no original intention). Now after twenty years, it has been abundantly proved that I have been occupied. Judged overall, there has been a long agony of effort, the more strenuous because not rewarded and not encouraged. Every one who knows about it says, "He ought to rest for a few years" (tho they do not exactly mean "he ought to rest on his laurels"). In any case, if any one asks me, "What are you doing these days?" I find that I can answer with equanimity, "Nothing"—not mentioning the verses I keep writing by a kind of reflex, for they are nothing.

I always wrote with the hope of making money, at the same time as I jealously reserved the right to write "as I pleased," and I have hundreds of times had the sinking feeling of seeing a work becoming non-saleable under my pen. I have made almost no money by writing—I have been driven to, and learned, other expedients to achieve decent poverty—and now I have learned not to count on anything. Consequently I could now cheerfully write for money, for I would think of the money and not of writing for money; I say I "could," but I do not know how to. When I get the chance I cheerfully ask for what seem to me to be large sums, what the market will bear, far beyond what my effort is worth, for I admit that it is worth nothing. Also it is interesting to me to see how works of mine are more saleable after ten or fifteen years: my disappointing spite-work of the past becomes a commodity in the present, others have caught up with and learned to share my old disaffection. I am paid for my persistent name, altho my name on a work is a signal to disregard the work.

My works have no social audience, This is inevitably so because social groups are interested in the works that enhance their identity or solve their problems; but I am niggardly of enhancing the others or paying attention to their wants, just as I am niggardly with my own wants. Yet just because it is the kind of work it is, I find to my surprise that I have a loving audience of isolated persons. They have no public words to express their appreciation—the words and the organs of publicity belong to the groups I disappoint. Instead from time to time they become intimate with me. So I garner friends and flatterers, sexual friends and disciples. Beneath my fears of isolation and loneliness, a nature communicates itself that is childlike eager, and young people come to me as I to them. My public is restricted precisely to the circle of my close or potentially close acquaintances, and publication has meant not publication at all but the wider circulation of a kind of private letter. What is the message of this letter? and what, correspondingly, do we say to one another when we meet closely and kiss? what ideas do we share? Always nothing. There are not only no public words but also no private words. There is of course a tacit agreement on the unwanted, but that is not something to discuss when face to face, for we do not have a circle of spite. I am embarrassed if a friend praises what I write, just as I am annoyed that the public does not praise it. I presume that what my friends and I share, or hope to share, is a belief in possibility. Possibility! But in fact what we do share is dumb, impersonal, animal touch; and that is very well. Certainly we are not yet to the point of simple contact, without "sharing" it or being "personal" or "impersonal"; but one cannot come to that point as a reward of being a writer.

From time to time I learn, with a shock, that I am feared. I presume that this is the meaning of prestige, as Franz said it well enough.

> After a man is dead, it can be seen whether his contemporaries harmed him more or whether he did the more harm to his contemporaries; in the latter case he was a great man.

Correspondingly, the kind of admiration I have won is well expressed in the letter of an editor (who is not an intimate friend), "Your argument is coercive." He does not want to print it but he must. But of course this is what I have communicated: I have let it coerce me too. I have seduced him, I have seduced myself.

So I have been describing the rewards of being a writer, that have alleviated the pressures of my career and brightened my prospects of resting on my laurels. All this is, of course, nothing but an illustration of Freud's remark about artists: frustrated in his need for money, respect, and love, a man becomes an artist and so indirectly wins for himself money, fame, and love. He wins it by giving up his immediate goals and resigning himself to a public role, a career, that establishes with the others a distant relation, not what he wants at all; nevertheless thru this role his vitality speaks out and makes an effect. I have carried out this performance in a grudging and unmagnanimous way, and my rewards too have been grudging. They are enough (I am grudging with myself).

But the chief reward I have gotten during twenty years is one that Freud does not mention: a sense of justification, or better, the absence (or avoidance) of the issue whether or not I am justified— if once it is felt as an issue, it is likely impossible to feel justified (but I really know nothing about it, for I have not arduously experienced such an issue). My attitude toward my career, and my mode of composition as a writer, precisely prevent such an issue from arising: for on the one hand I continually let my inner excitement and my responses to the world express themselves and drain themselves away, and on the other I nullify myself, I keep out of the way. Thus I experience little discontinuity with whatever else there is, it makes no counter-claim against me. And being justified in this way, it has not been hard for me to bear the other pressures of myself and society, to treat them with even a certain blithe spitefulness. Indeed, writing even these pages I have fallen into the familiar rhythm, been buoyed on the currents of thought, and have become more cheerful and careless.

Unfortunately this serene sense of justification exists only with the activity itself or with the sense that I can embark on it, for I am a writer. How shall I cope with the problem if I come to rest on my laurels? A couple of days ago I decided with pleasure to disburden myself of my unwanted effort; I had a right, I felt, to rest on my laurels. Soon I knew I was powerless and cut off, I had failed and a nameless claim was made against me. Then if I picked up a piece of prose written by no matter whom, I was moved to envious wonder at the steady pace of it, at the ease with which each sentence communicated something to the reader, at the skill with which the author was achieving something that he wanted. He did not wander (he never surprised). I felt too guilty to weep, too ineffectual to try again.

III.

I have the feeling that I am inhibiting myself from writing a major work. (So people have often told me, but I was unwilling to believe it. Also, I feel that I don't want to write anything, but perhaps to do something else. More generally, I feel that I don't want anything, I hardly want.

It would be a major work if I began on something I wanted to write, rather than beginning with just something or other and sneaking into writing; then I would have both more control and more desire. (I have been sneaking into writing as I do into sexual play or asking for a job.) To write the wanted work is to make one's master-piece, in the old sense: the work that is no longer apprentice-work, externally authorized.

Now that I could perhaps write this work, however, I find that I hardly want to write anything, or at least do not want to *write* it.

I have been telling myself that I am waiting for others to commission me, to mobilize me to action; but this craving for "external" authorization has in fact lapsed along with "my own" wants. And the very distinction between the "external" and "my own" is now a false one: it existed as a mechanism to set the one against the other—what "they" tell me to do against what "I" want—in order to nullify both and allow the unauthorized activity, the work that "wrote itself."

"I" was not guilty of it if "I" did not do it. Then punished, I have always felt aggrieved innocence; and others have responded, have not questioned my good intentions, and have let me off easy. (In the actual misdeed, both sides have been silent accomplices.)

"My own" wants have been a mixture of my desire to participate in the group-goals and my refusal or defiance of participating in them. Given this clinch, I have omitted wanting but have acted anyway. Instead, I have re-admitted wanting subterraneously as that which "comes to" me, "writes itself." Many strong motives and even excellent ideas have come to me in this way; I have often let them, so to speak, act me out as if they were mine.

But I have lacked conviction in them; I did not affirm them but only performed them. I did not know myself whether I wrote in earnest or play. When I came to suffer for something and did not recant, I took it as a proof that I must have been in earnest (tho perhaps it was a proof only that I was stubborn). I have sometimes implored others to try to refute me in order that I might come to belief or disbelief in my own words; but mostly people have responded with silence.

Meantime, against the words that came to me and that I told to myself, there was the overwhelming torrent of the words that were everywhere being said in society. They drowned out the voice that rose in me and made it hard for me to recognize it as my own, or learn it as my own. Even if the voice of the consensus agreed mostly with what I was saying, it confused me. I have always had such agreement, either of experts or of a special group or of the ancients, for I have not written anything very novel. But this did not bolster me up, for I would not willingly participate with the others, so could not draw on the courage of numbers. Indeed, on the contrary, public opposition has given me courage to speak a little louder, to preserve myself from utter destruction. Yet this has never hardened me to be a rebel, tho naturally people assume that I am a rebel; for to be a rebel would again be a bona-fide social role, a kind of participation.

I have found it delicious when I was being most outrageous, to be quoting Aristotle or Spinoza and feeling that I was most orthodoxly innocent. This does not mean that I was using them; they were my masters. But I could not practice what we preached.

While I was writing something, I disbelieved it. This does not mean that I was lying; for I should have been pleased to express the opposite opinion, but I could not find any evidence for it. I disbelieved it because *I* was writing it, and because I was *writing* it. If I read my opinion expressed by another, I would breathe, "Yes! yes!" with excitement, but still without conviction. And the result, I confess, has been that I regard those who agree with me as not persons at all, but merely transitory phenomena like myself; they are only my intimates. (But if they are dead, they—and we—are masters.)

During brief periods I have lived in small face-to-face communities with like-minded people, not merely my intimates for we were also the constituted authorities. There was no opposition between what the others authorized and what I would authorize— for even if we disagreed, we disagreed as intimates. Then it seemed to me that I could write something that *we* wanted; it would be something that, in a small community, would make an immediate difference to our feeling and practice (and my own feeling and practice). This roused in me great hope of doing a major work. But in fact I have soon been exiled from those communities.

I am at a loss, in our great city, how to do anything at all that could make an immediate difference in our feeling and practice (and so in my own feeling and practice). Therefore I have ceased to want anything, I do not know what we want.

No no! I know it well, the subject of that inhibited work that we want, but I refuse to tell it to myself, for fear that I might write it down and make a difference in at least my own feeling and practice.

I have begun to invade the area of writing with my guilt, fear of consequences because it is *my* action. Therefore, just in order to be safe, I must write more effectually or not at all.

Goodman wrote this essay in the late summer of 1951, for his fortieth birthday (September 9). It was not something that one could easily publish if one were not famous—or if one were famous at fifty, a decade later. Therefore Goodman never published it. He probably never expected to publish it, but it was nonetheless intended as a public statement. Its themes are characteristic of Goodman's attitude toward his own work at this time and through most of the Fifties.

The
Politics
of
Being
Queer

In essential ways, my homosexual needs have made me a nigger. Most obviously, of course, I have been subject to arbitrary brutality from citizens and the police; but except for being occasionally knocked down, I have gotten off lightly in this respect, since I have a good flair for incipient trouble and I used to be nimble on my feet. What makes me a nigger is that it is not taken for granted that my out-going impulse is my right. Then I have the feeling that it is not my street.

I don't complain that my passes are not accepted; nobody has a claim to be loved (except small children). But I am degraded for making the passes at all, for being myself. Nobody likes to be rejected, but there is a way of rejecting some one that accords him his right to exist and is the next best thing to accepting him. I have rarely enjoyed this treatment.

Allen Ginsberg and I once pointed out to Stokely Carmichael how we were niggers, but he blandly put us down by saying that we could always conceal our disposition and pass. That is, he accorded us the same lack of imagination that one accords to niggers; we did not really exist for him. Interestingly, this dialogue was taking place on (British) national TV, that haven of secrecy. More recently, since the formation of the Gay Liberation Front, Huey Newton of the Black Panthers has welcomed homosexuals to the revolution, as equally oppressed.

In general in America, being a queer nigger is economically and professionally not such a disadvantage as being a black nigger, except for a few areas like government service, where there is considerable fear and furtiveness. (In more puritanic regimes, like present day Cuba, being queer is professionally and civilly a bad deal. Totalitarian regimes, whether communist or fascist, seem to be inherently puritanic.) But my own experience has been very mixed. I have been fired three times because of my queer behavior or my claim to the right to it, and these are the only times I have been fired. I was fired from the University of Chicago during the early years of Robert Hutchins; from Manumit School, an offshoot of A. J. Muste's Brookwood Labor College; and from Black Mountain College. These were highly liberal and progressive institutions, and two of them prided themselves on being communities. —Frankly, my experience of radical community is that it does not tolerate my freedom. Nevertheless, I am all for community because it is a human thing, only I seem doomed to be left out.

On the other hand, so far as I know, my homosexual acts and the overt claim to them have never disadvantaged me much in more square institutions. I have taught at half a dozen State universities. I am continually invited, often as chief speaker, to conferences of junior high school superintendents, boards of Regents, guidance counsellors, task forces on delinquency, etc., etc. I say what I think is true—often there are sexual topics; I make passes if there is occasion: and I seem to get invited back. I have even sometimes made out—which is more than I can say for conferences of S.D.S. or the Resistance. Maybe the company is so square that it does not believe, or dare to notice, my behavior; or more likely, such professional square people are more worldly (this is our elderly word for "cool") and couldn't care less what you do, so long as they don't have to face anxious parents and yellow press.

As one grows older, homosexual wishes keep one alert to adolescents and young people more than heterosexual wishes do, especially since our society strongly discountenances affairs between older men and girls or older women and boys. And as a male, the homosexual part of one's character is a survival of early adolescence anyway. But needless to say, there is a limit to this bridging of the generation gap. Inexorably I, like other men who hang around campuses, have found that the succeeding waves of freshmen seem more callow and incommunicable and one stops trying to rob the cradle. Their music leaves me cold. After a while my best contact with the young has gotten to be with the friends of my own grown children, as an advisor in their politics, rather than by my sexual desires. (The death of my son estranged me from the young world altogether.)

On the whole, although I was desperately poor up to a dozen years ago—I brought up a family on the income of a share-cropper—I don't attribute this to being queer but to my pervasive ineptitude, truculence, and bad luck. In 1945, even the Army rejected me as "Not Military Material" (they had such a stamp) not because I was queer but because I made a nuisance of myself with pacifist action at the examination and also had bad eyes and piles.

Curiously, however, I have been told by Harold Rosenberg and the late Willie Poster that my sexual behavior used to do me damage in precisely the New York literary world. It kept me from being invited to advantageous parties and making contacts to get published. I must believe Harold and Willie because they were unprejudiced observers. What I myself noticed in the 30's and 40's was that I was excluded from the profitable literary circles dominated by Marxists in the 30's and ex-Marxists in the 40's because I was an anarchist. For example, I was never invited to P.E.N. or the Committee for Cultural Freedom. —When C.C.F. finally got around to me at the end of the 50's, I had to turn them down because they were patently tools of the C.I.A. (I said this in print in '61, but they lied their way out.)

To stay morally alive, a nigger uses various kinds of spite, which is the vitality of the powerless. He may be randomly destructive, since he feels he has no world to lose, and maybe he can prevent the others from enjoying their world. Or he may become an in-group fanatic, feeling that only his own kind are authentic and have soul. There are queers and blacks belonging to both these parties. Queers are "artistic," blacks have "soul." (This is the kind of theory, I am afraid, that is self-disproving; the more you believe it, the stupider you become; it is like trying to prove that you have a sense of humor.) In my own case, however, being a nigger seems to inspire me to want a more elementary humanity, wilder, less structured, more variegated, and where people pay attention to one another. That is, my plight has given energy to my anarchism, utopianism, and Gandhianism. There are blacks in this party too.

My actual political stance is a willed reaction-formation to being a nigger. I act that "the society I live in is mine," the title of one of my books. I regard the President as my public servant whom I pay, and I berate him as a lousy employee. I am more Constitutional than the Supreme Court. And in the face of the gross illegitimacy of the Government—with its Vietnam War, military-industrial cabal, and C.I.A.—I come on as an old-fashioned patriot, neither supine nor more revolutionary than is necessary for my modest goals. This is a quixotic position. Sometimes I sound like Cicero.

In their in-group, Gay Society, homosexuals can get to be fantastically snobbish and a-political or reactionary. This is an understandable ego-defense: "You gotta be better than somebody," but its payoff is very limited. When I give talks to the Mattachine Society, my invariable sermon is to ally with all other libertarian groups and liberation movements, since freedom is indivisible. What we need is not defiant pride and self-consciousness, but social space to live and breathe. The Gay Liberation people have finally gotten the message of indivisible freedom, but they have the usual fanaticism of the Movement.

But there is a positive side. In my observation and experience, queer life has some remarkable political values. It can be profoundly democratizing, throwing together every class and group more than heterosexuality does. Its promiscuity can be a beautiful thing (but be prudent about V.D.)

I have cruised rich, poor, middle class, and petit bourgeois; black, white, yellow, and brown; scholars, jocks, Gentlemanly C's, and dropouts; farmers, seamen, railroad men, heavy industry, light manufacturing, communications, business, and finance; civilians, soldiers and sailors, and once or twice cops. (But probably for

Oedipal reasons, I tend to be sexually anti-semitic, which is a drag.) There is a kind of political meaning, I guéss, in the fact that there are so many types of attractive human beings; but what is more significant is that the many functions in which I am professionally and economically engaged are not altogether cut and dried but retain a certain animation and sensuality. H.E.W. in Washington and I.S. 201 in Harlem are not total wastes, though I talk to the wall in both. I have something to occupy me on trains and buses and during the increasingly long waits at airports. At vacation resorts, where people are idiotic because they are on vacation, I have a reason to frequent the waiters, the boatmen, the room clerks, who are working for a living. I have something to do at peace demonstrations—I am not inspirited by guitar music— though no doubt the TV files and the FBI with their little cameras have pictures of me groping somebody. The human characteristics that are finally important to me and can win my lasting friend-ship are quite simple: health, honesty, not being cruel or re-sentful, being willing to come across, having either sweetness or character on the face. As I reflect on it now, only gross stupidity, obsessional cleanliness, racial prejudice, insanity, and being habitually drunk or high really put me off.

In most human societies, of course, sexuality has been one more area in which people can be unjust, the rich buying the poor, males abusing females, sahibs using niggers, the adults exploiting the young. But I think this is neurotic and does not give the best satisfaction. It is normal to befriend and respect what gives you pleasure. St. Thomas, who was a grand moral philosopher though a poor metaphysician, says that the chief human use of sex—as distinguished from the natural law of procreation—is to get to know other persons intimately. That has been my experience.

A common criticism of homosexual promiscuity, of course, is that, rather than democracy, it involves an appalling superficiality of human conduct, so that it is a kind of archetype of the inanity of mass urban life. I doubt that this is generally the case, though I don't know; just as, of the crowds who go to art-galleries, I don't know who are being spoken to by the art and who are being bewildered further—but at least some are looking for something. A young man or woman worries, "Is he interested in me or just in my skin? If I have sex with him, he will regard me as nothing": I think this distinction is meaningless and disastrous; in fact I have always followed up in exactly the opposite way and many of my lifelong personal loyalties had sexual beginnings. But is this the rule or the exception? Given the usual coldness and fragmentation of community life at present, my hunch is that homosexual promiscuity enriches more lives than it desensitizes. Needless to say, if we had better community, we'd have better sexuality too.

I cannot say that my own promiscuity (or attempts at it) has kept me from being possessively jealous of some of my lovers—more of the women than the men, but both. My experience has not borne out what Freud and Ferenczi seem to promise, that homosexuality diminishes this voracious passion, whose cause I do not understand. But the ridiculous inconsistency and injustice of my attitude have sometimes helped me to laugh at myself and kept me from going overboard.

Sometimes it is sexual hunting that brings me to a place where I meet somebody—e.g., I used to haunt bars on the waterfront; sometimes I am in a place for another reason and incidentally hunt—e.g., I go to the TV studio and make a pass at the cameraman; sometimes these are both of a piece—e.g., I like to play handball and I am sexually interested in fellows who play handball. But these all come to the same thing, for in all situations I think, speak, and act pretty much the same. Apart from ordinary courteous adjustments of vocabulary—but not of syntax, which alters character—I say the same say and do not wear different masks or find myself suddenly with a different personality. Perhaps there are two opposite reasons why I can maintain my integrity: on the one hand, I have a strong enough intellect to see how people are for real in our only world, and to be able to get in touch with them despite differences in background; on the other hand, I am likely so shut in my own preconceptions that I don't even notice glaring real obstacles that prevent communication.

How I do come on hasn't made for much success. Since I don't use my wits to manipulate the situation, I rarely get what I want out of it. Since I don't betray my own values, I am not ingratiating. My aristocratic egalitarianism puts people off unless they are secure enough in themselves to be also aristocratically egalitarian. Yet the fact I am not phony or manipulative has also kept people from disliking or resenting me, and I usually have a good conscience. If I happen to get on with some one, there is not a lot of lies and bullshit to clear away.

Becoming a celebrity in the past few years, however, seems to have hurt me sexually rather than helped me. For instance, decent young collegians who might like me and who used to seek me out, now keep a respectful distance from the distinguished man. Perhaps they are now sure that I *must* be interested in their skin, not in them. And the others who seek me out just because I am well known seem to panic when it becomes clear that I don't care about that at all, and I come on as myself. Of course, a simpler explanation of my worsening luck is that I'm growing older every day, probably uglier, and certainly too tired to try hard.

As a rule I don't believe in poverty and suffering as a way of learning anything, but in my case the hardship and starvation of my inept queer life have usefully simplified my notions of what a good society is. As with any other addict who cannot get an easy fix, they have kept me in close touch with material hunger. So I cannot take the Gross National Product very seriously, nor status and credentials, nor grandiose technological solutions, nor ideological politics, including ideological liberation movements. For a starving person, the world has got to come across in kind. It doesn't. I have learned to have very modest goals for society and myself: things like clean air, green grass, children with bright eyes, not being pushed around, useful work that suits one's abilities, plain tasty food, and occasional satisfying nookie.

A happy property of sexual acts, and perhaps especially of homosexual acts, is that they are dirty, like life: as Augustine said, *Inter urinas et feces nascimur*, we're born among the piss and shit In a society as middle class, orderly, and technological as ours, it's good to break down squeamishness, which is an important factor in what is called racism, as well as in cruelty to children and the sterile exiling of the sick and aged. And the illegal and catch-as-catch-can nature of much homosexual life at present breaks down other conventional attitudes. Although I wish I could have had my parties with less apprehension and more unhurriedly, yet it has been an advantage to learn that the ends of docks, the backs of trucks, back alleys, behind the stairs, abandoned bunkers on the beach, and the washrooms of trains are all adequate samples of all the space there is. For both bad and good, homosexual life retains some of the alarm and excitement of childish sexuality.

It is damaging for societies to check any spontaneous vitality. Sometimes it is necessary, but rarely; and certainly not homosexual acts which, so far as I have heard, have never done any harm to anybody. A part of the hostility, paranoia, and automatic competitiveness of our society comes from the inhibition of body contact. But in a very specific way, the ban on homosexuality damages and depersonalizes the educational system. The teacher-student relation is almost aways erotic.—The only other healthy psychological motivations are the mother-hen relevant for small children and the professional who needs apprentices, relevant for graduate schools.—If there is fear and to-do that erotic feeling might turn into overt sex, the teacher-student relation lapses or, worse, becomes cold and cruel. And our culture sorely lacks the pedagogic sexual friendships, homosexual, heterosexual, and lesbian, that have starred other cultures. To be sure, a functional sexuality is probably incompatible with our mass school systems. This is one among many reasons why they should be dismantled.

I recall when *Growing Up Absurd* had had a number of glowing reviews, finally one irritated critic, Alfred Kazin, darkly hinted that I wrote about my Puerto Rican delinquents (and called them "lads") because I was queer for them. News. How could I write a perceptive book if I didn't pay attention, and why should I pay attention to something unless, for some reason, it interested me? The motivation of most sociology, whatever it is, tends to produce worse books. I doubt that anybody would say that my observations of delinquent adolescents or of collegians in the Movement have been betrayed by infatuation. But I do care for them.—Of course, *they* might say, "With such a friend, who needs enemies?"

Yet it is true that an evil of the hardship and danger of queer life in our society, as with any situation of scarcity and starvation, is that we become obsessional and one-track-minded about it. I have ‹certainly spent far too many anxious hours of my life fruitlessly cruising, which I might have spent sauntering for other purposes or for nothing at all, pasturing my soul. But I trust that I have had the stamina, or stubbornness, not to let my obsession cloud my honesty. So far as I know, I have never praised a young fellow's bad poem because he was attractive. But of course I am then especially pleased if it is good and I can say so. And best of all, of course, if he is my lover and he shows me something that I can be proud of and push with an editor. Yes, since I began these reflections on a bitter note, let me end them with a happy poem that I like, from *Hawkweed:*

We have a crazy love affair
it is wanting each other to be happy.
Since nobody else cares for that
we try to see to it ourselves.

Since everybody knows that sex
is part of love, we make love.
When that's over, we return
to shrewdly plotting the other's advantage.

Today you gazed at me, that spell
is why I choose to live on.
God bless you who remind me simply
of the earth and sky and Adam.

I think of such things more than most
but you remind me simply. Man,
you make me proud to be a workman
of the Six Days, practical.

On balance, I don't know whether my choice, or compulsion, of a bisexual life has made me especially unhappy or only averagely unhappy. It is obvious that every way of life has its hang-ups, having a father or no father, being married or single, being strongly sexed or rather sexless, and so forth; but it is hard to judge what other people's experience has been, to make a comparison. I have persistently felt that the world was not made for me, but I have had good moments. And I have done a lot of work, have brought up some beautiful children, and have gotten to be 58 years old.

Previously unpublished; an earlier version of this essay, titled "Memoirs of an Ancient Activist," was published in *WIN*, V (November 15, 1969).

My
Psychology
as
a
"Utopian
Sociologist"

I.

When I think of what I know and the
books I have studied, I am astonishingly blank in modern sociology; I hardly know the names of the authors, e.g., Parsons or
Merton. This is perhaps partly their blame; they are too metho-
dological, not enough involved. Comte, Marx, Durkheim, Veblen,
etc.—whom I know as much as I tend to know things—were more
political and moral. But clearly it is mainly a psychological problem of my own, since I am convinced that intelligent doctors do not
waste their talents on nothing. The case is that I do not grasp their
subject matter, it does not interest me. How is this?

I *am* interested, I am even one of the authors, in social psychology. I take this to be the extension—by projection, identification, and other mechanisms—of primary interpersonal relations into the wider secondary environment. Thus, a man's attitude
on the job may be like his pre-adolescent family life; or behind the
charismatic leader is the infantile father; or the public feeling about
war and the bomb is importantly grounded in primary masochism
and creative block. These are propositions in social psychology.

Sociology is something different; let us try to derive it. Men
are inherently social, share action and sentiment, and affect one
another: this is the subject matter of psychology and social

psychology. But suppose that the accumulation and interplay of these group relations come to existing facts that overshadow personal and group psychology and strongly determine the behavior of their members just as members of groups, whether riding on a bus or in the institutions of society. Such behavior is the main substance of the social scene, of history, politics, and economics. We can analyze such group behavior, make models of it, treat it statistically, make predictions. We have a science of sociology.

Where in this subject matter, and in the science of this subject matter, do I sign off? I strongly experience shared activity; but it is at the second proposition, the overshadowing of the social psychology by group relations in which the persons are structured, that I lose touch with what is going on. In my own primary relations as son, father, friend and lover, I have been so little satisfied, I have so many unfinished situations, that I resist becoming further involved in events that would reduce me to a unit that may be counted in or out without being able to react on the total and its laws. I fail to experience myself in groups that I cannot immediately try to alter by personal decision and effort.

I understand, of course, that my primary dissatisfaction is our average human condition. But whereas most people seem to respond by inhibiting their unsatisfied needs and throwing themselves all the more into conformity and mass action, for comfort and for abreaction, it is just this that I resist. Rather, I keep alive my close needs and withdraw from group interplay that for me would be superficial.

The result of what I do is disastrous in both my life and thought. By living all contacts too personally, I lose the advantages and the accepted techniques of simply belonging. My thinking, therefore, has a certain radical irrelevance and insubstantiality. Since I resist existing in the usual areas of history and society, I am not serious about most people's *actual* plight in the world; but I am a good teacher, because I seriously address each individual's potentialities.

No doubt my failure in these things is appropriate to me as a creative artist, for we artists do personally and idiosyncratically initiate, and we stay with, our close conflicts. Artists are difficult to summate or manipulate sociologically. There is likely no possible sociology of creative action. But there is plenty of social psychology, if this allows, as it should, for novelty as a crucial principle of behavior. Indeed, in *Gestalt Therapy* I define psychology as the study of creative adjustments.

At the same time, when I do not matter-of-factly confront the "big" realities as limiting conditions for others, I become conceited and a coward in myself, and for the others I am a bore who expects the impossible. Paradoxically, my withdrawal from being a sociological unit as if in the interests of maintaining my creative integrity—though I do not need to rationalize it in this way, for I am secure in my integrity—becomes in me an evident lack of personal dignity. Since I fail to take the others in their actual plight, with the corresponding techniques, I do not, I do not know how to, assert myself as an equal in the social milieu, whether at the corner tavern or in the elections. Being above it, I cower beneath it. I doubt that this is a general dilemma of artists; it is my own problem. An artist can have the dignity of his art and speak as an equal from that position. I have the grandeur and responsibility of art, but I get from it no dignity—and little joy.

Most people seem to be in a neurotic situation the contrary of mine. They are not enough in touch with their personal inventiveness, so they conform like sheep, for one must structure one's experience somehow. But they have more humility, courage, and dignity in their secondary group dealings. May I say that this same amalgam seems to me to characterize modern sociology: it combines natural historical and group situations and neurotic inhibitions and errors, and treats them as one social reality.

I must, however, make the obvious and now much repeated observation: that at present the major group relations—whether we look at the standard of living, the job-holding in organizations, or the front politics that has no place for rational persuasion—are uniquely empty of human meaning to the point of metaphysical absurdity; so that the common man, the healthier artist, or myself, all are equally out of contact with "society," for one cannot touch nothing or share in nothing.

Then, to sum up these reflections on my coldness to modern sociology, let me mention three factors:

(1) My own unfinished interpersonal situations, keeping me from group belonging.

(2) The unsociological nature of all original creative behavior.
(3) The unique emptiness of the major group activities in America at present.

II.

Nevertheless, I am political beyond the average man in the sense of having a lively concern, and engaging in action, for the common welfare as such. How is this? Let us examine the details of my concern—my patriotic concern, for I feel it as such. They are such as belong to a man with the relation to sociological groups that I have been describing.

(1) They are isolated and desperate, therefore quixotic, attempts to impose on people something better, about which they couldn't care less. This follows from my not taking seriously their actual plight and limitations.
(2) I am concerned not for material improvement or safety, but for conservation or innovation in our culture and humane ideals. I feel myself and my colleagues to be in special touch with the holy spirit.
(3) In the face of the general absurdity, I consider it reasonable to propose things "gratuitously," by arbitrary voluntary decision, without needing party or historical warrant; or, what comes to the same thing, using all human existence as a warrant.

Of these points, the first is merely personal to me and of no literary interest. But I think that points two and three do give a useful and relevant motivation for action in our times. Again let me offer my meaning concretely.

Recently I tried to stir up some protest in the university and the publishing world on the issue that the wave length of our Discoverer satellite "has been withheld for unexplained reasons of military security." (*New York Times*, March 6, 1959.) Now, the tack I took in this was that it was a shame that the grand and ingenuous enthusiasm of the people, of my own children, for the adventure of space, should be thus debased to the level of the cold war and business as usual. I was not moved by the horror of war as such—though I am a pacifist. Rather, that we must not lose the ideal feelings that make life worth living; and the ideal of science is tainted by secrecy.

Similarly, I waxed indignant enough to speak publicly against a statement of Dr. William Kvaraceus (*New York Times*, Feb. 10, 1959) that the teaching of geometry should be curtailed because it is too hard for most kids and so it increases delinquency. Again, my tack was that we owe a duty to *geometry as such*, to Euclid, Archimedes, Newton, and we must promote it no matter what the consequences. Though indeed, I would argue, the social consequences of the doctor's proposition are also calamitous, for the root of delinquency is in the kid's dumb but accurate perception that our present society is not worthy of a man's effort, and the doctor would strip it still further of the lovely sciences that are worthy of a man's effort.

I turn the same attitude against my political friends. At the height of the protest against the Russian censoring of Pasternak, a usual group of us held a meeting on the issue. I insisted that any attempt to discuss it in itself was effectually a cold-war maneuver, so I proposed—and had so written the press—that the censorship of Pasternak, the recent collapse of the Dublin An Tostal because of opposition to O'Casey and Joyce by the Catholic hierarchy, and the suppression of some early Chaplin slapstick by the village of Hicksville should be treated as equally significant and blameworthy. This would raise our protest to the proper philosophical plane. My proposal managed to sabotage the meeting. (Let me say that William Phillips and Mary McCarthy supported me.)

III.

The existential absurdity of our society appears as increasing means and increasing impracticality, increasing communication and information and increasing superstition and ignorance, increasing socialization and increasing communal anomie, etc.; but however we consider it, it invites "arbitrary" utopian intervention, for there is no doubt that the usual procedures are self-contradictory. My own experience, however, makes me dissent from the French existentialists; I do not find myself personally or religiously in an "extreme situation." Both my animal and spiritual values are unquestionably worth while and justified. (Incidentally, the French psychologizing seems to me to be primitive and melodramatic. They do not have the technique to stay closely in contact with everyday emergencies and anxiety—a contact which yields hard but manageable expedients; therefore they believe that life can be touched only by catastrophes.)

Positively, the content of my own "arbitrary" proposals is determined by my own justified concerns. I propose what I know to be my business. These are definite and fairly modest aims; whether or not they are practicable remains to be seen. For instance, in 1958, inspired by reading some documents of the American Revolution, I resolved to "do something for my country," just to be more proud of her, and I conceived the following little program of tasks to work at as much as I can.

(1) I want to transform the physical training and play periods in the public schools according to the principles of character analysis and eurhythmics. The aim is to unblock and animate, so that school becomes a place of excitement and growth. Such techniques must be directed at the repressions in each child, they cannot be stereotyped; and they require cultural invention by the group. The chief obstacle seems to be the anxiety in the teachers and administration. My concern is natural to anyone who has been maimed in his own upbringing, as I have. My hope is to get on some local school board and effect the change.

(2) To my heart the most dismaying object in American life is the eighteen-year-old who says that he has no ambition to work at anything in particular. This is a problem of vocational guidance, but precisely not the kind we usually get. The task is not to fit the youth into some useful place in the economy, but to find what work will bring him out, be his vocation. If there is no such job, then do something about *that,* not him. My concern in this springs from my erotic urgency toward these youths, which is to have them as ideals fulfilling my own unused youth; that is, to be productive citizens in a practical community.

(3) I want to do something for the man-made landscape, especially of the country towns. Traveling in Europe, I have been struck with dismay at how ugly, shapeless, and neglected our own small places usually are; whereas in Ireland, England, France, Italy, every small place has a shape and often a uniqueness. I am

not sure of the grounds of my concern about this. As an artist I believe that the sensuous scene is, of course, important for its people. But besides, I am a regionalist, even a local regionalist. The centralizing uniformity of America seems to me to be insulting to all of its people, depriving every place of its own fancy and spirit.

(4) I want to restore the reality of our freedom of speech. The merely legal freedom has come to mean little. The Russians have their commissars and we have our feudal lords of the networks and the mass press. Our system is such that a wise, eccentric, or minority voice is deafeningly drowned out by sheer quantity, there is no need for "censorship." The letter columns of the *New York Times*, for instance, carefully screen out anything controversial; the very news, e.g., about Cuba, is withheld—from us—till it is safe for "security," and long hours of the few TV channels are stamped with corporate images, though they are public property. Naturally, this has me by the throat as a man of letters.

I have reported these incidents and this little program in order to illustrate a kind of political attitude, with obvious weaknesses and strengths. The weaknesses seem to me to be: irrelevance to the issues that are in fact agitating people; a frigid emphasis on ideal values and profound aspirations, by-passing immediate needs and dangers; and a certain fastidiousness that makes solidarity difficult. Yet by and large I am not impressed that those who are better socialized to our present society are wise and brave or, indeed, altogether sane. On balance I do not think it would be an advantage to identify with them more than I do. It is better to follow my own genitals, heart, and head, family and friends.

This apologia was written first as an answer to a query from *Anvil* magazine (Winter 1960) to Arthur Miller, Lionel Abel, Harold Rosenberg, and Goodman: "Is there a drift away from politics on the part of writers? Does the writer have an obligation to political commitment? Is there a conflict between art and political commitment?" The turning of the question into his own narrower concern as social critic was part of Goodman's initial response, and Goodman revised chiefly for style when he reprinted the essay in *Utopian Essays* under the present title.

Manlike my God I make, nor fear
to be an idol's fool, for
    so hard I think of man the thought
    crumbles into absolute

un-Nature. Oh, and He will save
me in the little work and love
    I lust in day by day until
    my name He elects to call.

VI

WHAT
IS
MAN?

Notes
from
a
Journal

Why are we so well behaved? It seems to require so few in society to deter the rest. I can think of two factors. First, it is not the present threat or risk that deters, but childhood fear and guilt that were implanted when disproportionate strength was indeed brought to bear: the policeman is papa and mama writ large, so we are still disproportionately small. A psychopath is relatively free of these particular internalized fears, so he calculates only the present risk, which is often not great. But for most, a small deterrent keeps the old time spasm of fear from thawing out; we remain in a state of deep freeze; and so a few easily prevent the happiness of all. Second, this frigidity is pervasive in institutions which are inflexible and unfunctional, and most institutions are that way. This makes direct and spontaneous action extremely awkward; it cuts down the possibilities in the environment, so that it really is too difficult, or at least too much trouble, to act out. The world is not enough "for us," in the present. Or more accurately, the world that *is* for us is most easily encountered, in the present, precisely by resignation, frustration, complaint, rebelliousness, symbolic satisfactions, symptom-formation.

234   ["If I bring up the sexual problem of the boys, some will say

'Stick to your woodwork.' "—But what is woodwork? The case of the lad who cannot hammer on the outbreath, withholding his aggression. They want skill & strength but do not speak of aggression, anger, & risk. They want beauty but do not speak of eros. Also, what is the education *for?* certainly not to make carpenters, but citizens, etc. . . . . "I have never before heard you speak eloquently."—This is the difference between a real problem & a neurotic problem; by a real problem I mean one that *I have* to cope with, so *must* be persuasive.]

: Impotence is positive, a cutting off of feeling, and you cannot explain a positive effect by a negative cause. It is not that the queer boy is not attracted to the girl, but that he begrudges giving her anything. His "homosexuality" is irrelevant except in so far as he regards it as a further grounds of resentment: "Mama won't let me enjoy myself as I wish."

["The Psychoanalyst & Society": shall he be "therapist" in ordinary company? shall he marry? etc. thru the list of questions that would apply to the cloth. But this is presumptious in the way the problem is first set: the distinction is as if there were a prophetic vocation; there is none. A man should be as compassionate & wise as he can in society, & not otherwise with his patients. If others expect him to be other than his ordinary self, that is their lookout.]

: Phases: (1) Threshold of perception or fantasy, (2) passage into muscular action. Both these require a prior accumulation of latent energy. The passage into muscular action is known as "will." There is an interval during which the "idea" does not change, but much energy must be added to it till the result of overt behavior. In this context, however, we must also contrast deliberateness and spontaneity. In deliberateness much energy is extrinsically employed in inhibiting other activity, in *paying* attention rather than being "distracted" (attracted elsewhere). In spontaneity, it is as if we were already well toward the phasic change of state, so to speak "over the hump"—and so in spontaneous action there is little "idea"; the idea does not continue to be energized, and the energy of the idea itself merges into the overt act. E.g., orgasm is murky.

: Awareness is simple presentness, both perceptual and motor. Experience, in Aristotle's sense of the grounds of inductive truth, is present memory and habits. Consciousness is limitation of presentness to the subvocal and the safe perceptions, and the confining of motor response to the deliberate and the delaying, excluding the stronger passions which are motoric. Fantasy and dream are largely pure consciousness. Hope is largely fantasy and merely conscious, but the unlimited present component in hope is faith, in the fixed attitudes of ambition, determination, confidence, risking. In its most precise form, rather than in its fixed attitudes, faith is always "groundless," although *a posteriori* its grounds are generally apparent.

: Under sedation, I have a moment psychotic to the point that I think, "I am losing my grip and they'll put me away." The conditions seem to be these: (1) sleeping pills that don't work, (2) pain and fear, (3) inability to get attention to ask for help, (4) being deprived of my usual security measures of smoking and masturbating. I cannot smoke because there is an oxygen tent in the ward; I cannot masturbate because I have no genital feeling. My floor signal is broken. It is a busy day on that floor of the hospital. My mind strays and I realize that there is a cosmic plot against me, swiftly taking away my resources and neatly trapping me by the simplest means. "Whom God wishes to destroy, he first makes mad." So swiftly to this point! Obviously I live with little reserve of strength—yet I do feel the moment with a certain bleak humor for its simple technique.

: The three roots of love are lust, taking care of somebody, and feeling secure from anxiety during excitement. Normally, these should enhance one another, pleasure leading to affection and protection, gratitude and confidence unblocking feeling, and so forth. Instead, they usually seem to embarrass one another. Secure lust threatens to make us lose ourselves, and we panic. It is hard to wish those we love to be free and strong. Those we feel easy with are not exciting.

: When I consider the long lineage: Paris manned Oxford, and Oxford Cambridge, and Cambridge Harvard, and Harvard Yale, and Yale Chicago, etc., I realize that I am not a scholastic nor a university man—though I ceremonially defend them. I am a humanist, that kind of Renaissance free-lance. At present I seem to be seeking a different lineage: Charcot to Freud, Freud to Reich, and so forth; but I am significantly unable to belong to it. In fact, I was born fatherless.

: Buddha is awareness. By awareness we come to non-attach-ment, and by non-attachment we can temper and escape our wretchedness, and reactively create the compassionate world. But indeed there is that of which we are unaware, and towards this our attitude is Faith. We hope in it as providential. Such are the Jewish and Christian religions. Now the choice between a therapy of awareness and a religion of faith is an empirical question; it depends, for instance, on the quantity of one's misery, the amount of opportunity that there seems to be, the degree to which one's childhood has preserved or destroyed one's animal faith. The psychology works both ways: The high born and happy—Gotama —can settle for awareness without seeming to be shamefully avoiding experience; but the wretched must hope for a total mira-culous transformation, miraculous because it is so out of touch with what they experience, namely Jesus on the Cross; it is the substance of things unseen. Or on the contrary, those who have lost confidence in the possibility of an aggressive and creative change must content themselves with ordering their errors and desires, and they pray for peace; but those who have been more lucky can still believe in a New Heaven and New Earth. Luck is the grace of the holy spirit, that gives sense to the glancing present as it comes to be; it is God's favoring countenance.

Or we can ask, what is the metaphysical status of pain? If pain is, objectively, chaos—causing the confusion of form and the sensory excesses that we experience as ugliness and pain—then *either* creative love transforms it into New Heavens and New Earth, *or* it remains lurking there as pain, to which we ineluctably return when we cease being distracted by our illusions. This is an empirical question.

: If a man becomes quickly and unreasonably angry when he is frustrated, you may suspect that his desire for the thing is shallow; he is forcing himself to seek it against his nature. He's touchy because he has to keep down his own rebellion.

: The structure of passivity is that in the developing feeling there is an unchanging "objective" element. The structure of activity is that an objective element is destroyed.

: The patient is sitting in a noble pose, legs crossed, small of the back straight and supporting, head up, freely breathing from the midriff—and then she begins to laugh. At first her laughter is anxious, the relief of tension. But then the laughter deepens and becomes spontaneous. It is the Homeric laughter. "What fools these mortals be!"

: There are two states that balk me as a therapist: (1) Jealousy. I empathize completely. I can predict the next sentence and the course of resentment, anger, fear, and grief. I even know how to alleviate suffering by holding oneself more erect and lessening depression (the mind goes blank). But I have no perspective. I do not know how to drain energy from the insanity. It is with the patient as with myself, we are forced to rely on time and chance and flattering rationalizations and resolutions. (2) Blocked blank inability to speak or have a next thought or feeling. Here my bother is just the contrary. I often have to deal with this state and recognize it, but I have no empathy with it, I do not believe it. It leaves me out, and I don't know how to woo him forth. I myself can always think of something—except just when I am balked. I can write something even when I am balked.

: A difference between dream and waking is that the waking world is "real," it has a feeling of possible public validation. It is not that we feel dream as fantasy, we do not. Rather, it is peculiarly conscious, phenomenally complete, not theorized or theorizable. Waking is real just in that it presents the possibility of being doubted, of its reality being questioned. Dream is not questioned, though often, dreaming, I feel that the whole thing can be turned off. But this is *not* done by pinching myself, by questioning this part or that part, but precisely by waking.

: I get a vague signal to shit; I have the theory that it's good to perform animal functions without delaying; I go and shit; and *then* I get a belly-ache. It's the same with everything I do: I cruise for sex because of a vague dissatisfaction and a strong ideal ("sex is grand"); if I find anybody, I get a hard on; then, when the bout is all over and gone, I lust. Now no doubt this is neurotic, a defense against dangerous excitement, operating by safe controllable thoughts, which are also domesticated as "justified." Yet instead of just brushing my character off in this way, let me regard it as a viable psychological type, in the manner of Jung. Different characters have different styles of first contact, whether thought, conation, or feeling. What matters is that the experience is total in the end. Next, let me try to notice in which situations I begin one way and in which another. What are the structures of the various sequences?

[I have to do 2 things apparently incompatible. (1) Simply disregard evil, folly, prejudice, lethargy, provoking timidity; cheerfully assume that you aim at the sensible & pleasant—rousing, of course, first your disbelief (& disregard), then your irritation, but finally without a frontal fight—you're laughing at yourself. This is right behavior—I always have done it when at my best. (2) But it is too thin in content. I must learn to take seriously your world as it is for you—& richly for me;—*not* glibly bypass it, and yet use it without either acquiescence or frontal onslaught. God is in the world, not in my soundest intuitions. . . . Perhaps my difficulty is that I do not understand the conventional motivations (my "psychopathic personality"). I haunt the bars, the fringes, etc., because I understand the simple passional motives there; but of course I am very thinly engaged there. The psychotherapeutic situation seems to be the only one where I am animatedly engaged.]

: There are three theories of pain, (1) as a feeling the "opposite" of pleasure, (2) as the excess in any sensation, (3) as a specific perception with its own sensory nerves. Physiologically, the last is the case. But we must then ask, "What is the specific object of the perception of pain?" as color, solidity, pitch, heat are specific objects of specific organs. Is the painful an objective property of the environment? It is the chaos or unorganizability-for-the-organism of the environment; that is, it is the contrary of the esthetic. Or it is the brute factuality of the environment, contrary to purposiveness or ideality. Such an answer is at once compatible with the other two theories of pain. Chaos is the material cause, excess is the efficient cause, and unpleasantness (inactivation) the formal and final cause. But if this answer is valid, the occurrences and varieties of pain must be used as evidence of the nature of things, a painful idea. To be sure, most common pains are proprioceptive, intra-organic, but this does not sweeten the picture.

: Grief, so that in a blink it is dark from the horizon to the pole; and then jokes and bizarre actions; and somewhere, as if in the background but growing stronger, the high and clear music of Paradise. To start from a gloom as uncompromising as melancholia, till there is a delicate psychosis. . . . Related to this, no doubt, is that I laugh, and even heartily laugh, at only what is scrupulously real and accurate, without exaggeration. But when I write what is funny to me, most readers take it as serious; and when I'm most serious, they think I'm joking, for "he can't mean that." Sometimes I can almost portray the impregnable frustration of my gloom, and I break down by becoming still more accurate till it's a joke. But the clear high music comes from I know not where. I guess it's the same as the voice of the Dog in Kafka's story, "torn from his chest."

: After Nietzsche and Jekels, I usually trace compassion to a refusal of injury to oneself. But the thought of Melanie Klein is also very valuable when she speaks of "reparation" for one's own destructive action, especially an infantile wish taken as real. The child sees that in fact Mama is not destroyed; his wish has not been a reality; there she is good as new. This humbling but salving experience gives him joy and security. The compassionate man works toward this experience of Repair.

Reparation-compassion is a means of buying off retaliation. I am compassionate so that "some one" will not take revenge on me.

: A feeling that is not deeply repressed—if you tempt it too overtly or in a way that he cannot deny noticing, he reacts with angry defense, projection, counter-attack. But if the stimulus is covert or is felt as a "suggestion" and partly induced by himself, he responds by yawning and perhaps lightly napping. As Freud would put it, the repressed draws the cathected object down toward itself. Ordinarily his jaw is squared against the threat, and his teeth are grinding; now his jaw relaxes and he yawns. Since for various reasons I touch on the not-deep-repressed, I am surrounded by yawners. But I am also boring—perhaps for the same reason. "Is he yawning because he is interested or because he is uninterested?"

: Continuing functional needs, like breathing and sensing, that require no initiative, are accompanied by only mild feeling. Recurring appetites, like hunger and excreting, build up tension that must be attended to and give pleasure in the satisfaction and strong unease in deprivation. Sexual lust and learning, which are more sporadic and require complicated initiative in the environment, are strongly motivated by longing and strong pleasure, boredom and interest.

"Desire" is different in kind from need, appetite, lust, and interest. It is immediately stimulated not by felt scarcity which appropriates or seeks out satisfaction in the environment, but by an external or internal image or an ideal to be fulfilled. It is sometimes initiated by the initiating self prior to felt need. In the neurotic behavior of greed, there may be no need at all, but the desire acts as if to answer a conceit of starvation.

Thus the counsel of ethical perfection has usually been to diminish desire, to make life simpler and happier. This in no way involves asceticism or renouncing appetite. (By rule and discipline, ascetics mistakenly try to disattach themselves from satisfying needs; they try not to initiate or be pleased at all.) Happiness enjoys, but it does not seek out enjoyment.

Nevertheless, desire does have a positive life-furthering function. It attaches needy feelings and behavior to activity that has otherwise become meaningless through frustration, discouragement, and resignation. Desiring, one has to walk abroad and seek for stimulation when stimulation has become dulled. Because of frustrations and punishments, curiosity is inhibited, adventure is feared, there is no surplus of animal spirits. But desire urges us on; it is a kind of memory of a past that was less resigned.

: In the nature of the case, desire is usually deceitful and ineffectual—hope is almost always so. Being ideal, it is out of touch with the present and what is possible. It is a poor guide, a bad provider, an augmenter of disappointment and misery. Everything that the Buddha says is certainly the case. But desire is nature's way of our making the most of a bad deal in a difficult field.

[I shy away from the individual psychology of the persons, and go into these general cultural thoughts (1) as if I were ashamed of psychology (2) because I am resigned to be alone with my thoughts, and lonely thoughts are general thoughts.]

: Let me try to contrast the homosexuality of America and Italy. In America there underlies more of the normal homosexuality of ages 6 to 12, the gang "overcoming the Oedipus complex," and exploring first among the like. At adolescence there is a strong and combative reaction to this, but it is superficial, and what underlies can be released for the "educational" homosexuality of antiquity, conformity to a model. On the other hand, because of the general anti-sexuality and the spiteful mothers there are serious problems about all sexuality as such. In Italy it is different. There seems to be less free growing up and almost no adolescence. Then there is little normal homosexuality, but rather a regressive feminine-identification on the part of some, and "active males" who enjoy any sexual outlet whatever (phallic types). So far as I can see, this development has no cultural value whatever. In general in Italy, any sexuality is acceptable, but the equal cooperation that transcends oneself seems to be rare. On the other hand, since Italian early childhood is better and warmer than ours, they have more capacity for enjoyment and more resiliency in difficulties, they are less "neurotic." Nevertheless, one rarely meets a man, one who has developed into manhood the hard way by alienation and overcoming alienation. The majority are mama's boys. Such things must have been otherwise during the Renaissance, or it is unthinkable.

: Under present urban conditions, it is hard to define Marriage of our American-European kind without finding neurotic components in the essence: ties of infantile dependency, fear of abandonment, jealousy, conceit, super-ego, Oedipus complex. It is hard to conceive of an aware and independent person as being "married," even though one might start by rationally choosing monogamous marriage as an economy of energies, the most efficient way of managing one's time and feelings. The chances of life soon confuse and dissolve such a merely prudent choice. There is always looming a more attractive and somewhat practical opportunity. It seems to be the play of non-rational clinging, resentment, guilt, dependency, need to imitate one's own parents, that preserves the marriage. The prudential advantages look like a "secondary gain of illness." But in a society where everybody is pretty impractical, a healthy man might paradoxically find himself frustrated and left out just on statistical grounds, because he does not get the secondary advantages of remaining married!

Marriages get a more rational meaning by being obliged to real necessities, primarily the children, that must be coped with unquestionably. These limit the working of the underlying fantasies that wreak havoc with the happiness of the partners. Objective necessity provides a workable and sharable tie. And in the course of time, too, those shared necessities become a fund of shared memories and experience, unsoured by hurt feelings and with demonstrable achievements. This is a rational bond of union, a friendship.

Let us distinguish two levels of irrationality in marriage. (1) More superficially, the way in which the partners are suckers for each other's manipulations. This is likely what gets them to marry in the first place, for it is only with this one partner that either can become involved and feel anything at all. When the going gets rough at this level, the irrationality can often be worked through and the persons be made aware of what they habitually do to each other. (2) This means working down toward the underlying non-rational level, of jealousy, fear of abandonment, the Oedipus complex. The person says, "I see that we are bad for each other, but I cannot leave him (her) anyway." At this level there are several cheerful possibilities: there may be a diminution of the energy of the neurosis by working out unfinished needs when the superficial barriers to contact have been eliminated; there may be a compromise in which the marriage survives as a home base for outside exploration—"I am reconciled to my parents since they let me have fun and friends"; there may be growth through simple aging and increasing *self*-justification—"I can do what I want since I have spent so many years doing what I must."

Confronted with persons who cannot abide their marriage, try to find out if there is ever *any* real satisfaction that they get from each other, occasionally a pleasant shared meal, agreement on the children, a moment of teasing, a moment of feeling protected, a good fuck once a month. If there is this much, say three good hours a week, it is probably best to try to keep the couple together. It means that there is no inexorable positive principle of separation—e.g., somebody else whom one of them might marry; and to have something, in a lonely and difficult world, is better than nothing at all. There is no doubt—it leaps to the eye as we look about—that in most cases married couples would for a time be healthier and happier if they separated; but they would be less real; and when the feeling of emptiness begins to irk, they would marry again even more foolishly.

We must then speak of the "normal neurosis" of marriage (as we speak of "normal jealousy," etc.). The normal neurosis has important secondary gains, which are enhanced by the fact that it is epidemic and that everybody concurs in its rationalizations: "A husband has no right to—you cannot blame her if—"

Perhaps the concept of "Normal Neurosis" is the defining mark of an "Institution." It is the non-rational system that seems to be, and is taken as, a law of nature, and so it generates its own persistence. If the permanence of an Institution is threatened, there is at once anxiety and a fear of emptiness. It is believed that except in the Institution, a particular social function could not be carried on, though indeed it might be carried on better. As if bridges could not exist without tolls, or children be born and reared without marriage licenses, or education occur without schools. Wherever there is an Institution, like Marriage or the School System or the State, look for the repression and transference.

[Fundamentals of psychology: after a long slightly chilly walk, I have a bowl of pretty good hot soup. Then I find myself singing.]

[Twice this week I have "explained" to patients—contrasting their balkiness to my disposition to come across—that I am nearer to the angels. Now what the devil do I mean by doing that?]

: "I do it because I want to."—Who are you to want? by what right? "I'll show you." This is the good answer. If he makes good his will because you can't stop him, he has established a sovereign political right. Or further, if he will try to do it anyway, to death, like the tigress defending her cubs beyond reason or fear, then his action is self-justifying, because he can only rationally be dealt with if the action is respected as his right. Self-justification is given by grounding his claim outside the realm of moral discourse, in some ineluctable behavior.

But what about compulsions? for the compulsive ineluctably acts what is countered by the ineluctable rational will of those who are socially stronger. The question must again be answered by the test of strength. If his action willed in the teeth of reason and custom in fact unsettles the social opposition, causing paralysis, shame, love, etc. in those who would stop him, then he avoids blame. But he is merely compulsive if he begins to have inner doubts. He is self-justified when he rouses their inner doubts.

: How to explain the extraordinary attention and esteem that are given to things that are not necessary and not, finally, very interesting, the Arts, War, Crime? First, there is the psychoanalytic explanation: In these the repressed or inhibited finds expression in a setting of necessity, explanation, policy, etc., that gives justification. In War and Crime we can do or watch what we otherwise forbid. But secondly, if we consider growth as the normal function of an organism, there will always be a pressure toward what seems useless and gratuitous, and even "not very interesting," since its meaning is still future. The growth proves itself as Culture. The gratuitous creativity of one man then gives a justified activity, learning, to the others, to catch up by informing themselves. Who listens to Beethoven does not incur the risk and guilt of being Beethoven, but everybody agrees that he has the duty to know Beethoven. A creative society is one that fosters, seeks out, and immediately responds to strange excellences. It gives a social justification where there is not a necessitous justification. This simple message, Foster Excellence, is what I must tell people. Even if it hurts. . . .

: A "minority" exists because of a psychic boundary, that makes a real or fancied distinction *relevant,* and the anxious clustering and self-identification of the "majority" to keep on the right side. The minority is always a repressed part of the majority. Prejudice is not merely a projection of the repressed *onto* the minority, but indeed, it creates the minority *qua* minority and maintains it in being. Thus, the minority is always right in its demands, for it is moral and psychological wisdom for the majority to accept the repressed part of itself. "Class," on the other hand, implies a more conscious alienation and banding together, when there are clashing interests and it is *profitable* for one class to keep another in existence. "Enemies," finally, are not very different from the non-human and could be annihilated.

Censorship is directed against the minority. Its aim is to keep the repressed in repression.

There are minorities of religion, color, morals, and manners. In the first centuries of the Roman Empire, color did not seem to constitute a minority. During the North African dominance, for instance, there must have been many colored people around. Were Tertullian and Augustine colored? Interestingly, I do not know. I do not recall any mention of color *prejudice*—the nearest is in Virgil's pastoral, "even though I am black." Nor was there much prejudice on this account in the middle ages, though during the Crusades the colored were Enemies. Throughout these periods, however, religious minorities existed and were oppressed.

When and under what circumstances are particular minorities called into existence? An obvious circumstance is that a group cannot adapt itself to a change of fortune and creates a scapegoat. Internal tension and anxiety are heightened, producing a feeling of worthlessness, which is then projected to lessen the pressure.

: Prediction is not the "confirmation" of an hypothesis, but its meaning, for truth is not the description of a state of things but the orientation of an ongoing activity. Truth is structured faith. By confirmation we mean encouragement that we're going the right way, we are well oriented. Thus, with a patient I do not have a "diagnosis" but a kind of vaguely articulated prediction of behaviors in the session which, as they come to be, make me press on with more confidence. For the principle of Operationalism I would substitute something like reasoned-history-plus-prediction. When I have any success, it does not occur to me that I know (or have known) anything about the case; but I boast that I am a "good technician," I can get on confident paths and bring something about.

[It is neurotic to have "thoughts" that you try to "express" in speech; one simply talks & it makes sense because of good habits, present context, desire to communicate, etc. (The "thinking" is fear of ridicule or being punished or shamed; and more deeply, because of a deeper hostility & contempt, turned against the self.) Yet there must be a normal, natural use of this "thinking." Plato calls thinking an "interior dialogue"—e.g., the exploring self confronting that part of the self identified with the object being studied, & the two trying to come to terms. . . . The principle that the neurotic must be a weak or isolated use of the natural, must never be forgotten. (I give many examples in *Gestalt Therapy*.) It's H[ughlings] Jackson's "Do not explain a positive effect by a negative cause." Or more generally, Darwin's resolution after a gaff, "Never in a scientific matter to rely on the principle of exclusion." So Freud's explanation of the neuroses first had *meaning* when he could show the mechanisms operating in normal life, history, folklore. Unfortunately he tended to imply that the normal was somewhat batty, rather than risking the conclusion that the "normal" had been much too narrowly conceived, and "reality" was not what it was taken as.]

: Let me return to the idea of the power that is in a thing making it exist. This is the power added to it to make it break into existence; and that it then *exerts* just because the thing exists and must be coped with. When Wm. Reich distinguishes 3 layers, the "polite superficial," the "repressed character," and the "biological core," he habitually under-rates the surface. We can see in our present organized society how just this polite presentness dominates and shapes everybody's behavior because there it is.

Reich rightly rates the middle layer, because indeed people act with a catastrophic response since they are cut off from a satisfactory present actuality. And whatever vitality is released by bypassing the surface behaves according to his model of the organism as pulsating bladder. But he then extrapolates this bladder behavior to be the "biological core." I doubt that it is a core and that it is biological.

The chief trends of my own thought—natural potentiality, background and figure, creator spirit, strength and value welling from the real task, open experiment, naturalist rather than scientist—all are about the "power that is in the existing." I sit secure in this position, it proves itself in many problems, yet I cannot define it. I cannot get it "out there" to point at, and of course it is not "out there" to point at. What do I want? Do I want to eat it? touch it? say it? measure it? What I want is, first, a crucial experiment.

Most of the notes printed here were collected in *Five Years*, Goodman's rewriting of the journal he kept from 1955 to 1960. In the original notebooks the entries range very widely in subject matter. Goodman rearranged them thematically, and considerably rewrote them (chiefly expanding their sketchier ideas) for *Five Years*. In these selections I have not followed Goodman's own categorization of entries, adding some from "Method," "Society," etc., and omitting many he included under "Psychology"; and I have printed the original notebook versions (in brackets) when those were fuller or more interesting than the revised text.

What
Is
Man?
Eight
Lectures

I.

*T*he pervasive subject-matter of any investigation is "What is the case?"

Since we have cases available for experiment, let us ask, "What is man?"

We seek in whole-analysis the parts that are articulated in making up the structure of the whole. But in doing so, our predecessors tend to start with big parts (cf. Rorschach) that are indeed parts of the whole, but then to generate the whole in terms of those parts. (There ought to be terms proper to the whole that are meaningless for the parts, as "degrees of rotation" applies to an angle but not to its lines.) Aristotle starts with complex of soul-and-body; is this prima facie in the immediate experience? Or again, Angyal generates personality out of organism-and-environment.

Some form of the hypothetico-deductive method is necessary. Yet as it is scientifically used, they cut off from the immediate at the beginning and then in the end have to show that what they have constructed is relevant to the case. But let us proceed more like the naturalists: there is a whole experience not homogenous nor chaotic, but some of it fairly bright, some vague, some blank, some dark, some problematic. To keep this whole from the beginning as we explore in it.

The phenomenologists bracket off an area for attention, ready at every moment to drop the brackets. Consider this as a method of refinement: how much can we bracket off and still have the essential experience?

Describe to an understanding Martian what it is to be a man, how we men are. We would bracket off our idiosyncracies.

Let us ask: some one is coming up the street you assume to be a man: what could he do or fail to do that would deceive your expectation that he is a man? E.g., if he suddenly flew? That would depend on how he flew. Most likely we would expect there is some device and want to be let in on it, etc.

Movement, breathing, etc. The mannequin is not a man, we have been deceived. How is the fakir in suspended animation a man?

Gross form, persisting. He looks like a man. Is a talking dog a man? We would behave as tho he is, trying to conceal our mirth or embarrassment, answering his question, etc.

Expectation of a response if we try to get something across to him, tho not necessarily the response we desire. The response has to make "sense." Now let us compare our expectation of the man and the thinking-machine. (We agree that even an expert might err in taking one for the other.) Gross form is not a good criterion: if we had X-ray and microscopic vision we would see the man also as wires and tubes.

Consider a machine that answers to everything and correctly; or in which is built a random element that makes for occasional unpredictable errors. We must try to distinguish the random from the indefinite. The random is systemically definable (in a meta-system), it is what follows some rule *not* the rule of this system. The immediate projected feeling, expecting it to be a man, is that it is perverse.

It must answer *back* and not merely reflect like a mirror. If you lived with a person who answered to every whim just as you pleased, it would not be a man. Contrariwise, if there were man-like beings around and no matter what one did, they did not respond but merely re-acted: e.g., kick them, they are physically affected but do not otherwise give a sign; first one would feel insulted and rejected, but then as if there were no man. The dog is not up to continuing responses; it is human-like as far as it can go, but beyond a point we lose our expectation.

The questions and answers need not be verbal; there is a difference between a physical reaction and a shared physical meaning.

Presence of a disembodied communicant: we should implore him to reveal himself and so make more animal communication possible.

A solid impinging among the creatures of a flatland. If somehow he could convince one of them that he is possible, then they would be imperfect solids: that is what it would be to be a man.

II.

Human as reachable, communicable with, for both response and initiation.

We must include subvocal commands, etc.: walking down the street not going to talk to anybody, but you would not undress because of their communication. Or alone in the room: plans, responsibilities, shall I call up so and so?

Is this human, what is the state of experience that brackets this off? Aristotle's: Man is a political animal, otherwise he is either a beast (wolf-boy) or a god.

Or we could distinguish "social" (the reachable) from "human"; then "human" might be how to integrate the "social" and this other condition.

Consider Robinson Crusoe. Make him very non-neurotic, so as not to be driven to suicide by loneliness and frustrated hopes. Is he a man? Moment at which he "gives up" the present social aim, perhaps shaken out of his funk by needing to protect himself from a hurricane to avoid pain.

He will go thru a phase of talking to himself, drawing on the subvocal, like the old men who talk to themselves on the street. This might go to insanity—for there is no present limiting object to make an integration with. Infantile regression.

He becomes a naturalist: the stars, the seasons. A good observer with plenty of time might come to identify the Morning and the Evening Star. But this is really high grade communication:

he would starve for pencil and paper. (So Kropotkin or Cervantes in jail.)

Perhaps it would be non-social if it were non-discursive intelligence, like the medieval angels. (The fact that the parts are spread in time does not seem essential, for each observation might simply fall into place in the intelligible pattern.) The angel does not say "I wonder why" or "let's look for it."

Insightful behavior seems non-communicative: the monkey learns to get the banana by putting the sticks together, he knows this and can repeat it. But he has an organic need—so perhaps Crusoe could become a naturalist to avoid the hurricane, etc. So Frazer: magic is primitive science, needful control.

Does not all sensation have an Other? Its intention or organizing object. Then Crusoe would still be communicating when looking at the seasons, etc. But perhaps to stretch the notion of communication thus far is inconvenient. We need not consider sensation as an interchange of organ and object; this is a sophisticated abstraction.

· Can we distinguish sensation and perception? It is possible to withdraw its "thereness" from an Object (the cup is there) and so make it a "mere sensation" in a pattern; but perhaps this is to give perceptual reality to the pattern itself, ultimately the oval of vision. We must go into this further.

If Crusoe has some non-social resource, then it is also available to us. So Aristotle (and in a way Spinoza) makes Theoria the highest ethical goal. It would surely make for happiness, because its objects are universal and available. But is this only a convenient transcendence of the social response (all knowledge social); we then think of the philosopher's last page as a symptom: a synthesis of his power and of what wards off his irk.

Buber considers the primary perception as a Thou, prior to I or it. The object reveals itself.

III.

Notion of the object revealing itself as a Thou compared to Lewin's "valence."

What is curiosity? ("How does it work? why so-and-so?")

The Freudian conception of obsessive asking because the real question: "Where do the babies come from?" is unanswered. Again, the necessity to be grown-up, to satisfy a social conception of oneself as one who knows (imitation).

But it seems as if there is an original spontaneous asking. Even if the object is questioned in this way, as tho it were a person. When Mathew Ready [Goodman's eight-year-old son] is simply puzzled and grasps the answer he merely says "Mm" and it is settled, not as if there were an obsessive Why.

(This question of an irreducible curiosity is logically very important for our question, What is Man? For if there is something irreducible at this level, it is likely part of the essence.)

Curiosity is the necessity to perceptualize; to turn sensation into perception, on the assumption that there is a difference between sensation and perception. This is fundamentally what Kant is saying: the refutation of idealism, to think is to *have* a world, and Kant then describes the categories and motions of going from sensation to perception. (Or from dialectic, the possible forms of judgment, to science, the application of the categories.)

Under what conditions does curiosity arise? As mama says to the child, "If you leave your shoes there, the tide will come up"—and then he watches the tide.

Is puzzlement the motive of curiosity? What is a problem? It seems there must be goal (drive) and difficulty (means). The pseudo-problems attacked by modern positivism are those where there is no available means for decidability, at least to take a few steps. (So Kant demolished such problems by showing the contradictoriness of scientific means for their solution.)

But evidence can be shown of intelligent inquiry where there does not seem to be a problem. Experiments of chimpanzees who figure out the slot-machine to see it work. This seems to be "play." But what then is "play"? One extreme of answer is "practice in war-games and domesticity," the other is "to exercise the powers as they develop" (acting to avoid the tension of growing pains).

(Our activity here, on the question "What is the case?" is not, on the part of PG, bona fide curiosity, to find out the answer, but rather to allay superstition and prejudice, to increase non-verbal and non-intellectual freedom.)

IV.

(Our method seems to be similar to the Platonic anamnesis: we know the answer somehow and bring up our hypotheses against this implicit standard, hoping to get a definite remembrance that we can formulate.)

Again on sensation vs. perception: (1) is perception the human as such? (2) does perception imply communication, (a) as dialogue between the revealer and the revealed-to? (b) as the "public world" making interpersonal communication possible?

Does perception entail responsibility—e.g., to look and listen, to answer in the dialogue? Is this the human factor?

Or perhaps it is human to be able to distinguish sensation and perception, the first being a withholding of the body-reaction to stimulus, the second an attending to the stimulus as a revelation. Perhaps an animal feels, e.g., the itch and drive of hunger—*sees* a moving object, that must be pursued, compulsively pursues always self-stimulating but without felt connection with the object; but when he catches and eats, the whole process stops, the tension relieved.

(Is this a satisfactory account of animal behavior? It is if it saves the appearances and if one doesn't care what the case is. Obviously the implicit aim of the behaviorists who affirm it is to extend it first to infantile, then to all behavior. Their conviction is that then psychology will be a science.)

Case of sensation in infants: seeking the nipple as a warm area to match mouth as warm area, so that the experience goes below the threshold of stimulation.

Observation that 9-12 year-olds have no feeling for the 3-dimensional (aptitude for "spatial relations"); this seems to indicate a weakness in perceiving; and this aptitude correlates highly with "general intelligence."

The possibility that there is no distinction between sensation and perception, despite the apparent experimentability of the difference: Attending to the sensation-stimulus is to make it a figure against the ground of the rest of the body; it is then a kind of perceived object of attention. It might be said that fine-art is the organization of this pure sensation as object.

The moment of saying, and responsibility answering the experimenter, "*I* am stimulated, there is a disturbance going on that I will report" seems already to imply a public world.

Is there responsibility to look at Buber's self-revealing tree in bloom? One says, "It is more human to respond," "less human to have to ask, Shall I? or not to respond at all." Probably the non-response is due to a counter-drive: it is "neurotic." Shall we then make 4 classes: beasts, gods, men, neurotics? But we at once recognize the counter-drives as human.

Peter Bell: "A primrose by a river's brim a yellow primrose was to him and nothing more"—that is, he was not human. This seems to bring up limiting the perception.

What is the responsibility at this level? We must first distinguish it from socially-introjected obligation, tho it might be the grounds of that. Is anything added to "look and listen" by saying "must look and listen"; compare a falling body, do we add anything by saying "it must fall," in the manner of the ancients, "it is tending toward the center of the earth its proper place"? But concerning the falling body, we use Occam's Razor and save the appearances with as few hypotheses as possible; is Occam's Razor applicable to every subject-matter? (In general, we may consider the theories of the ancients as important projections of high-grade men.)

Does "play" involve a must in this way? Distinction between fooling-around and art, which is demonstrably responsible (to the tradition, to clarity, etc.)

V.

Talking to self, equated to Plato's "thinking is an interior dialogue," as relating of one's past to the confronting present— "recognition" and recollection.

Going back to the Martian of our first discussion: to tell the understanding Martian "what is it like to be a man." We may either start by explaining how we are "animals" and how "different," or more directly let this distinction develop.

We Eat: this must be explained as related to an urge and also as "something we do at stated intervals, with or without urge." So we Move—"by desire or avoidance," or described behaviorally simply as "toward or away." We "have Bodies," as abodes of pleasures and urges, or as something we feel as heavy or sick.

In general we will find this conflict of "urge to" and "ought to." It is certainly human to be prone to this conflict; also tolerant of this conflict. We have the capacity to "interrupt" for partial behavior.

We Laugh. Distinction from smiling (related to suckling): social laughing out loud is a shattering, and a continuance after something has been shattered. So in the Freudian theory of wit: the force of the shattering is given by the repression broken and the libido freed.

Again, given the awareness of death and the need to avoid its paralyzing anxiety, we laugh. Why otherwise reproduce or otherwise go on?

What is it to have a body? Urges of body. Pleasure in body. Tool. Easily available and manipulable close object (dog and tail). Sickness of body (as unpleasure, as pain, as betrayal-incapacitation). Also, we *have* bodies as, e.g., something to decorate and so objectify ourselves.

VI.

More information to the Martian: "We cannot define us, that is man." Means, "we don't know," "we are fucked up," "will change, either as don't yet know or will make-find-out" (so Sartre).

Fucked up: We don't see ourselves as others see us; perhaps this means we have "subjective and objective" natures. We are confused: by the excessive subtlety or by the great variety of differences. These parts do not "add up." Confusion as a feeling that it "ought to make sense"—betrayal by the body.

(Too much absence of confusion or dark area is likely highly neurotic.)

Confusion: Is it a confused picture or no picture? Alternatives of contradictory (incompatible) or incommensurable parts.

What is the dynamic description of confusion? Agitation; tugging-nagging; longing-reaching and tears of frustration. Behind all these seems to be a feeling of Vortex gathering momentum. And the Vortex is indefinable since explosive.

(If we say that "over-control" is neurotic and not human, we must say it is human to be prone to this neurosis, equivalent to a constitutional original sin.)

We Dream. The dream is more clear than the waking confusion: it does not "ought to make sense"; but also it has less feeling of the body. (Under hypnosis, to suggest a body-motion, bringing a part of the musculature into the dream, results in great fatigue, keeping the rest of the muscles from following along and causing waking.)

Are men "different"? Some think they are basically different, others they are basically (omitting conditioning) the same; best, perhaps, is Kafka's "indissoluble alliance" of communication making for society and culture, without prejudgment of samenesses or differences.

VII.

"We men know we die." (1) We grow old, (2) this makes the living urgent.

Aging as a loss of powers, death as the powers lost. Cocteau's "You can see death daily in the mirror."

Death as a cutting-off suddenly. The expression "I died a thousand deaths," as in shame, means vanishing from the scene: there is hoped to be no next moment. So taking an anesthetic or falling asleep, in pain: does this imply that a waking-up is expected, recovered? Is death as such always avoided?

What of ordinary falling-asleep? Say, "If you fall asleep you won't wake up again"—then we rally from sleeping, to what? fearful of what?

There seem to be two distinct elements: (1) Missed opportunity—"I never did get paradise." This goes back to the child sent up to bed out of the company. To resign from it is a liberating letting-go: it's not for me, why nag myself?

(2) Or unfinished situations, unfulfilled possibility, the work interrupted in process. This involves frustration, frustrated and so weeping.

The hero has not "missed opportunity" for he has his opportunity *in* the action he is performing. (The possibility of this heroic transcendence of death seems to be historically conditioned: thus Washington is beyond death, DeGaulle not; but Trotsky is. Modern life allows for no martyr; contrariwise, then, there is every effort to preserve youth by cosmetics and hygiene.)

Things pertaining to death, like funerals, are "different," awesome, magical. Death is "great," like the grown-ups.

"Man acts as if he could do something about dying": he has the delusion of immortality; or perhaps he is immortal.

Immortality is clearly a reaction-formation, to both the unfinished (we enter paradise) and to the missed (we do bear-witness or stand for something). The question is whether the reaction-formation is "true." Case of [Goodman's early-dead friend] Charles Wallis's articles: when he was alive, they seemed promising, very imperfect; after he was dead, they were excellent, idiosyncratic, they were what they were. It would be salutary to treat our living friends somewhat as if they were dead, as if they meant themselves; and then also to treat the self as dead. (The martyr's choice is not to die but between a slow death and no death.)

In psychotherapy we aim to change the changeable weakness and to come to the by-us unchangeable source of strength. This is "to be saved."...A man is "untimely dead" when in this process; or again when the strength is still potential. So Mozart was not untimely dead, but Schubert was.

VIII.

Confronted with death: (1) own grief, (2) other's grief, (3) close one's grief.

Private and conventional devices to cushion the grief. The child's first comment, "I'll get the house"; later, "how old was Uncle R.?" The chief mourner, on hearing the news, blanks out affectively, and goes into routine details; notifying, funeral arrangements, haggling.

The petty details of life, which are means of living on, rouse great disgust and rage in those who are more open to accept the grief. But one's own grief is acceptable if one can let it take over the whole picture—till mourning is complete—otherwise there is a painful friction between the old and the not-yet.

The wake, giving candy, etc., as means of seducing back life.

Wailing of the unconscious-imago when the parent dies: "it is not I who am crying. I feel silly, I don't know why I am crying."

Is there a great distinction between the thought of one's own death and the experience of the other's death with its threat to oneself? To Kierkegaard this was a great difference, to Buber no difference, for we take ourselves as the social band.

(One's own pain is bearable by letting it take over; the child's pain is unbearable to us if we must "do something" and are helpless. The animal sneaks off by itself.)

(Rilke's "youthfully dead and heroes" are not to be grieved for; they have not messed up the primal meaning, or have fulfilled it in a seized opportunity. In Wordsworth's "There was a boy" we feel that the poet has transcended the grief for both himself and the boy, but grieving in himself; so the society makes immortal.)

We must, with Schilder, distinguish out the fear of *dying*. This seems to be panic of choking and is met by the fight for life; whereas the fear of death is met by reaction-formations.

The question "If you had six months to live?" is generally met by "I should continue as at present, but with a little less foolish caution" (which would then be better dropped anyway). Where there would be a great change, we can imagine the story that acting out the change the man will not die after all.

These notes were prepared for a series of seminars Goodman gave in the Fall of 1954 to a group of Gestalt Therapy trainees.